# LEGAL ENVIRONMENT

## BUSINESS LAW AND BUSINESS ENTITIES

ASPEN COLLEGE SERIES

# LEGAL ENVIRONMENT

## BUSINESS LAW AND BUSINESS ENTITIES

**Brian J. Halsey**, J.D., LL.M., CISSP
*Associate Professor of Business Law*
*West Chester University of Pennsylvania*

**June McLaughlin**, J.D., LL.M., LL.M.
*Assistant Professor of Business Law/Paralegal*
*Irvine Valley College*

Wolters Kluwer
Law & Business

Published by Wolters Kluwer Law & Business in New York.

Wolters Kluwer Law & Business serves customers worldwide with CCH, Aspen Publishers, and Kluwer Law International products. (www.wolterskluwerlb.com)

To contact Customer Service, e-mail customer.service@wolterskluwer.com, call 1-800-234-1660, fax 1-800-901-9075, or mail correspondence to:

Wolters Kluwer Law & Business
Attn: Order Department
PO Box 990
Frederick, MD 21705

Design and book composition by Keithley & Associates, Inc.

Printed in the United States of America.

1 2 3 4 5 6 7 8 9 0

ISBN 978-0-7355-6810-5

Library of Congress Cataloging-in-Publication Data

Halsey, Brian J., 1971–
    Legal environment of business : business law and business entities / Brian J. Halsey, June McLaughlin.
        p. cm. — (Aspen college series)
    Includes index.
    ISBN-13: 978-0-7355-6810-5
    ISBN-10: 0-7355-6810-3
1. Business law—United States.  2. Business enterprises—Law and legislation—United States.  I. McLaughlin, June, 1963–  II. Title.

    KF390.B84H35 2011
    346.7307—dc23
                                                            2011019729

# About Wolters Kluwer Law & Business

Wolters Kluwer Law & Business is a leading global provider of intelligent information and digital solutions for legal and business professionals in key specialty areas, and respected educational resources for professors and law students. Wolters Kluwer Law & Business connects legal and business professionals as well as those in the education market with timely, specialized authoritative content and information-enabled solutions to support success through productivity, accuracy and mobility.

Serving customers worldwide, Wolters Kluwer Law & Business products include those under the Aspen Publishers, CCH, Kluwer Law International, Loislaw, Best Case, ftwilliam.com and MediRegs family of products.

**CCH** products have been a trusted resource since 1913, and are highly regarded resources for legal, securities, antitrust and trade regulation, government contracting, banking, pension, payroll, employment and labor, and healthcare reimbursement and compliance professionals.

**Aspen Publishers** products provide essential information to attorneys, business professionals and law students. Written by preeminent authorities, the product line offers analytical and practical information in a range of specialty practice areas from securities law and intellectual property to mergers and acquisitions and pension/benefits. Aspen's trusted legal education resources provide professors and students with high-quality, up-to-date and effective resources for successful instruction and study in all areas of the law.

**Kluwer Law International** products provide the global business community with reliable international legal information in English. Legal practitioners, corporate counsel and business executives around the world rely on Kluwer Law journals, looseleafs, books, and electronic products for comprehensive information in many areas of international legal practice.

**Loislaw** is a comprehensive online legal research product providing legal content to law firm practitioners of various specializations. Loislaw provides attorneys with the ability to quickly and efficiently find the necessary legal information they need, when and where they need it, by facilitating access to primary law as well as state-specific law, records, forms and treatises.

**Best Case Solutions** is the leading bankruptcy software product to the bankruptcy industry. It provides software and workflow tools to flawlessly streamline petition preparation and the electronic filing process, while timely incorporating ever-changing court requirements.

**ftwilliam.com** offers employee benefits professionals the highest quality plan documents (retirement, welfare and non-qualified) and government forms (5500/PBGC, 1099 and IRS) software at highly competitive prices.

**MediRegs** products provide integrated health care compliance content and software solutions for professionals in healthcare, higher education and life sciences, including professionals in accounting, law and consulting.

Wolters Kluwer Law & Business, a division of Wolters Kluwer, is headquartered in New York. Wolters Kluwer is a market-leading global information services company focused on professionals.

*For my beloved Jennifer, Emma, Grace and Caroline. This text is as much yours as it is mine. We built it together.*

—BJH

*To my students, who continuously teach and inspire me.*

—JM

# Summary of Contents

# Contents

**CHAPTER 4**

# Contracts in Action 53

# Preface

*Legal Environment: Business Law and Business Entities* is different from the traditional textbook. Not different in the underlying information in text, but rather in the way that material is conveyed to the students. In three words, our goal for the text was to produce a tool that is *clear*, *affordable*, and *effective*.

In our years of teaching the Legal Environment of Business and related courses, we noticed that many legal environment and business law texts were unnecessarily complicated and quickly alienated students. Many textbooks focus on the basic theory without application, or the opposite—application without an understanding of why. That, and the basic approachability problem of the law (it is seen as something scary and "out there"), can shut students off quickly. We seek to avoid those pitfalls with our text.

One of the strongest features of the text is its approachability. It covers all the major subject areas of the legal environment in an easy to understand and concise manner. The basic concepts are explained clearly and simply, without either pandering to the readers or overwhelming them with material more appropriate to a graduate or law school level course. The concepts are reinforced by cases and hypotheticals within the text that allow for practical application of the legal concepts discussed in each chapter.

We are also aware that many texts include information that the professors and students never touch in class. We personally know many professors who assign large texts but pick and choose from within the text for course coverage. This included yet bypassed information causes the cost of the text to increase, yet it adds little to nothing to the course experience. By excluding that information we are able to provide an affordable alternative, reduce waste and support sustainability, and provide the material that professors actually teach in the classroom.

The text is divided into two natural sections. Chapters 1 through 9 are traditional Legal Environment subjects that we suspect virtually every professor will address in their semester, while Chapters 10 through 17 cover concepts that are more traditional Business Law subjects that most, but not all, professors address in their courses. The bifurcation also accommodates multiple-semester courses with an obvious break between subjects, and courses at higher academic levels that require clear and concise material that is beyond the introductory level.

All chapters have the following features:

**Learning Objectives**  The learning objectives set out the important points that students should absorb from each chapter. We drafted these objectives in a simple question format for clarity.

**Introduction**  Each chapter has a short introduction that clearly presents the chapter's coverage.

**Ethics Box**  Law divorced from ethics, and business removed from ethics, are recipes for scandal and for harm to our society. As professors we have a duty to show our students how the three (law, business, and ethics) are interrelated. Ethical concerns are an integral part of the law today—and many classroom debates start on discussions of where and how ethics relates to the law. In order to foster that debate and to impress on the students the importance of this interdependence, we include in every chapter ethical questions, including a separate ethics box that includes source material and a corresponding ethics question.

**Useful Web Sites**  In each chapter are links to web sites of relevance to the chapter material. Many links are to government web sites that contain forms relevant to the chapter coverage. Other links are to general interest web sites that foster classroom discussion. Additional web sites links are included in the instructor's manual and on the accompanying course web sites.

**Chapter Summary**  The chapter summary debriefs the students and explains why the material they just learned is important to the classroom discussion.

**Exercises, Questions, and Hypotheticals**  At the end of each chapter are multiple exercises that require students to apply, outside of the text, some of the concepts from the chapter. Questions review and reinforce the chapter material, and the hypotheticals require practical application of the law.

**Sample Cases**  Each chapter includes a couple of fact patterns based on real cases. The sample cases include citations to the full cases for more in-depth coverage and discussion. Redacted versions of the sample cases also appear in the supplemental materials provided online.

**Marginal Definitions**  Each chapter includes highlighted concepts in the body of the text, and corresponding short definitions in the margins that reinforce those concepts. The margin definitions are also a useful teaching tool and outline to chapter coverage.

**Appendix**  We realize that many professors begin legal environment of business courses and business law courses with political science—an introduction to the structure of government and the various sources of law. Therefore, the Appendix at the end of the book contains the text of the federal Constitution. We also realize that many professors spend significant time on contract law issues. To assist, we included on the web site that accompanies this text not only the Constitution but also a redacted version of the Ohio Code's UCC Articles 2 and 9 that includes the more important Code sections. These statutes are reflective of the laws of most states, and provide an excellent teaching tool to reinforce how basic contract law principles translate to the real world of business.

**Key Terms**  The text includes a detailed glossary of key terms that contains clear, short definitions of every important concept covered in the text.

**Instructor's Manual**  The instructor's manual includes explanatory material, additional resources, sample exercises and exams, sample syllabi, and various other enhancements.

**Online Resources**  An additional feature unique to this textbook will be free Loislaw web access for students and faculty—a feature rare for an undergraduate textbook. Students may use their Loislaw account for research projects, to access additional resources, and to complete course assignments.

A course web site at http://aspenlegalcollege.com/books/legal_environment includes sample customizable PowerPoint presentations, and additional course material.

## Acknowledgments

The authors would like to thank the staff at Wolters-Kluwer for their efforts and patience in the development of this text. In particular, we wish to express our appreciation to Betsy Kenny for her many valuable insights during the review and editorial process.

We would like to thank the following reviewers, whose suggestions, criticism, and observations have helped us write an accessible and enjoyable text:

Michael Boyer, *University of Alaska Southeast*
Carol Brady, *Milwaukee Area Technical College*
Loretta Calvert, *Volunteer State Community College*
Whitney Glaser, *Manatee Community College*
Jason Harris, *Augustana College*

Lizzette Herrera, *University of San Diego*
Linda Wilke Heil, *Central Community College*
Christie Highlander, *Southwestern Illinois College*
Will Mawer, *John Massey School of Business*
Brian McDuffie, *Florida State College*
Kemberly Murphy, *Sanford-Brown College*
Lorrie Watson, *Orangeburg-Calhoun Technical College*

**Brian J. Halsey**
South Coventry, Pennsylvania
**June McLaughlin**
Irvine, California

*June 2011*

**PART I**

# THE LEGAL ENVIRONMENT

# Overview of the U.S. Legal System

**LEARNING OBJECTIVES**

You will be able to answer the following questions after reading this chapter:

1. What are caselaw, statutory law, and administrative law?
2. What is the role of the Constitution in U.S. government?
3. What are federalism and the federal system?
4. What are the three branches of government and their functions?
5. What are civil law and criminal law?

## INTRODUCTION

The United States has a legal system that allows the theory of **Capitalism** to function within stable, reasonable, defined limits. Every student of the legal environment of business needs to have an understanding of how this balance between the state and business works in practice. This chapter discusses the basic governmental structures that channel, define, and limit many human activities, including those of business.

**Capitalism:**
An economic system that relies on competition in the free market and on the private ownership of goods and the means of production of goods.

## COMMON LAW AND THE ENGLISH ANTECEDENTS OF U.S. LAW TODAY

The United States and most countries that were once British colonies inherited the English **Common Law** System. The common law system relies on precedent—what other courts have done in similar situations and circumstances. Really it is about fairness. For instance, if there was a dispute in rural England in the Middle Ages between farmers about who owned a pasture, the judge would look to see how other judges had resolved such disputes. He would look for other cases that had facts in common with the case that he was

**Common Law:**
A system of law originating in England in the medieval period that is derived from judicial decisions.

deciding, and then he applied the law and logic the judge had used in that previous case to the case he was deciding now. That law—the common law—was not created by Parliament or by decrees from the King.

Instead, it was essentially created as cases came before courts, and those courts then looked to what had been decided before for guidance and "precedent." The system was inherently fair because in theory everyone was treated in the same way. Over time a large body of this judge-made caselaw grew up—each case building on the ones that came before it. Caselaw and its role in the U.S. legal system will be analyzed in detail in Chapter 2.

## SOURCES OF LAW

Law in the United States comes from four principal sources. The Constitution provides the baseline legal framework for U.S. government. Statutory law is made by legislatures. The federal **Congress** and the legislatures of the 50 states are the major legislatures in the United States. Administrative law is created by federal and state agencies that are charged by the legislatures with fulfilling the statutory law created by the legislatures. Caselaw is created by judges as they interpret state and federal constitutions, statutory law, and administrative law and apply it to real-world cases.

**Congress:**
The governing assembly of the U.S. federal government.

## RELATIONSHIPS BETWEEN SOURCES OF LAW

How do these four principal sources of law relate to each other?

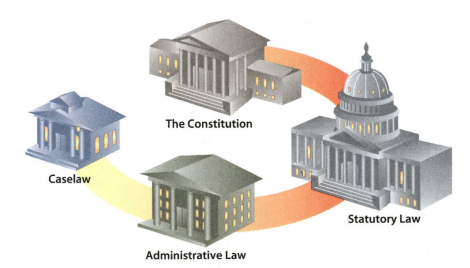

**The Constitution**

**Caselaw**

**Statutory Law**

**Administrative Law**

**Figure 1-1**
Sources of Law

## United States Constitution

The **Constitution** provides the framework within which the government and laws of the United States can operate. It is important to understand that the Constitution is the basic law of the land—all other laws must be authorized by the Constitution and must operate within the bounds of what the Constitution says that the government can and cannot do.

**Constitution:**
The foundational document of the federal government and of each state government.

The United States Constitution is unique in that it is not like the constitutions of many other countries. In many other countries, it is assumed that the government inherently may do whatever it wishes and is only constrained by the privileges granted to the people in that country's constitution. In the United States, by contrast, the Constitution is based on the premise that all power rests in the people, and by mutual consent the people have granted the government the power to make laws within specific parameters outlined in the Constitution itself.

This concept is also one of the reasons why the U.S. Constitution is so short. The framers of the Constitution in 1787 were setting out the basic goalposts of what the government can and cannot do. Reading the Constitution today (including all 27 Amendments) will take a very short time—the Constitution, when printed, is only a dozen or so pages long.

Of course, all the law that is in force today does not fit on those 12 pages. But by design the writers of the Constitution knew that future generations would need more than the basic framework. So they provided a tool, right within the Constitution itself, to fill in the blanks. That tool is Congress, with its power to make statutory law.

## Statutory Law

The Constitution creates the United States Congress. Congress has the power, derived from the Constitution, to make laws. These proposed laws must be passed by both houses of Congress: the House of Representatives and the Senate. Then the proposed law (called a bill) must be signed into law by the President in order for it to become enforceable law. The President also has the option of rejecting the proposed law. This rejection is called a veto. Congress may override the President's veto and the bill may still become law if two-thirds of both houses of Congress vote in favor of the law.

These laws passed by Congress are called **Statutory Law**. Any laws passed by a state legislature are also called statutory law—here, the state legislature mirrors the role of the federal Congress,

**Statutory Law:**
Law created by the governing assembly of the federal government or a state government.

and the state governor mirrors the role of the President. Though it has the power to make laws, Congress cannot pass a law on any subject it wishes, without any limitation. The Constitution limits what government can do—and no statute can contradict or go beyond the powers granted to the government in the Constitution itself. A law that does contradict or go beyond the powers granted is **Unconstitutional** and is not enforceable.

## Administrative Law

Congress creates statutory law, but it is not expert in everything and cannot think of every conceivable situation that might arise as a result of the statutory laws that it has created. It knows this.

The solution? Congress, in a way, "outsources" to **Administrative Agencies** the writing of the rules and regulations that are needed to enforce the laws that it has passed. The administrative agencies then interpret, implement, and enforce the law through further administrative rules and regulations. These administrative rules and regulations are **Administrative Law**.

Administrative agencies are common today, and most people in the United States have dealt with them in one way or another at some point in their lives. Administrative agencies exist at both the state and federal levels. Examples of these agencies at the federal level are the Internal Revenue Service, the Environmental Protection Agency, and the Federal Communications Commission. There are hundreds of these agencies in the country. At the state level the Department of Motor Vehicles (driving) and the state Department of Revenue (taxes) are the administrative agencies that are familiar to most citizens.

Administrative agencies function as follows: Suppose that Congress passes a law that requires all vehicles sold in the United States to emit no carbon dioxide. The statutory law that creates this requirement is rather specific, but the members of Congress, not being engineers, have probably not included information about how these emissions should be reported or verified or engineered. But—knowing this—Congress delegates the responsibility for filling in the blanks in this new emissions control law to an administrative agency: the Environmental Protection Agency (the EPA). For this example, jurisdiction could also easily fall to the federal Department of Transportation.

The EPA then tries to fulfill the orders it has received from Congress by drafting new administrative rules and regulations that set out how vehicles must be tested before they are placed on the market. The agency makes rules about how the results must be

**Unconstitutional:**
Status of any law, rule, caselaw decision, or regulation that goes outside the permitted bounds of government set out by the United States Constitution or a state constitution.

**Administrative Agencies:**
Agencies of the executive branch of federal and state governments.

**Administrative Law:**
Rules and regulations created by the administrative agencies.

## Sample List of Federal Administrative Agencies*

Advisory Council on Historic Preservation (ACHP)
www.achp.gov

African Development Foundation  www.adf.gov

Agency for International Development (USAID)
www.info.usaid.gov

American Battle Monuments Commission
www.abmc.gov

AMTRAK  www.amtrak.com

Appalachian Regional Commission  www.arc.gov

Architectural and Transportation Barriers Compliance
Board  www.access-board.gov

Ballistic Missile Defense Organization  www.mda.mil

Bureau of Alcohol, Tobacco, & Firearms
www.atf.treas.gov

Bureau of Arms Control
www.state.gov/www/global/arms/bureauac.html

Bureau of Engraving & Printing  www.bep.treas.gov

Bureau of Labor Statistics  www.bls.gov

Bureau of the Census  www.census.gov

Bureau of Transportation Statistics  www.bts.gov

Centers for Medicare and Medicaid Services
www.cms.gov

Central Intelligence Agency (CIA)  www.cia.gov

Chemical Safety and Hazard Investigations Board
(USCSB)  www.chemsafety.gov

Commission on Civil Rights  www.usccr.gov

Commodity Futures Trading Commission (CFTC)
www.cftc.gov

Consumer Product Safety Commission (CPSC)
www.cpsc.gov

Corporation For National Service (CNS)  www.cns.gov

Defense Advanced Research Projects Agency
www.darpa.mil

Defense Information Systems Agency  www.disa.mil

Defense Intelligence Agency  www.dia.mil

Defense Logistics Agency  www.supply.dla.mil

Defense Nuclear Facilities Safety Board
www.dnfsb.gov

Defense Security Service  www.dss.mil

Defense Threat Reduction Agency  www.dtra.mil

Drug Enforcement Administration
www.usdoj.gov/dea

Environmental Protection Agency (EPA)  www.epa.gov

Equal Employment Opportunity Commission
www.eeoc.gov

Export-Import Bank of the U.S.  www.exim.gov

Farm Credit Administration (FCA)  www.fca.gov

Federal Accounting Standards Advisory Board
www.fasab.gov

Federal Aviation Administration  www.faa.gov

Federal Bureau of Investigation  www.fbi.gov

Federal Communications Commission (FCC)
www.fcc.gov

Federal Deposit Insurance Corporation (FDIC)
www.fdic.gov

Federal Election Commission (FEC)  www.fec.gov

Federal Emergency Management Agency (FEMA)
www.fema.gov

Federal Energy Regulatory Commission
www.ferc.fed.us

Federal Highway Administration  www.fhwa.dot.gov

Federal Housing Finance Board (FHFB)
www.fhfb.gov

Federal Labor Relations Authority  www.flra.gov

Federal Maritime Commission  www.fmc.gov

Federal Mediation & Conciliation Service
www.fmcs.gov

Federal Mine Safety & Health Review Commission
www.fmshrc.gov

Federal Railroad Administration  www.fra.dot.gov

Federal Reserve System  www.federalreserve.gov

Federal Retirement Thrift Investment Board
www.frtib.gov

Federal Trade Commission (FTC)  www.ftc.gov

Food & Drug Administration  www.fda.gov

General Accounting Office  www.gao.gov

General Services Administration (GSA)  www.gsa.gov

Ginnie Mae  www.ginniemae.gov

Institute of Museum and Library Services
www.imls.gov

Inter-American Development Bank  www.iadb.org

Inter-American Foundation  www.iaf.gov

Internal Revenue Service  www.irs.ustreas.gov

International Bank for Reconstruction & Development
www.worldbank.org

International Labor Organization  www.us.ilo.org

International Monetary Fund  www.imf.org

International Trade Commission (USITC)
www.usitc.gov

Legal Services Corporation  www.lsc.gov

Medicare Payment Advisory Commission
www.medpac.gov

*from http://www.usa.gov/Agencies/Federal/All_Agencies/index.shtml

continued on next page >

Merit Systems Protection Board www.mspb.gov

National Aeronautics and Space Administration (NASA) www.nasa.gov

National Archives and Records Administration (NARA) www.nara.gov

National Bioethics Advisory Commission www.bioethics.gov

National Capital Planning Commission www.ncpc.gov

National Commission on Libraries and Information Science (NCLIS) www.nclis.gov

National Council on Disability (NCD) www.ncd.gov

National Credit Union Administration www.ncua.gov

National Endowment for the Arts http://arts.endow.gov

National Endowment for the Humanities www.neh.gov

National Geospatial-Intelligence Agency www.nga.mil

National Highway Traffic Safety Administration www.nhtsa.dot.gov

National Institute of Justice www.ojp.usdoj.gov/nij

National Institute of Mental Health www.nimh.nih.gov

National Institute of Standards & Technology www.nist.gov

National Institutes of Health www.nih.gov

National Labor Relations Board www.nlrb.gov

National Mediation Board www.nmb.gov

National Oceanic & Atmospheric Administration www.noaa.gov

National Park Service www.nps.gov

National Science Foundation (NSF) www.nsf.gov

National Security Agency (NSA) www.nsa.gov

National Skill Standards Board www.nssb.org

National Technology Transfer Center (NTTC) www.nttc.edu

National Telecommunications Information Administration www.ntia.doc.gov

National Transportation Safety Board www.ntsb.gov

Neighborhood Reinvestment Corporation www.nw.org

Nuclear Regulatory Commission (NRC) www.nrc.gov

Occupational Safety and Health Review Commission www.oshrc.gov

Office of Federal Housing Enterprise Oversight www.ofheo.gov

Office of Government Ethics www.usoge.gov

Office of Personnel Management (OPM) www.opm.gov

Office of Special Counsel www.osc.gov

Office of Thrift Supervision www.ots.treas.gov

Organization for Economic Cooperation & Development www.oecdwash.org

Organization of American States www.oas.org

Overseas Private Investment Corporation www.opic.gov

Pan American Health Organization www.paho.org

Patent & Trademark Office www.uspto.gov

Peace Corps www.peacecorps.gov

Pension Benefit Guaranty Corporation (PBGC) www.pbgc.gov

Postal Rate Commission www.prc.gov

Railroad Retirement Board (RRB) www.rrb.gov

Securities Exchange Commission (SEC) www.sec.gov

Securities Investor Protection Corp. www.sipc.org

Selective Service System (SSS) www.sss.gov

Small Business Administration (SBA) www.sba.gov

Smithsonian Institution www.si.edu

Social Security Administration (SSA) www.ssa.gov

Substance Abuse & Mental Health Services Administration www.samhsa.gov

Surface Transportation Board www.stb.dot.gov

Tennessee Valley Authority www.tva.gov

Trade and Development Agency www.tda.gov

U.S. Citizenship and Immigration Services www.uscis.gov/portal/site/uscis

U.S. Customs Service www.customs.gov

U.S. Fish and Wildlife Service www.fws.gov

U.S. Forest Service www.fs.fed.us

U.S. Government Printing Office www.gpo.gov

U.S. Institute of Peace www.usip.org

U.S. Marshals Service www.usdoj.gov/marshals/

U.S. Office of Government Ethics (USOGE) www.usoge.gov

U.S. Treasury www.treas.gov

United States Holocaust Memorial Council www.ushmm.org

United States Postal Service (USPS) www.usps.gov

United Nations Information Center www.unicwash.org

Voice of America (VOA) www.voa.gov

Walter Reed Army Medical Center www.wramc.amedd.army.mil

White House Commission on Remembrance www.remember.gov

White House Fellows www.whitehousefellows.gov

Women's History Commission www.gsa.gov/staff/pa/whc.htm

reported (what forms, to what address, by what deadline, and so forth). These new rules are laws—administrative laws—that must be obeyed by those affected by the laws.

The EPA in this is example is adding another layer of detail to the law. The law started with the small surface area of the Constitution, grew bigger with statutory law authorized by the Constitution, and now grows bigger still with administrative law authorized by the statutory law.

## Caselaw

Growing up out of the common law, **Caselaw** is judge-made law that fills in the blanks in all the other sources of law. Congress sometimes is not clear in its intent. Often new legal issues arise that were never contemplated by Congress or by state legislatures. In recent years, issues like same-sex marriage and adoption, surrogate motherhood, and the like all have made the front pages of the news as novel legal issues at the state level. And these issues, for the most part, had no statutory law or administrative law or clear constitutional guidance to help the parties involved come to a resolution of the question. So the courts in each of these cases have stepped in to clarify what the law actually is. In the process, that clarification—the court's holding—becomes law, too. That decision of the court that can be applied to other cases like it is called caselaw.

Courts also act as guardians to ensure that no statutory law or administrative rule or regulation is contrary to the constitution. See Chapter 2 for further discussion of this role of the courts.

**Caselaw:**
Judge-made law coming out of the common law tradition.

## FEDERALISM

One of the first issues that a business and its advisers must understand is that every transaction is subject to many different laws. Those laws come from multiple sources. The nature of U.S. government, with its system of **Federalism**, ensures that in any given transaction, at least two sets of laws apply—and maybe many more. Federalism is a system in which political and legal authority is split between a central government and other units of government that together make up the whole. In the United States, the national federal government headquartered in Washington, D.C., is the central government, and the 50 states (and the territories and District of Columbia) make up the lesser political units that are part of the national whole.

**Federalism:**
A governmental system in which political and legal authority is split between a central government and other units of government that together make up the whole.

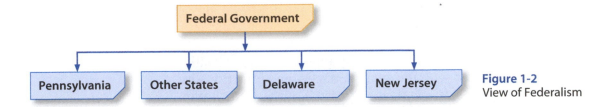

**Figure 1-2**
View of Federalism

## Federal Law

Federal law is the law made by the U.S. national government in Washington, D.C., and by its representative agencies and courts throughout the country. Remember that federal law stems from four sources—the Constitution; the statutory laws passed by Congress; the administrative rules and regulations written by agencies such as the Internal Revenue Service, the Federal Communications Commission, the Environmental Protection Agency, and the rest of the alphabet soup of federal agencies; and the judge-made caselaw to fill in the blanks in the other three primary sources of law.

Federal law virtually always applies to the entire country (with the exception of some federal district and circuit court decisions, discussed in Chapter 2). Thus, when Congress passes a statutory law, it will apply in essentially the same way to a Maine resident as to a Montana resident.

## State Law

State law is made by each of the 50 states. Each state has its own constitution, statutes passed by the state legislature, administrative rules and regulations made by state agencies, and caselaw generated by state courts. The important thing to note about state law is that it only applies in that particular state. Thus, Pennsylvania law has no bearing on Hawaii law, and California law has no impact on Tennessee law.

However, under the Full Faith and Credit Clause of the federal Constitution, "full faith and credit shall be given in each state to the public acts, records, and judicial proceedings of every other state." This means that certain actions recognized under the laws of one state are required by the Constitution to be recognized by the other states. For instance, if someone left her home state for a trip to Nevada, obtained a divorce there during the trip, and then returned to her home state, the home state would be obligated to recognize the divorce, even if the divorce would not have been valid under the home state's laws. The Full Faith and Credit Clause does not require one state to change its laws to match those of another, but it does require it to recognize most actions taken under another state's jurisdiction.

## Supremacy

The concept of **Supremacy** means that when federal law and state law are at odds with each other, federal law will control the situation—it is supreme—and state law will not be applied.

Many areas of the law are inherently federal, some are traditional state law subjects, and some areas of the law are governed both by state and by federal governments. For instance, military matters, diplomacy, treaties, postal service issues, securities law, foreign trade, and other areas like them are exclusively federal, and states rarely if ever are involved in lawmaking in these areas. Other matters, like family law (divorce and child custody, for instance, or the requirements to form a corporation in good standing in a given state) are almost always handled by the states themselves.

In other cases there is an overlap of jurisdiction. For instance, in many criminal matters a person could commit one illegal act and be found guilty of both a federal crime (prosecuted by the federal government) and a state crime (prosecuted by the relevant state).

It is important to understand this concept of federalism as it applies to business law—as federal law will be consistent across the country. State business law, although basically similar throughout the country, has important variations between jurisdictions. In practice, it is important to know that the law in state A is not necessarily the law in state B. The business owner or its legal advisers must act accordingly.

## Separation of Powers

At both the state and the federal level, there are three branches of government. All three have a role in the lawmaking process. The three branches are the **Executive Branch**, the **Legislative Branch**, and the **Judicial Branch**.

Traditionally, the legislative branch is the federal Congress or the state legislatures. The legislative branch makes the law, the executive branch enforces the law, and the judicial branch interprets the law.

However the reality is that the separation of powers doctrine blurs quite often, and each branch of the government ends up doing a little of the functions of another branch. For instance, the legislative branch (Congress) can only make statutory laws with the signature of the head of the executive branch (the President). The

**Supremacy:**
A legal concept under which federal law controls if federal and state law are in conflict.

**Executive Branch:**
The branch of government headed by the President at the national level and by governors at the state level. The executive branch is responsible for enforcing the laws.

**Legislative Branch:**
The branch of federal and state governments made up of Congress and the state legislatures, respectively. The legislative branch is responsible for making the laws.

**Judicial Branch:**
The branch of government made up of the courts at the state and federal levels. The judicial branch is responsible for interpreting existing law.

legislative branch also maintains oversight ("Congressional Oversight Committees," for instance) over executive branch agencies in some circumstances—thus keeping an eye on enforcement and the legislative functions exercised by the executive branch.

The executive branch, aside from enforcing the law, also makes law through a variety of tools. It makes law through the President's signing of or veto power over congressional bills. It makes law through the rules and regulations written by the administrative agencies (which are part of the executive branch). Those same administrative agencies have administrative law courts that act as informal courts within the agencies to decide matters before the matters go on to the judicial branch. The decisions by these administrative law courts also have the force of law.

The judicial branch is primarily meant to interpret the law made by the legislative and executive branches. It also ensures that none of the actions by these branches (or the courts) violate the Constitution. However, the judicial branch, by the very act of interpreting the law, creates new law, an inherently legislative function.

Thus, the lines between all three branches of government quickly become blurred. Where the lines lie can become the subject of controversy, too—both between the branches, and between political parties.

## CIVIL LAW

The law is divided into many different areas. The basic division is between **Civil Law** and criminal law. Civil law covers everyday activity, and violations of civil law are punished by fines, monetary damages, and other enforcement tools that do not involve the criminal court system of crime and punishment. An an act could violate both criminal law and civil laws at the same time. Civil law is meant to ensure the smooth functioning of the society by providing basic rules that all parties to any given transaction will know the other side will respect. And if the other party does not respect those rules, the harmed party can turn to the government to enforce the rules. Civil law is the foundation of business law and commerce in our society.

Of the many different areas of civil law, several directly affect business law and the legal environment of business. Among them are contract law; the Uniform Commercial Code and law of commercial paper; bankruptcy law; employment law; real property law; tort law; agency law; employment law; mergers, acquisitions, and antitrust law; and international law. Any and all of these areas of law could have an impact on a single business transaction.

**Civil Law:**
The law that governs the basic relationships between people and business in everyday noncriminal matters.

## ETHICAL ISSUES

● ● ●

Administrative agencies are by definition part of the executive branch that enforces the law. They also have rulemaking powers and even have their own courts within their agencies. Is it appropriate for these agencies to act in a legislative or judicial manner when they are part of another branch of government? Are there constitutional separation-of-powers issues involved, and how do administrative agencies address this potential problem? Do you see any ethical issues with this solution?

## CRIMINAL LAW

**Criminal Law** deals with crimes against society. Crimes are punishable by simple tools like fines (as in civil law), monetary restitution, probation, jail terms, and even death in some cases. Although this text does not deal with criminal law specifically, where criminal law is relevant it will be mentioned.

**Criminal Law:**
The law that governs the behavior of individuals and the safety of the society as a whole.

## CHAPTER SUMMARY

There are four major sources of law: Constitutional Law, Statutory Law, Administrative Law, and Caselaw. The United States operates under a federal system, where under the doctrine of supremacy the national federal government makes law for the entire nation, while individual states, within their borders, make law, too. When there is a conflict between state and federal law, federal law always controls. In both state and federal governments, there is a separation of powers between the legislative, executive, and judicial branches. However, the separation of powers between the branches is often blurred when one branch performs some of the functions of another. The law is also divided into the basic areas of civil and criminal law. It is important to understand the way in which all these areas of law function together and to determine what law applies in order to make appropriate business decisions.

### Relevant Web Sites

http://www.usa.gov/
http://www.usa.gov/Agencies/Federal/All_
   Agencies/index.shtml
http://www.whitehouse.gov/

http://www.senate.gov/
http://www.house.gov/

## Exercises

1. Find three administrative agencies at the federal level and three agencies at the state level in your state and describe what those agencies do.
2. Identify your federal senators and congressperson.
3. Identify the Chief Justice of the United States Supreme Court and of the supreme court of your state.
4. Search the Internet for a case in which a federal law has overridden a state law because of the doctrine of supremacy.
5. Identify two areas of law that are exclusively managed by your state government, and two areas of law that are exclusively managed by the federal government.
6. Find a real-world example of a dispute that would be classified as civil law. Find a real-world example of a dispute that would be classified as criminal law.
7. Explain in a one-page memorandum why a legal framework is necessary for a business to function successfully in a capitalist economy.
8. Explain in a one-page memorandum the importance of the common law and caselaw.
9. Explain what feature distinguishes the United States Constitution from all other foreign constitutions.
10. Explain the advantage of a federal government as opposed to a unitary government.

## Questions

1. What is the doctrine of supremacy?
2. What government (your state or the federal government) has the power to make treaties?
3. Is corporate formation usually governed by state or federal law?
4. What does it mean for a law to be "unconstitutional"?
5. What does it mean for administrative agencies to perform aspects of the executive, legislative, and judicial functions of government?

## Hypotheticals

1. The federal Congress passes a bill and the President signs it, creating a new statute. Several of the opponents of the new statute claim that the statute is beyond the power of the federal government. What type of legal argument should they make against the statute, and where should they make it? Why?
2. If California votes to legalize recreational marijuana use, and federal law states that such use is illegal, what is the status of users of recreational marijuana within California? Explain.
3. Martin receives his driver's license at age 16 in Pennsylvania, and then while he is still 16 he drives into New Jersey. In New Jersey the minimum driver's age is 17. Has he broken the law? Explain.
4. Your state legislature passes a statute signed by the governor that creates a new agency that is required to write rules regarding the use of widgets within the state. The agency has the power to impose fines for violations of the rules. The agency also holds hearings on the misuse of widgets. What branch of the government does the agency belong to? What types of powers is the agency exercising? Explain how this is or is not constitutional.
5. The governor of California goes on a trade junket to a foreign country, and after a successful trip announces a trade agreement. The trade agreement's terms provide that California and the foreign country will eliminate all tariffs on goods traded between them. Does California's governor have the authority enter into this trade deal? Explain.

## Sample Cases

1. Congress passed and the President signed the Controlled Substances Act, which criminalized the use or misuse of certain controlled drugs. Oregon passed its Death with Dignity Act, which allowed medical doctors to prescribe controlled drugs to terminally ill patients to end their lives, in contradiction to the provisions of the Controlled Substances Act. Was the

Controlled Substances Act meant to preempt Oregon's Act?

*Gonzales v. Oregon*, 546 U.S. 243 (2006).

2. The Environmental Protection Agency (EPA) maintained that it had no authority to regulate carbon dioxide as a pollutant under powers given to it by Congress in the Clean Air Act. Twelve states and some local governments sued the agency in order to require the agency to regulate carbon dioxide as a pollutant. Could the EPA be forced to regulate carbon dioxide under the Clean Air Act?

*Massachusetts v. Environmental Prot. Agency*, 549 U.S. 497 (2007).

## Key Terms

**Administrative Agencies:** Agencies of the executive branch of federal and state governments. The administrative agencies are charged with enforcing the laws created by the executive branch of the government. These agencies sometimes exercise judicial power, having their own courts. They also exercise legislative power when they draft administrative rules and regulations under the direction and oversight of the legislative branch.

**Administrative Law:** Rules and regulations created by the administrative agencies. These administrative laws cannot contradict statutory law or the constitution.

**Capitalism:** An economic system that relies on competition in the free market and on the private ownership of goods and the means of production of goods. The theory of capitalism relies on the reinvestment of profits combined with the competition that results because of the free market. This combination results in increases in wealth for the owners of the capital. Legal restraints on the early excesses of capitalism have tempered the extreme inequities that can and have resulted from unregulated capitalist behavior and have allowed the increase in wealth to spread from the owners of the means of production themselves to the society at large.

**Caselaw:** Judge-made law coming out of the common law tradition. The decision made by a judge in a court case serves as precedent for other cases like it within that same jurisdiction. In that way, later cases are treated in the same manner as prior cases. Caselaw also can interpret the constitution, statutory law, administrative law, and prior cases from the deciding court or courts that are of a lower rank than the deciding court.

**Civil Law:** One of two basic divisions of the law that governs the basic relationships between people and business in everyday activity. Violations of civil law are punished by fines, monetary damages, and other enforcement tools that do not involve the criminal court system of crime and punishment.

**Common Law:** A system of law originating in England in the medieval period that is derived from judicial decisions. It is the basis of the legal systems in most countries that were colonized by England, including the United States (except Louisiana—which had French roots), Canada (except Quebec—which also has French heritage), Australia, and New Zealand. The common law system relies on judge-made law from similar cases in similar circumstances, so that the law in the jurisdiction is applied in "common" to all.

**Congress:** The governing assembly of the U.S. federal government. Congress is composed of two houses, the House of Representatives and the Senate. Each state sends two senators to Congress. Each state also sends representatives to Congress based upon the state's population. Congress is created by the United States Constitution and is empowered to create statutory law.

**Constitution:** The foundational document of the federal government. State governments also have constitutions. The United States Constitution is unique in that it generally provides limits on what the federal government can do, and it provides that all other rights, including the rights specifically listed in the Bill of Rights (the first ten Amendments to the Constitution), belong to the people (private individuals and state governments). All laws passed in the United States must conform to the limits of the Constitution, else they are unconstitutional and cannot be enforced.

**Criminal Law:** One of two basic divisions of the law that governs the behavior of individuals and the safety of the society as a whole. Violations of criminal law are punishable by fines, probation, community service, imprisonment, and even death, depending on the severity of the crime.

**Executive Branch:** The branch of government headed by the President at the national level and by governors at the state level. The executive branch is responsible for enforcing the laws.

**Federalism:** A governmental system in which political and legal authority is split between a central government and other units of government that together make up the whole. In the United States power is split between the 50 states and the national federal government.

**Judicial Branch:** The branch of government made up of the courts at the state and federal levels. The judicial branch is responsible for interpreting existing law, although the very act of interpreting the law makes new caselaw.

**Legislative Branch:** The branch of federal and state governments made up of Congress and the state legislatures, respectively. The legislative branch is responsible for making the laws.

**Statutory Law:** Law created by the governing assembly of the federal government or a state government.

**Supremacy:** A legal concept under which federal law controls if federal and state law are in conflict.

**Unconstitutional:** Status of any law, rule, caselaw decision, or regulation that goes outside the permitted bounds of government set out by the United States Constitution or a state constitution. Unconstitutional laws, rules, caselaw, and regulations are not enforceable.

# The U.S. Court System

## INTRODUCTION

The U.S. court system is one of the three branches of government. The court system forms the judicial branch of government. The other two branches are the executive and legislative branches. Each of the three branches, however, exercises some of the powers of the other two branches. It is very important to understand the relationship of the judicial branch to the government as a whole. It is also crucial to grasp the functions of the judicial branch internally in order to have a clear picture of this interrelationship.

## THE PLAYERS IN A LAWSUIT

Each person in a lawsuit has a role to play. A **Lawsuit**, or case, is a real-world matter heard before a court, wherein one side is seeking money or property—or in some criminal cases, imprisonment—from the other side. U.S. courts do not issue **Advisory Opinions**, which are opinions about hypothetical situations ("Judge, what do you think would be the result if this happened someday?"). Instead, U.S. courts only take, hear, and decide a case if there is a **Matter in Controversy**. In other words, the court only acts on real cases.

**Lawsuit:**
A matter that is heard before a court, wherein one side is seeking damages from, or punishment of, the other side.

**Advisory Opinions:**
Hypothetical opinions issued by courts when there is no matter in controversy. U.S. courts do not issue advisory opinions.

**Matter in Controversy:**
A real-world issue for a court to decide in a lawsuit.

17

The **Judge**—or Justice, as a judge is called at the highest-level court in a jurisdiction—is generally considered to be the "umpire" of the case. The judge makes sure that each side follows the rules. The judge also makes **Rulings** about issues of law that come up during the case. That is, the judge decides if X law applies, or Y law, or if a particular statement can be heard by the jury, or if that bit of evidence must be excluded. In almost all cases the judge does not decide the facts of the case—he or she merely guides the process of finding the facts. But the rulings the judge makes about the law become law themselves that can be used in future cases.

The **Jury** is an old institution—one that is specifically mentioned in concept in the **Magna Carta**. Juries are "triers of fact." The concept behind the jury is that anyone accused of a civil or criminal transgression has the right to be listened to, to be heard, by his or her peers. Initially intended as a right for nobility, the right expanded over time to include the entire population. The term **Peers**, today, usually means people of legal age who are randomly selected from the community in which the court has jurisdiction. As triers of fact, juries determine just that—facts. They decide, for example, if person A ran a red light, or person B intentionally killed another person, or if business C intentionally dumped toxic waste in a marine sanctuary. They are guided through this process by the judge's rulings of law as the "umpire."

The procedural system for trying lawsuits in the United States and in most countries that came from the English tradition is the **Adversary System. Attorneys** are advocates for the two sides in any given lawsuit—or for multiple sides in those lawsuits that have more than two parties. As an illustration of the latter, think of a multiple-car collision, or a contract dispute involving four companies. In these cases each party to the collision or the contract is represented by a different attorney. The attorney's job is to best represent his or her client's positions before the judge and the jury. The attorney presents the legal arguments that are best for the client to the judge and presents the best factual arguments for the client's case to the

**Judge:**
An officer of the court who acts as the "umpire" of a case, in order to ensure that procedure is properly followed and the law is enforced.

**Rulings:**
Decisions issued by a judge regarding issues of law that come up during the case.

**Jury:**
The finders of fact in a lawsuit.

**Magna Carta:**
A "great charter" signed in 1215 by John of England that granted, among other rights and privileges, the right to judgment of the accused by a jury of peers.

**Peers:**
In a legal context, those on a jury drawn from a representative group of the citizenry of legal age and without a legal disability (a felony conviction, for example) in the jurisdiction where the trial takes place.

**Adversary System:**
The procedural system for trying lawsuits in which each side through its attorney presents its respective legal case in the best possible light to the judge and jury as neutral decision makers.

**Attorneys:**
The professional advocates for one side or the other in a legal transaction or lawsuit. Attorneys, like judges, are officers of the court. They are subject to a code of ethics and legal restrictions on their advocacy. For instance, they may not knowingly lie, they may not misrepresent law or facts, and they may not assist in the commission of a crime or its cover-up.

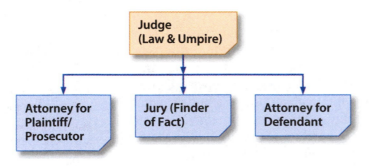

**Figure 2-1**
Roles in a Lawsuit

jury. Attorneys are required to comply with a **Code of Ethics**. They cannot lie, misrepresent the law, or hide **Evidence** from the judge, jury, or other side of the lawsuit.

This does not mean that an attorney cannot argue cases that he or she personally finds to be distasteful. So long as there is a reasonable basis for the position taken by the attorney on behalf of his or her client, the attorney may take and argue and defend that position, regardless of the attorney's personal beliefs.

In arguing their clients' positions in a lawsuit, attorneys present evidence to the judge and jury. Relevant evidence is evidence that will help prove or disprove an issue presented in a case. But not all relevant evidence is admissible. That is, not all evidence will be considered by a judge or jury in a trial. Only evidence that is permitted by the rules of evidence is admitted. Admissible evidence is made up of the facts, figures, objects, and testimony that a judge and jury are permitted to consider when making a decision about a case.

As discussed above, there are at least two sides in every lawsuit. At the criminal level, the **Prosecutor** is the representative of the government on one side of the lawsuit. The government, on behalf of the people of the jurisdiction, brings criminal charges against the **Defendant**. In criminal cases, the defendant is the business entity (for example, a corporation) or the person who is accused of breaking a criminal law or causing damages to the plaintiff in a particular case. At the civil level, the **Plaintiff** is a person, business entity, or even the government bringing a civil claim that alleges that the plaintiff was harmed in some noncriminal way that requires compensation. There is also a defendant in civil cases—the person or entity accused of causing the wrongs against the plaintiff.

## CAUSES OF ACTION

A plaintiff or prosecutor may not bring a lawsuit against a defendant for frivolous reasons. This happens, of course, but the legal process is designed to try to weed out these **Strike Suits**. There is an old saying that "you can sue anyone for anything." That is true. But getting a lawsuit through the court system all the way past judge and jury to a positive result for the plaintiff's side in the lawsuit is a different matter altogether.

Each lawsuit brought by a plaintiff or prosecutor must have a **Cause of Action**. A cause of action is, really, a preapproved reason to sue that is set out by caselaw or statutory law. For instance, if the law states that a plaintiff may successfully recover money damages for a breach of contract if the plaintiff proves A, B, and C, the plain-

**Code of Ethics:**
A code, sometimes called a code of professional conduct, for attorneys that requires them to operate with strict limits on behavior in order to maintain the integrity of the legal profession, the legal process, and the legal system itself.

**Evidence:**
Facts that are related to a case.

**Prosecutor:**
An attorney who acts as the representative of the government in bringing criminal actions against defendants as a part of the adversary system.

**Defendant:**
The party who is accused of breaking a criminal law or causing civil damages to the plaintiff.

**Plaintiff:**
The party (either the government or a private person) who brings a civil lawsuit to court for the redress of damages.

**Strike Suits:**
A term used for baseless lawsuits.

**Cause of Action:**
A recognized reason to sue.

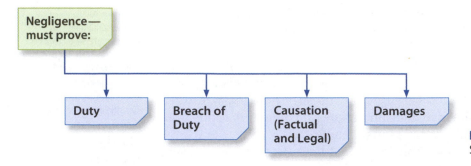

**Figure 2-2**
Sample Cause of Action

tiff must **Allege** facts when he or she first goes to court in a breach of contract action. That is, the plaintiff must make claims of facts that if proven, will meet the requirements of A, B, and C. The facts of the particular cause of action must be alleged properly to get into court—and to stay in court. In order to actually win at the end of the case, the plaintiff must prove those alleged facts. There are hundreds of causes of action. They vary by state, but books are available in each jurisdiction that are filled with each of the elements of the causes of action available in a given jurisdiction.

**Allege:**
To assert that a given fact is true or false.

## BURDEN OF PROOF

The standard on **Burden of Proof** in U.S. court systems is that it lies with the plaintiff or prosecutor. That is, in a criminal case a criminal defendant in almost all cases never has to prove that he or she did not do something illegal. The prosecutor must prove that the defendant *did* commit an alleged act. In almost all civil cases the plaintiff must also prove that a fact occurred. For instance, in a breach of contract case a plaintiff needs to prove that a contract was breached by the defendant. The defendant does not need to prove that she did not breach the contract. Of course, a strong defense is advisable, but the tough job of proof falls squarely on the shoulders of the party who is bringing the lawsuit. There are some limited circumstances (for example, in many tax cases) in which the burden of proof is on the defendant. But these are exceptions to the general rule.

**Burden of Proof:**
A term used to describe a party's duty to prove any given element of a cause of action.

## STANDARDS OF PROOF

There are **Standards of Proof** that must be met in order for a plaintiff or prosecutor to be successful in a lawsuit. The standard of proof varies based on the type of lawsuit.

**Standards of Proof:**
A term describing the balancing test required to determine if the side holding the burden of proof on any given element of a case has actually met that burden.

In civil cases, the standard of proof is generally **Preponderance of the Evidence**. That is, a plaintiff in a lawsuit must prove each element of a cause of action (for example, breach of contract or negligence) by the preponderance of the evidence. What does this mean? It means that a jury, when it looks at all the facts laid before it at the trial, must find that at least 50.1 percent (just over half) of the evidence for every single element of any given single cause of action points in the factual direction that the plaintiff needs it to point in order for the plaintiff to win the lawsuit. Because multiple causes of action may be brought in any given lawsuit, a plaintiff may lose on some causes of action by not meeting the burden of proof, but still win the lawsuit by proving other causes of action instead.

In criminal cases, the standard of proof is **Beyond a Reasonable Doubt.** The beyond a reasonable doubt standard sets a very high bar. Essentially, it means that a prosecutor in a criminal case must prove that all the elements of a given crime (for example, embezzlement) actually occurred, and that no reasonable person could doubt that they occurred. This standard is much higher than the 50.1 percent standard of a civil case. Although there is no percentage found in the law to use for determining guilt beyond a reasonable doubt, a good unofficial rule of thumb is that a prosecutor needs to prove that it is 99 percent likely that the crimes that the prosecutor say were committed by the defendant actually were committed.

Note, however, the word *reasonable*. **Reasonable** is a word that occurs multiple times in the law. It is key. Is it *possible* that a given criminal defendant accused of embezzlement didn't actually commit the alleged crime despite overwhelming evidence that he did so, and that space aliens from Mars actually spirited in and stole the embezzled funds? Yes. Is a reasonable person going to believe that claim? No. There are millions of possible explanations that could be used to explain away any alleged criminal's guilt. But only a few may be reasonable.

There is a third standard—that of **Clear and Convincing Evidence.** The clear and convincing evidence standard lies between the

**Preponderance of the Evidence:**
A balancing test used in most civil cases whereby plaintiffs have met the standard of proof if 50.1 percent of the evidence on a given issue points in their favor.

**Beyond a Reasonable Doubt:**
A balancing test used in criminal cases whereby the prosecution has met the standard of proof if all of the evidence on a given issue supports the prosecution's argument, with no room for a reasonable person to doubt the prosecution's version of events.

**Reasonable:**
A term used to describe what a common person, at that place, at that time, would consider to be plausible and logical.

**Clear and Convincing Evidence:**
A balancing test used in certain high-stakes civil cases whereby plaintiffs have met the standard of proof if a strong majority of the evidence on a given issue is in their favor.

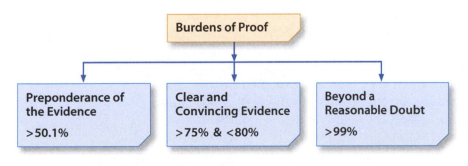

**Figure 2-3**
Burdens of Proof

preponderance of the evidence standard and the beyond a reasonable doubt standard. It is used in civil cases in many states when the stakes of the lawsuit are especially important—for example, in cases involving fraud or will contests. It is a standard of proof that requires the jury—the "trier of fact"—to be convinced that not only does the majority of the evidence point in one direction or another but also that the evidence is convincing in a particular direction, that it is highly probable or reasonably certain. Even though there is no percentage test for the clear and convincing evidence standard, it is easy to visualize it as a 75 percent to 80 percent test—where the preponderance of the evidence test is at 50.1 percent, the beyond a reasonable doubt test is at 99 percent, and this standard is in the middle of the other two.

## COURT STRUCTURES

There are at least 52 court structures in the United States (the reality is that there are many more than that). Each of the 50 states, the District of Columbia, and the national federal government all have individual, independent judicial branches with their own court structures. Virtually all of these court systems are set up in a similar manner.

It is easiest to understand the court system by reviewing the federal courts first, and then extrapolating to the states. In the federal court system, as in all court systems, there is one **Court of Original Jurisdiction.** A court of original jurisdiction is the court that first hears a case when it enters the judicial system.

**Court of Original Jurisdiction:**
The court in a jurisdiction that first hears a lawsuit. A court of original jurisdiction is a trial court.

There are usually courts below the courts of original jurisdiction—for example, traffic courts, and justices of the peace—but such courts have very limited authority, and in cases coming before these courts, there is an automatic appeal right from the court's decision, and the lower court's decision plays no role in the lawmaking procedure discussed here.

These courts of original jurisdiction are always **Trial Courts**. In the federal system they are called District Courts. Trial courts are typically composed of a judge and a jury. Before them appear advocates (attorneys) for both sides, and the plaintiffs and defendants in any case. Trial courts are the courts that most people think of when they think of "court," or when they watch law-related movies and television shows. Generally the trial courts are the first to hear any given case. Some minor cases are heard by lower courts such as justices of the peace, district magistrates, traffic courts, and similar courts.

**Trial Court:**
A court, typically composed of a judge and a jury, that tries both law and fact. It is the court of original jurisdiction in almost all cases.

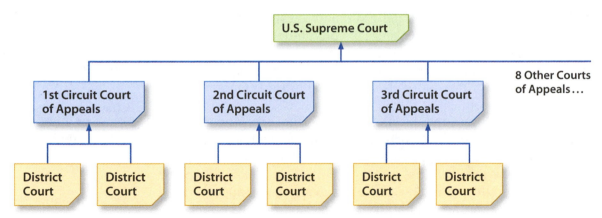

U.S. Supreme Court

8 Other Courts
of Appeals...

1st Circuit Court
of Appeals

2nd Circuit Court
of Appeals

3rd Circuit Court
of Appeals

District
Court

District
Court

District
Court

District
Court

District
Court

District
Court

**Figure 2-4**
Schematic of Federal
Court Scheme

As noted previously, the judge decides issues of law both before and during the trial, and except in nonjury trials—which are rare and are usually requested by a criminal defendant—the jury decides issues of fact. This distinction is very important in the court system.

At its most basic level, a jury's finding of fact is not something that can be changed later on in the process by an **Appeal**—a request to a higher court to reconsider all or part of a lower court's decision. That is why, for example, if a jury decides in a criminal case that a corporation accused of a certain crime actually did not commit the crime based on certain facts, that is the end of the subject. What the jury says happened, for all legal intents and purposes, happened. It might not be what *actually* happened, but for legal purposes it is presumed to be the truth.

**Appeal:**
A request to a higher court by an aggrieved party in a lawsuit to correct errors of law made by the judge at the lower court.

The decisions of the judge in a trial court are focused on the implementation and interpretation of the law. In making those decisions and interpreting the law, there are times when the judge is incorrect. When the judge makes mistakes, the judge's decisions are appealable to the next higher court in the judicial system. What this means is that one of the parties in a lawsuit can go to the next higher court (pursuant to certain time limits and other rules) and tell the court that, for example, the judge made a mistake of law that compromised the party's case, or that the judge mistakenly kept information from the jury that would have led the jury to decide the facts in a different way.

Furthermore, in this way the findings of facts by a jury can also be overturned in many cases. The findings of fact are not questioned in and of themselves, but the basis for the jury's findings of facts—evidence and legal rulings by the judge—is questioned.

There is an important exception to this rule—if a criminal defendant is found "not guilty" (no one is ever found "innocent" by a jury), there is a constitutional prohibition against trying that defendant twice for the same crime. This prohibition is called the rule against **Double Jeopardy** and is a constitutional protection provided in the Bill of Rights. So, if an obviously guilty criminal defendant is found factually "not guilty" by a jury, the prosecution has few, if any, grounds for appeal of the jury's decision.

In short the loser (and it is almost always the loser who appeals) of a lawsuit who can allege (claim) that a judge made errors of law in the lawsuit can then ask the next higher court up the appeals chain to review those alleged errors. The **Appeals Court** will review all the appropriate evidence, and make a decision. An appeals court will not review the facts as a jury has decided them, because the judges on these courts are also only dealing with legal rulings.

Appeals courts have no juries. They do not hear testimony from witnesses. In most cases a panel of three judges selected from the many (sometimes 11 or 12) judges on that appeals court will sit in a courtroom, hear lawyers for both sides argue their cases regarding the particular issue that is being appealed, review the record of the trial court, and then make a decision several months later. It is a far different atmosphere than that in a trial court. If a question before the court is especially important, all the judges on that court will sit and hear the case (not just three) and decide the case "en banc."

In the federal system the district courts are all part of one of 11 numbered **Circuit Courts** or the District of Columbia Circuit. Each of these circuit courts is the first avenue of appeal for the district courts in its geographical area. The U.S. Court of Appeals for the Federal Circuit also hears appeals from the district courts as well as other appeals, but its jurisdiction is based on subject matter, not geographic location. Decisions of each of the circuit courts are all appealable to the United States Supreme Court. The Supreme Court's jurisdiction covers the entire United States.

## LAW AND EQUITY

Historically, there was a difference between **Courts of Law** and **Courts of Equity**. Courts of law were run by the King in England. Their primary solution to disputes in civil cases was the award of money damages to one side or the other. Courts of equity were usually run by the church in England. Their primary tool in lawsuits was the award of property.

However, as time went on, it became clear that the appropriate relief in any given lawsuit might be either legal or equitable remedies. Sometimes money damages were in order, but at other

**Double Jeopardy:**
Being prosecuted twice for the same alleged crime, prohibited by the Fifth Amendment to the U.S. Constitution. The clause reads: "nor shall any person be subject for the same offence to be twice put in jeopardy of life or limb."

**Appeals Court:**
A court superior to the court of original jurisdiction in any given court structure. The appeals court hears issues of law, not facts. It has no jury, and it decides matters by the majority vote of multiple judges hearing the case.

**Circuit Courts:**
The appeals-level courts in the federal court system.

**Courts of Law:**
Courts historically controlled by the king in England. Law courts generally gave money damages in civil lawsuits.

**Courts of Equity:**
Courts historically controlled by the church in England. Equity courts generally gave other forms of legal relief besides money in lawsuits (for example, injunctions, property, etc.).

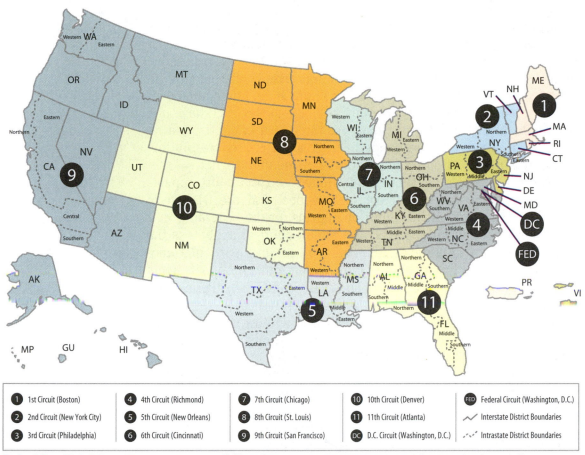

| | | | | |
|---|---|---|---|---|
| **1** 1st Circuit (Boston) | **4** 4th Circuit (Richmond) | **7** 7th Circuit (Chicago) | **10** 10th Circuit (Denver) | **FED** Federal Circuit (Washington, D.C.) |
| **2** 2nd Circuit (New York City) | **5** 5th Circuit (New Orleans) | **8** 8th Circuit (St. Louis) | **11** 11th Circuit (Atlanta) | Interstate District Boundaries |
| **3** 3rd Circuit (Philadelphia) | **6** 6th Circuit (Cincinnati) | **9** 9th Circuit (San Francisco) | **DC** D.C. Circuit (Washington, D.C.) | Intrastate District Boundaries |

Derived from United States Government map available at http://www.uscourts.gov/uscourts/images/CircuitMap.pdf

**Figure 2-5**
Circuit Court Map

times property damages, or an injunction, or something else besides cash was appropriate. So in the United States most courts have been consolidated into courts of law and equity, so that the courts may hear many different kinds of cases, and have the power to provide many different solutions to any given problem that comes before the court. Of course, specialized courts are still available in certain types of cases. Tax and bankruptcy courts are specialized, as are chancery courts in some states. Chancery courts hear business-related cases. Admiralty courts hear cases that involve ships, shipping, and transportation.

## FEDERALISM AND COURTS

Federalism, the division of power among the states and the federal government, plays a role in the court system, too. It works on two levels, at both the federal level and the state level.

At the federal level, each district court has geographical jurisdiction over a specific area of the country. As the federal court of original jurisdiction in a given region, the district court hears, with a few minor exceptions, all the federal cases that arise in that geographical area. Some district courts cover an entire state, and some cover smaller areas. For instance, Delaware and New Jersey each have one federal district court. Pennsylvania has three district courts. Generally, the decisions that are made in the district courts are binding within that district, but are not binding outside that district.

The first appeals courts that hear federal district court appeals are the 11 numbered circuit courts of appeal and the District of Columbia Circuit. The U.S. Court of Appeals for the Federal Circuit hears cases for certain subjects. The circuit court of appeals is the appeals court for multiple district courts within in a particular geographical area. For example, the Third Circuit Court of Appeals hears appeals from the district courts in Delaware, New Jersey, Pennsylvania, and the U.S. Virgin Islands. Circuit court decisions are binding only on other courts in that circuit. This is why in a famous case in the early 2000s the Ninth Circuit Court of Appeals could decide that the reference to "under God" in the Pledge of Allegiance was unconstitutional, but that decision had an impact only on the states that were part of the Ninth Circuit. The rest of the country was not immediately affected.

The appeals court for decisions of all circuit courts is the U.S. Supreme Court. Its decisions, as noted above, are binding on the entire nation. The Supreme Court is the only court in the federal system that is established by the Constitution. The only cases the Supreme Court is required to hear are those regarding foreign ambassadors (that does not happen often) and disputes between states. One of the most recent disputes between states was a legal battle between New Jersey and New York over which state owned Ellis Island in New York Harbor. The Supreme Court was required to hear that case.

The Supreme Court is granted jurisdiction by Congress to hear the appeals from the lower federal courts, which Congress has created. But it is not required to hear these cases from the lower courts. Instead, appeals from the circuit courts are heard at the Supreme Court's discretion. The appealing litigant in a case files a **Writ of Certiorari**, which is basically a request to the Supreme Court to hear that case. The Supreme Court either decides to take the case ("grants cert") or declines to take the case ("denies cert").

**Writ of Certiorari:**
A formal request to the United States Supreme Court to hear a case.

Usually, the Supreme Court hears a very small percentage of the cases that are appealed to it. Most of the cases that are heard deal with legal issues that suffer from a "split in the circuits," where different U.S. circuit courts have decided differently on the same legal issue. In those cases, federal law is different in different regions of the country. The Supreme Court's decision then clarifies the law for the entire country. At other times the Court hears cases that have piqued the interest of the justices (as the judges are called on the Supreme Court) or that involve new issues of law. This choice is entirely discretionary by the Court and is a decision made by the justices themselves.

There are nine justices on the United States Supreme Court, and generally—absent sickness or a conflict of interest—all nine justices participate in every case the Court hears. All federal judges, in order to avoid outside public pressure on their decisions in individual cases, are nominated by the President, confirmed by the United States Senate, and serve for life unless they are impeached and removed for "high crimes and misdemeanors," an exceedingly rare occurrence.

This structure is essentially the same in each and every state. Most states have three levels of courts, starting with a court of original jurisdiction that functions as a trial court, and at least one and usually two layers of appeals courts above the trial courts.

There is an instance where federalism affects the state court system: State courts handle questions of law for their own state, usually working from the bottom at county-level trial courts up to statewide supreme courts. A state supreme court is the "court of last resort"—that is, the court with final say on issues of state law in that state. Those state law decisions only apply in that state. Idaho has little concern about the decisions of a state court in Wyoming. However, state courts sometimes hear cases that involve both state law and federal law. If the case begins in the state courts, after the state supreme court rules on the case, it is possible to appeal to the federal system regarding the federal law involved in the case. Therefore, it is possible to have multiple courts at both the state and the federal level successively involved in any given case.

## CASELAW AND PRECEDENT

> *It is a maxim among these lawyers, that whatever hath been done before, may legally be done again: and therefore they take special care to record all the decisions formerly made against common justice and the general reason of Mankind.*
> —**Jonathan Swift** in *Gulliver's Travels* (1726)

The reason that all of the previous discussion is important is that when judges sitting and deciding real-world cases make decisions of law, they are interpreting, clarifying, and filling in the blanks in the law that already exist. These new decisions of law are caselaw. This new caselaw is reported in **Legal Reporters** that are accessible to both legal professionals and the general public.

The new law that is developed by the court in its opinion is called the court's "holding." News listeners and watchers actually hear of new court holdings in everyday news reports. A news program might report, "The Supreme Court decided that the death penalty cannot be administered to people who committed their crimes under the age of 18." Note that statement. There is nothing included in it about the particular case at issue, or what happened in that case, although the assumption can be made that someone younger than 18 committed a crime, was convicted and sentenced to death, and then appealed the case. What is included is the precedent— what the public and legal professionals can use in later cases that involve children under age 18 who are accused of capital crimes. Because this was a United States Supreme Court case, it applies to the entire country.

Caselaw is used as **Precedent** in future cases with similar issues. The courts, later on, can use those decisions made by prior courts in prior lawsuits as decision-making tools. The relationship between precedent, federalism, and the structure of the courts is important. If a legal finding is made by the highest court in the jurisdiction, it applies to the entire jurisdiction. Therefore, state or federal Supreme Court cases apply to the entire state or country, respectively. All lower courts in that jurisdiction must follow the higher court's decision as law.

If, however, the caselaw stems from a lower court in a jurisdiction, generally it is binding on all courts in that jurisdiction. But caselaw precedent can be **Overruled** by courts at the same level or above in that jurisdiction or, in the case of state cases, by a federal decision to the contrary in the federal circuit in which the state court sits or by the United States Supreme Court.

Another important concept is **Judicial Review,** under which the courts review statutes, administrative rules and regulations, and other acts of government when those laws are brought before them in a lawsuit. The courts review these laws to determine if they violate the Constitution. The limits of judicial review are always controversial, but the basic theory behind it is a long-established part of U.S. constitutional law.

Court decisions from other states are not mandatory law in any given state. Rather, they are **Persuasive Law**. Although the courts in a state may look to what courts in other states have done, there is no requirement that they follow those other states' decisions. For

**Legal Reporters:**
Books that contain written opinions of appeals courts that may be used as precedent in later cases.

**Precedent:**
A legal decision that binds later courts in certain circumstances to follow the logic and legal holdings of a previous court in the interests of fairness, justice, and clarity.

**Overruled:**
A term used to describe the overturning or setting aside of precedent from one court, when it is voided and replaced by another precedent from the same or a higher-level court.

**Judicial Review:**
The power of the courts to review statutes, administrative rules and regulations, and other acts of government.

**Persuasive Law:**
Precedent that a court is not required to observe as binding law. In most cases persuasive law originates in another state.

## ETHICAL ISSUES

● ● ●

In an adversary system, in which there are attorneys whose duty is to advocate the best case for their client, there is always a tension between the need to present a client's case in a winning light and the ethical obligation not to lie, misrepresent the law, or hide evidence from the judge, jury, or other side of the lawsuit. How does the adversarial system create ethical dilemmas for attorneys in the courtroom, especially when the law and facts are clearly against their clients?

instance, when surrogate motherhood became an issue in the late 1980s, as new technology became available, many governments just did not have any statutory laws "on the books" or guiding caselaw precedent to provide relevant answers. So, as real controversies erupted, it fell to state courts to fill in the blanks. For example, state courts in New Jersey's famous "Baby M" case looked to California to see what that state's courts had done. It was guidance—New Jersey was not required to follow California's lead.

One of the skills of using caselaw is to be able to distinguish precedent from the facts of a given case. Say, for example, that precedent exists that is very harmful to a particular legal position. A skilled advocate will argue that in some way that precedent does not apply in this case or that is should be applied differently. Why? Because that apparent precedent only applied on Tuesdays during a Blue Moon, or it only applied to adults, not minors. Will an advocate always be successful? No—but the ability to distinguish precedent from the case at hand is a necessary part of the refinement of the law and of the adversary process.

## CHAPTER SUMMARY

The U.S. court system is one of the three branches of government: the judicial, executive, and legislative branches. A lawsuit is a real-world matter in controversy that is heard before a court. The judge issues rulings and ensures that all sides follow the rules. Juries are "triers of fact" in the case. There is always a plaintiff or prosecutor and a defendant. In this adversary system, attorneys are advocates for each side in a lawsuit.

Each lawsuit must be based on a cause of action, which is a reason to sue. The burden of proof usually lies with the party bringing the lawsuit. The standard of proof in most civil lawsuits is preponderance of the evidence. In some civil cases the standard is clear and convincing evidence. In criminal cases the standard is beyond a reasonable doubt. A court of original jurisdiction is the court that first hears a case when it enters the judicial system. These trial courts try both facts and law and have judges and juries. An appeal is a request to a higher-level court to reconsider all or part of a lower court's decision through the process of judicial review. Criminal cases in which the defendant is found not guilty are not appealable because of the principle of double jeopardy. Appeals courts have no juries and legal questions before them are decided by panels of judges. These appellate judges do not hear testimony from witnesses. There are multiple levels of courts in any jurisdiction. Most courts have been consolidated into courts of law and equity.

Federalism is important to understand, because it relates to the value of a case decision in a particular jurisdiction. New caselaw is reported in legal reporters that are accessible to both legal professionals and the general public. Caselaw is then used as precedent in future cases with similar issues. Precedent can be overruled by courts at the same level or above in a particular jurisdiction or by a federal decision in the federal circuit that encompasses that jurisdiction.

## Relevant Web Sites

http://www.uscourts.gov/Home.aspx
http://www.supremecourt.gov/
http://www.courtinfo.ca.gov/courts/supreme/
http://www.courts.state.pa.us/T/SupremeCourt/

## Exercises

1. Find the Web site for the judicial system in your state. Describe how the court system is structured in your state.
2. List all the current members of the United States Supreme Court.
3. Determine which federal circuit court has jurisdiction over your hometown.
4. Find an example of precedent from the United States Supreme Court that was later overturned by another Supreme Court case.
5. Find an example of a case in which a court provided relief in the form of both money and equitable damages.
6. List the elements of any civil cause of action in your state.
7. Determine what the court of original jurisdiction is at the state level for the area where your college is located.
8. Describe the role of the judge in a lawsuit.
9. Describe the role of a jury in a lawsuit.
10. Describe the role of the attorneys in a lawsuit.

## Questions

1. What is an advantage of the adversary system? What is a disadvantage?
2. What is the importance of federalism in the United States court system?
3. Why are courts permitted to be flexible, and how do they do it, if they are required to follow precedent?
4. Does the concept of judicial interpretation of all the law mean that the judges can make whatever law they wish? Explain.
5. Why are there different standards of proof for different types of cases?

## Hypotheticals

1. Emma is a criminal defendant. She appeals her conviction through her state court system all the way to the state supreme court, where her lawyers claim that her rights under both the state and federal constitutions were violated by the prosecution at her original trial. The state supreme court rules against her in finding that her rights were not violated. Does Emma have any further way to appeal? Explain.
2. The Eleventh Circuit Court of Appeals makes a ruling that directly affects what types of evidence are admissible in civil trials involving automobile accidents. To what states does that ruling apply? Why does it not apply in other states? Explain.
3. Reese is suing Logan for breach of contract because of a business deal that failed. What standard of proof should be used in the decision-making process in this case? Explain.
4. Hannah represents a client in a lawsuit. She finds two older cases that are very similar to her client's case. In those cases the court clearly lays out what the law is under the circumstances. Hannah checks, and both cases are good law. That is, the caselaw has not be overturned or superseded. One case is from the mid-level appeals court in Hannah's state, and one case is from the Supreme Court of a neighboring state. What case should Hannah use? Why?
5. Tessa kills a fellow motorist in an accident. She is tried by the state for manslaughter as the state claims that she acted criminally in causing the accident. The victim's family also sues Tessa for wrongful death in civil court. Tessa is found not guilty by the jury in the state criminal trial, but she is found liable by the jury in the civil trial. Both juries heard the same evidence. What legal concept can explain how the civil and criminal juries arrived at different verdicts? Please describe.

## Sample Cases

1. Philip Beachey was ticketed by a Pennsylvania police officer for flashing his high beams in daylight in order to warn oncoming traffic of a police traffic checkpoint. He was cited for violating 75 Pa. Cons. Stat. §4306(a), which provides that "[w]henever a driver of a vehicle approaches an oncoming vehicle within 500 feet, the driver shall use the low beam of light." Beachey claimed that the state legislature did not include "flashing" in the statute, and therefore it did not apply to him. Was he correct in his interpretation? Why or why not?

*Commonwealth v. Beachey*, 698 A.2d 1325 (Pa. Super. Ct. 1997).

2. Philip Beachey appealed the Pennsylvania Superior Court's decision to uphold his original conviction for flashing his high beams in daylight in order to warn oncoming traffic of a police traffic checkpoint. He argued that 75 Pa. Cons. Stat. §4306(a), which provides that "[w]henever a driver of a vehicle approaches an oncoming vehicle within 500 feet, the driver shall use the low beam of light," cannot be logically read without looking at another Pennsylvania statute, 75 Pa. Cons. Stat. §4302, which requires headlights only at night and during bad weather. Beachey claimed that the state legislature could not have meant for 75 Pa. Cons. Stat. §4306(a)'s prohibition against high beams to apply in daylight, because headlights are only required at night and in bad weather, and the high beams could not have blinded anyone in daylight. Was he correct in his interpretation? Why or why not? How does this case relate to the Superior Court version of the case discussed directly above?

*Commonwealth v. Beachey*, 728 A.2d 912 (Pa. 1999).

## Key Terms

**Adversary System:** The procedural system for trying lawsuits in which each side through its attorney presents its respective legal case in the best possible light to the judge and jury as neutral decision makers. The theory is that the truth will come from this give-and-take of arguments. The U.S. system is derived from England and is common to most of her former colonies.

**Advisory Opinions:** Hypothetical opinions issued by courts when there is no matter in controversy. U.S. courts do not issue advisory opinions.

**Allege:** To assert that a given fact is true or false in a lawsuit. An allegation is not yet proven. Proof that an allegation is true is determined by the trier of fact (usually a jury) in a case.

**Appeal:** A request to a higher court by an aggrieved party in a lawsuit to correct errors of law made by the judge at the lower court.

**Appeals Court:** A court superior to the court of original jurisdiction in any given court structure. The appeals court hears issues of law, not facts. It has no jury, and it decides matters by the majority vote of multiple judges hearing the case.

**Attorneys:** The professional advocates for one side or the other in a legal transaction or lawsuit. Attorneys, like judges, are officers of the court. They are subject to a code of ethics and legal restrictions on their advocacy. For instance, they may not knowingly lie, they may not misrepresent law or facts, and they may not assist in the commission of a crime or its cover-up.

**Beyond a Reasonable Doubt:** A balancing test used in criminal cases whereby the prosecution has met the standard of proof if all of the evidence on a given issue supports the prosecution's argument, with no room for a reasonable person to doubt the prosecution's version of events.

**Burden of Proof:** A term used to describe a party's duty to prove any given element of a cause of action. Usually the plaintiff or prosecution has the burden of proof and must provide evidence that facts supporting an allegation in a lawsuit did or did not occur.

**Cause of Action:** A reason to sue in a court of law. Each cause of action (there are thousands of types) has specific elements that must be alleged to remain in court, and proven in order for the plaintiff to recover.

**Circuit Courts:** The appeals-level court in the federal court system.

**Clear and Convincing Evidence:** A balancing test used in certain high-stakes civil cases whereby plaintiffs have met the standard of proof if a strong majority of the evidence on a given issue is in their favor. This standard falls between the preponderance of the evidence and the beyond a reasonable doubt standards.

**Code of Ethics:** A code, sometimes called a code of professional conduct, for attorneys that requires them to operate with strict limits on behavior in order to maintain the integrity of the legal profession, the legal process, and the legal system itself.

**Court of Original Jurisdiction:** The court in a jurisdiction that first hears a lawsuit. A court of original jurisdiction is a trial court.

**Courts of Equity:** Courts historically controlled by the church in England. Equity courts generally gave other forms of legal relief besides money in lawsuits (for example, injunctions, property, etc.).

**Courts of Law:** Courts historically controlled by the king in England. Law courts generally gave money damages in civil lawsuits.

**Defendant:** The party who is accused of breaking a criminal law or causing civil damages to the plaintiff.

**Double Jeopardy:** Being prosecuted twice for the same alleged crime, prohibited by the Fifth Amendment to the U.S. Constitution. The clause reads: "nor shall any person be subject for the same offence to be twice put in jeopardy of life or limb."

**Evidence:** Facts that are related to a case. Relevant evidence is evidence that will help prove or disprove an issue presented in a case. Admissible evidence is relevant evidence that will be considered by a judge or jury in a trial.

**Judge:** An officer of the court who acts as the "umpire" of a case, in order to ensure that procedure is properly followed and the law is enforced. The judge also acts as the interpreter of the law in the case and issues rulings that may act as new law and have precedential value. Judges are also called justices if they sit on the highest court of their jurisdiction.

**Judicial Review:** The power of the courts to review statutes, administrative rules and regulations, and other acts of government when those laws are brought before them in a lawsuit. The courts review these laws to determine if they violate the Constitution.

**Jury:** The finders of fact in a lawsuit. The jury is usually composed of 12 people of legal age in the jurisdiction, although numbers may vary.

**Lawsuit:** A matter that is heard before a court, wherein one side is seeking money or property, or in some cases punishment, from the other side. Lawsuits in the United States must be "real world," that is, there must be a matter in controversy for the court to decide.

**Legal Reporters:** Books that contain written opinions of appeals courts that may be used as precedent in later cases.

**Magna Carta:** A "great charter" signed in 1215 by John of England that granted, among other rights and privileges, the right to judgment of the accused by a jury of peers. Initially intended as a right for nobility, the right expanded over time to include the entire population.

**Matter in Controversy:** A real-world issue for a court to decide in a lawsuit.

**Overruled:** A term used to describe the overturning or setting aside of precedent from one court, when it is voided and replaced by another precedent from the same or a higher-level court.

**Peers:** In a legal context, those on a jury drawn from a representative group of the citizenry of legal age and without a legal disability (a felony conviction, for example) in the jurisdiction where the trial takes place.

**Persuasive Law:** Precedent that a court is not required to observe as binding law. In most cases persuasive law originates in another state.

**Plaintiff:** The party (either the government or a private person) who brings a civil lawsuit to court for the redress of damages and grievances.

**Precedent:** A legal decision that binds later courts in certain circumstances to follow the logic and legal holdings of a previous court in the interests of fairness, justice, and clarity.

**Preponderance of the Evidence:** A balancing test used in most civil cases whereby plaintiffs have met the standard of proof if 50.1 percent of the evidence on a given issue points in their favor.

**Prosecutor:** An attorney who acts as the representative of the government in bringing criminal actions against defendants as a part of the adversary system.

**Reasonable:** A term used to describe what a common person, at that place, at that time, would consider to be plausible and logical.

**Rulings:** Decisions issued by a judge regarding issues of law that come up during the case. That is, the judge would decide if X law applies, or Y law, or if this statement can be heard by the jury, or if that bit of evidence must be excluded in any given case. These decisions become new law and have precedential value in many cases.

**Standards of Proof:** A term describing the balancing test required to determine if the side holding the burden of proof on any given element of a case has actually met that burden.

**Strike Suits:** A term used for baseless lawsuits.

**Trial Court:** A court that is usually composed of a judge and a jury and that tries both law and fact. It is the court of original jurisdiction in almost all cases.

**Writ of Certiorari:** A formal request to the United States Supreme Court to hear a case.

# Contract Fundamentals

## INTRODUCTION

Contract law governs many of the relationships and transactions that businesses and businesspeople face on a daily basis. When a car is sold, when a shipment of goods is ordered and then delivered, or when software is installed, a contract is entered into. A **Contract** is an agreement or exchange of promises that is legally enforceable. That agreement can be broken when one of the parties to the contract does not do what he or she agreed to do. When that happens, the contract has been breached.

**Contract:**
An agreement or exchange of promises that is legally enforceable.

Occasionally, the breach can lead to a dispute that goes to court for resolution. Contract law guides courts on how to resolve those disputes. This chapter covers the four elements that every contract must have: mutual assent, consideration, legality of subject matter, and contractual capacity. If one of these elements is missing, a contract has not been properly formed and cannot be enforced in the courts.

## CONTRACT CLASSIFICATION

Contract classifications are helpful to determine whether a contract exists and what each party's obligations are under the contract. One way in which contracts can be classified is as bilateral or unilateral. A **Bilateral Contract** is created when both parties have made promises. This is the type of contract most people think about when two parties have exchanged promises to do something. For example, one person buys a used car from another individual and promises to pay the agreed-upon price for the car, and the seller of the car promises to deliver the car to the buyer. In contrast, a **Unilateral Contract** exists when one party promises to do something upon the satisfaction of a condition. When the specified thing happens, one party will perform some task. For example, suppose that a reward poster is put up regarding a lost cat. The poster says that payment of $75 will be made for the return of a lost cat named Muffy. When Muffy is returned, and only when she is returned, the $75 will be paid. The condition is the return of Muffy.

Contracts can also be classified as **Implied-In-Law** or **Quasi-Contract**. These contracts are implied by a court of law in order to resolve a contract dispute. An example of this kind of contract is the following: Your neighbor hires a local company to shovel his driveway when it snows. You do not have such a service. You shovel the snow on your driveway yourself. One winter, it snows several times. Each time the snowplow service comes and mistakenly clears your driveway instead of your neighbor's. You are aware of the mistake but do nothing to correct it. You do not notify your neighbor or the snowplow service. There is now a quasi-contract between you and the snowplow service. You will owe the snowplow service payment for services rendered. The snowplow service will only need to show that you knew that a mistake was made and you failed to correct it.

Finally, contracts can be classified as written or oral. An **Oral Contract** is formed when the parties promise to act by telling each other they will do so. There is nothing in writing. In most cases these contracts are just as binding as all other contracts.

## MUTUALITY OF ASSENT

In order to have a valid contract there must be **Mutuality of Assent**. Mutuality of assent requires a valid offer and a valid acceptance. There must be **Contractual Intent** on both sides to enter into the contract.

## OFFER

An **Offer** is a proposal by one party to another showing an intent to be bound by the terms of a contract. The offer must be communi-

**Bilateral Contract:**
A contract in which both parties make promises to each other.

**Unilateral Contract:**
A contract in which one party makes a promise and the other party performs in some way.

**Implied-in-Law Contract:**
A contract implied by a court of law. It is the same as a quasi-contract. The court will conclude that a contract exists based on what has transpired between the parties.

**Quasi-Contract:**
A contract implied by a court of law.

**Oral Contract:**
A contract created by verbal discussion but not memorialized in writing.

**Mutual Assent:**
A valid offer by the offeror and a valid acceptance by the offeree.

**Contractual Intent:**
The purposefulness of forming a contractual relationship.

**Offer:**
A proposal by one party to another showing an intent to enter into a valid contract.

cated. It can be communicated to anyone, even to an entity such as a corporation or limited partnership. For example, Tom offers to sell his computer to Eric for $150. Eric accepts and a contract is formed. The person making an offer is the **Offeror**. The person to whom the offer is directed is the **Offeree**.

A **Counteroffer** is the rejection of an offer and the creation of a new offer (the counteroffer). This exchange can continue back and forth until an agreement is either reached or an offer is simply rejected outright. An example of a counteroffer is as follows: Suppose that Bea's House Cleaning Service offers to clean Carol's house for $250. Carol rejects that offer and counteroffers that she would like the house to be cleaned for $150. The original offer is now invalid, terminated by the counteroffer. Bea's House Cleaning Service must accept or reject the counteroffer.

These examples of offers and counteroffers sound very much like negotiation. Sometimes these back-and-forth exchanges actually are negotiations or invitations to bargain and not true offers and counteroffers. The distinctions between all of these come to light when disagreements end up in court. Disputes of this nature concern whether an offer has been made or mere negotiation has taken place. Generally, the courts must consider evidence of the facts and circumstances surrounding communications between the parties. These can include the following:

1. The ordinary meaning of the language used. For example, was the word "offer" used?
2. Prior communications and dealings between the parties. For example, have they entered into other contracts?
3. The social relationship of the parties. For example, are the parties related?
4. Completeness of the terms of the contract. Has everything been spelled out expressly, leaving nothing out? If so, then this is most likely an offer.

A classic case that illustrates this process is *Fairmont Glass Works v. Grunden-Martin Woodenware Co.*, 106 Ky. 659 (1899). In this case there was an exchange of letters, leading to a dispute. A seller of mason jars received a letter from an interested buyer. The letter requested the lowest price at which ten carloads of mason jars could be purchased. (Letter 1) The mason jar company sent a letter to the purchaser quoting prices for various sizes of jars. (Letter 2) In a responding letter, the purchaser asked for delivery of ten carloads of jars. (Letter 3) The seller responded that it had sold out of all of its jars. (Letter 4) The purchaser filed an action for breach of contract. The court determined that because the letter from the mason jar

**Offeror:**
The party making an offer.

**Offeree:**
The party to whom an offer is made.

**Counteroffer:**
The rejection of an offer and the creation of a new offer.

company to the purchaser, Letter 2, contained quoted prices, it was an offer to sell at those prices. The seller's letter also contained the words "for immediate acceptance," leading the court to conclude that the letter was an offer rather than negotiation.

An exchange of offers may not be negotiation but rather just invitations to deal. In **Invitations to Deal,** the information advertising a willingness to sell is provided in order to entice people to consider buying. Examples of invitations to deal include advertisements, catalogues, or solicitations for bids to complete work like construction or building projects.

**Invitation to Deal:**
An act that looks like an offer but is simply an invitation to start the negotiation process or to come in and buy.

## Required Terms of an Offer

To be considered a valid offer, certain information must be contained in the communication. These terms include price, identification of the subject matter and parties, and time for performance. When these terms are missing, the parties may not have a mutual understanding of what the offer is about. Also, courts cannot easily determine whether an offer has been made when these terms are missing.

The price term of an offer is usually a dollar amount. The subject matter of an offer is the underlying focus of the contract. If the parties are trying to agree upon the delivery of widgets, the subject matter is widgets. Identifying the parties to a contract is usually straightforward. But it may get complicated when dealing with companies who have subsidiaries and foreign branches. In making the identification, always consider who is bound by the contract. The offer should include the time frame within which performance of the contract should take place. If no particular time is mentioned, then a reasonable time is presumed. Sometimes a contract includes the phrase *"time is of the essence."* This phrase means that the parties must perform exactly within the time frame as it is stated in the offer. If someone is late, the other party has the right to sue for breach. Usually, when time is the essence, one of the parties has multiple contracts that are interrelated. If one contract is not performed, the others are adversely affected.

## Revocation

Offers can be canceled or revoked before they have been accepted. The cancellation or **Revocation** of the offer must be communicated. It cannot be just thought or planned, without notification of the other party. Once the other party learns of the revocation of the offer, the revocation becomes effective.

**Revocation:**
The timely withdrawal of an offer.

## ACCEPTANCE

**Acceptance** is the other side of mutuality of assent. Acceptance is showing a willingness to be bound by the terms of a contract. The person who is able to accept an offer is the person who received the offer (the offeree). Also, under common law, the acceptance must be a mirror image of the offer. This is called the **Mirror Image Rule**, under which no terms of the offer can be changed in the acceptance. If the acceptance looks different from the offer, this failed acceptance will be considered a counteroffer that terminated the original offer and took its place. For an acceptance to be valid and a contract to be formed, the offeree must accept every term of the offer.

Acceptance must also be communicated. It cannot be just a thought or a unshared plan. Usually, acceptance will be made in the same form as an offer—via e-mail, letter, or conversation. Silence is generally not interpreted as acceptance. However, there are some circumstances where it might be. If the parties know each other well and have regularly done business together, then acceptance by silence may be interpreted as a **Course of Dealing**. A course of dealing describes how the parties have done business together in the past. If two parties regularly accept each other's offers by silence, then if a dispute arose, the court would gather evidence regarding their past transactions and conclude that it is reasonable for a party to consider silence as acceptance.

**Acceptance:**
Manifestation of assent to the offer proposed.

**Mirror Image Rule:**
The common law concept providing that no terms of the offer can be changed in the acceptance. If the acceptance looks different from the offer, it will be considered a counteroffer.

**Course of Dealing:**
How the parties have done business together in the past.

### Acceptance of the Unilateral Contract

A unilateral contract allows performance to function as acceptance. This performance must be with knowledge of the offer and the performance must be motivated by the offer. In the situation of the reward poster offering a reward to the finder of Muffy the cat, acceptance of that unilateral offer was delivery of Muffy to the distressed owner.

## CONSIDERATION

For a contract to be enforceable and binding on both parties, the contract must have valid consideration. **Consideration** describes the bargain that the parties strike when they exchange promises with one another. It is what each side gives to the other in the contract. For instance, if Frank agrees to buy 100 widgets from Marsha for $100, the consideration in this contract is the 100 widgets and the $100 dollars. Consideration does not have to be economic. It

**Consideration:**
The bargain of the contract—a benefit conferred by or detriment incurred at the request of the other party.

can also be the forbearance from acting when one has a legal right to act. There must be consideration flowing in both directions in a contract.

In order for consideration to support the contract, there must be a bargained-for exchange between the parties, and the subject matter of the bargain must have some kind of legal value. The value is thought of in legal terms. The value of the consideration is measured by some benefit that flows to the promisor or some detriment to the promisee, not in terms of money. The requirement of legal value ensures that the promises that are exchanged are not gratuitous.

There are some things that will not be sufficient consideration. These include past or moral consideration, token consideration, and preexisting legal duties. Consideration is best understood by example.

## Historical Development of Consideration

Consideration fits awkwardly into contract law. It is often difficult to understand even with many examples. It may help to take into account the historical development of the concept.

In general, in the United States, it is preferred that parties strike bargains and perform under the terms of their agreements without much interference from the courts. As a rule, courts try to uphold what parties agree to. The concept of consideration developed so that courts could distinguish an enforceable exchange of promises from gratuitous promises or gifts. Gifts and frivolous discussions have their place in the daily dealings between people. However, the courts should not be asked to enforce everything that has been agreed to or promised in jest.

In medieval England, promises to be performed in the future, **Executory Promises**, were not enforced. For example, on Monday, Farmer Jones promises to deliver hay on Friday to the town stable, run by Mr. Jennings. On Friday, the hay never arrives. Mr. Jennings has no legal recourse against Farmer Jones. At the time, the only way to make promises binding was to perform a ritual and make a seal in wax. Before the Industrial Revolution these seal-in-wax rituals had a legal meaning. They created the binding nature of the promises. The more solemn the signing ritual, the more seriously the contract was taken. Still, there was no legal means for enforcing the contract. There was only a right to recover if someone caused an injury through their actions.

As contract law developed the rituals gave way to the courts and the common law. Instead of solemnity through wax rituals, the simpler action of **Assumpsit** evolved and took its place. Assumpsit

**Executory Promises:**
Promises to be performed in the future.

**Assumpsit:**
A historical cause of action for recovery for breach of contract. It is based in tort law.

was originally an action in **Tort**, a civil wrongful act (other than breach of contract) causing harm or injury, for which relief may be obtained, usually in the form of damages. Tort law allows suits against people for misfeasance or malfeasance. Assumpsit emphasized each party's reliance on the other person to faithfully fulfill his or her duty to perform under the contract. Once the contract was formed, an expectation was created between the contract's parties. The expectation was that each person would perform properly under the contract. Over time assumpsit developed into a common action for commercial transactions.

The underlying concept in consideration, developing at the same time, was that a breach of contract was a form of theft or injury to property. It is because of the mixed heritage of consideration, property ideas, and tort law that there is confusion and ambiguity in court opinions when judges explain why a particular contract has consideration to support it but another contract does not.

**Tort:**
A civil wrongful act (other than breach of contract) causing harm or injury, for which relief may be obtained, usually in the form of damages.

## Bargained-For Exchange

The bargained-for element of consideration demands that a **Detriment** and a **Benefit** occur. The promise will bring about a detriment, and the detriment will bring about a promise. Each party gives something up (a detriment) and receives something in return (a benefit). It is a *quid pro quo*.

The California Civil Code has a section defining "consideration":

> §1605. Any benefit conferred, or agreed to be conferred, upon the promisor, by any other person, to which the promisor is not lawfully entitled, or any prejudice suffered, or agreed to be suffered, by such person, other than such as he is at the time of consent lawfully bound to suffer, as an inducement to the promisor, is a good consideration for a promise.

**Detriment:**
Something given up as a part of a contract (when referring to consideration).

**Benefit:**
Something received as a part of a contract.

## Adequate Consideration

Consideration can be as small as a peppercorn or a $1 bill. Consideration can be a large amount of money as well. In disputes courts must determine not if the consideration was adequate for the exchange of promises but whether the consideration was valid. The amount of consideration may indicate a gift or fraud, but it will not be measured for adequacy. An agreement may be enforceable even if it is supported by inadequate or unequal consideration.

A case illustrating this concept is *Batsakis v. Demotsis*, 226 S.W.2d 673 (Tex. Civ. App. 1949). The Court of Civil Appeals of Texas considered the value of consideration in an agreement to borrow money, executed in war-torn Greece.

In April 1942, Eugenia Demotsis was stranded in occupied Greece. German troops had been an occupying power for a year. The country had lost almost 300,000 civilians, mostly due to famine. There was inflation and starvation. Eugenia had assets in the United States. She had no access to the funds and her family was starving. Eugenia entered into a loan agreement with George Batsakis. Mr. Batsakis loaned Eugenia 500,000 Greek drachmas, worth $25. Eugenia had to repay Mr. Batsakis $2,000 if she was able to claim her assets in America. Eugenia survived the war and returned to

Peiraeus
April 2, 1942

Mr. George Batsaki,
Konstantinou Diadohou #7
Peiraeus

Mr. Batsakis:

I state by my present (letter) that I received today from you the amount of two thousand dollars ($2,000.00) of United States of America money, which I borrowed from you for the support of my family during these difficult days and because it is impossible for me to transfer dollars of my own from America.

The above amount I accept with the expressed promise that I will return to you again in American dollars either at the end of the present war or even before in the event that you might be able to find a way to collect them (dollars) from my representative in America to whom I shall write and give him an order relative to this. You understand until the final execution (payment) to the above amount an eight per cent interest will be added and paid together with the principal.

I thank you and I remain yours with respects.

The recipient,
(Signed)
Eugenia Demotsis

**Figure 3-1**
The Agreement

America to retrieve her assets. When Mr. Batsakis arrived to seek payment, Eugenia offered him $25. He sued to recover the $2,000.

The trial court found in favor of Mr. Batsakis for $750.00 plus interest. On appeal, the issue was whether there was adequate consideration for the contract to stand. If the consideration was not valid, Eugenia would have no obligation to repay, because there was no contract.

The appeals court stated that "mere inadequacy of consideration will not void a contract." There was a benefit and detriment. Mr. Batsakis did deliver to Eugenia 500,000 drachmas. The court found that both parties got what they bargained for out of the agreement. Also, the court would not consider the adequacy of the consideration, only that there was consideration to support the contract. The court ordered Eugenia to repay the $2,000 plus interest.

## Not Consideration

There are things that the law does not consider valid consideration. If someone has voluntarily performed or something has previously been given, it cannot then serve as consideration. This is called **Past Consideration**. For example, suppose that Carol gives Sally a ride home in her car. When they reach Sally's house, she offers Carol $7 for gas. Carol cannot enforce this promise because the consideration, the ride in the car, is in the past. Also, gifts are not consideration because there is no bargained-for exchange.

Illusory promises cannot be consideration. An **Illusory Promise** is one that is based on the whim of the promisor. For example, in the case of *Wood v. Lucy, Lady Duff-Gordon*, 222 N.Y. 88, 118 N.E. 214 (1917), the New York Court of Appeals considered whether a contract had adequate consideration. Lady Duff-Gordon was a "creator of fashions." Her name added to parasols and fabrics increased their value. Lady Duff-Gordon desired to take advantage of this situation. Mr. Otis Wood was hired to turn her fame into money. According to the court, they agreed that he was to have "exclusive right to place her endorsement on the designs of others." In return, Lady Duff-Gordon would receive one-half of "all profits and revenues" from any contracts made by Mr. Wood. This exclusive right would last one year and then go year to year thereafter.

Mr. Wood discovered that Lady Duff-Gordon had placed endorsements on dresses and millinery without his knowledge. He then began to withhold profits from her and then sought redress from the court. Lady Duff-Gordon argued in her defense that Mr. Wood was not bound by their arrangement. He never promised to do anything, so his promises were illusory.

**Past Consideration:**
Something that was done previously without expectation of payment or receipt of something in return.

**Illusory Promise:**
A promise that is based on the whim of the promisor but without the intention to really perform.

The court agreed that no promise was expressly made by Mr. Wood. However, the court pointed out that by 1917, contract law had developed beyond the point of "primitive...formalisms." Instead, the court could infer that Mr. Wood would make reasonable efforts to bring profits and revenues into existence. The court could infer that Mr. Wood would assume the duties of such an arrangement by his acceptance of an exclusive agency. The duties would be to seek out new endorsements for Lady Duff-Gordon. Therefore, Mr. Wood's promise was not illusory because the contract implied the condition of best efforts on Mr. Wood's part. Mr. Woods would make best efforts to generate profits through the placement of the Lady Duff-Gordon endorsement.

## LEGALITY OF THE SUBJECT MATTER

Contracts are only enforceable if they concern a **Legal Subject Matter**. Courts of law will not uphold agreements that have been crafted to break the law. The subject matter of a contract—what the contract is concerning—may be unlawful due to a statute, such as agreements relating to any criminal act, or unlawful as against public policy, such as contracts with illegally high interest rates. Parties may not be aware that their contracts involve illegal matters. Even if all of the other elements of a contract may be valid, if the subject matter is not legal, the court will find the contract unenforceable.

California Civil Code §1667, entitled Unlawful Contracts, is similar to the law of many states. It provides:

> That is not lawful which is:
> 1. Contrary to an express provision of law;
> 2. Contrary to the policy of express law, though not expressly prohibited; or
> 3. Otherwise contrary to good morals.

**Legal Subject Matter:** A requirement for the formation of a valid and enforceable contract, meaning that the purpose of the contract must be legal.

## PUBLIC POLICY CONSIDERATIONS

Contracts that violate public policy are void. Public policy can be determined by looking at what society has already made illegal. For example, polluting and racial discrimination are illegal. When a court is faced with a private contract between persons that allows someone to pollute, the contract can be found invalid as against public policy. Public policy can also be derived from a court's own sense of protecting some aspect of the public welfare. In circumstances where the matter is not addressed by statute, the court can weigh the interests of enforcing the contract and the parties' expectations against whatever public interest is involved. On that basis the court can refuse to enforce the contract.

## CAPACITY

Legal **Contractual Capacity** refers to the ability of individuals to enter into binding agreements that the law will uphold and enforce. A person who lacks capacity is considered to be unable to understand the consequences and ramifications of entering into a contract. A person who lacks capacity cannot understand his or her rights and obligations under a contract. Under the law, a person lacks capacity when intoxicated or under the influence of drugs, under the age of majority, or mentally impaired by a mental health issue or a disease of the mind such as dementia.

Historically, women were considered legally incapable of entering into a contract. Married women lacked capacity along with children and the insane. Consider the case of *Reed v. Reed*, 404 U.S. 71 (1971). In *Reed*, the Supreme Court of the United States ruled on an Idaho statute that permitted a probate court to choose an administrator of an estate based on gender.

Richard Lynn Reed, a minor, died in Idaho in 1967. Prior to his death, his parents had separated. Both parents sought appointment as administrator of the son's estate. The estate contained a few personal items and a small savings account. The probate court held a hearing and appointed the father as administrator of the estate. The probate court found that both parents were equally capable of being administrator. The court, however, cited Idaho Civil Code §15-314, which stated that "of several persons claiming and equally entitled to administer [an estate], males must be preferred to females."

The mother, Mrs. Reed, appealed the case to the Supreme Court. The Court found that the Idaho code provision violated the Equal Protection Clause of the United States Constitution. Under the Equal Protection Clause, part of the Fourteenth Amendment, states are allowed to treat people differently in their statutes. However, to be legal the different treatment must be reasonable and not arbitrary and must be related to the purpose of the legislation. If men and women are treated differently in a statute for no apparent reason, then the Supreme Court can strike that statute down. And the Court did determine that the different treatment between genders in Idaho was for no apparent reason.

> Clearly the objective of reducing the workload on probate courts by eliminating one class of contests is not without some legitimacy. The crucial question, however, is whether §15-314 advances that objective in a manner consistent with the command of the Equal

**Contractual Capacity:**
The legal ability of a person to enter into a contractual relationship.

Protection Clause. We hold that it does not. To give a mandatory preference to members of either sex over members of the other, merely to accomplish the elimination of hearings on the merits, is to make the very kind of arbitrary legislative choice forbidden by the Equal Protection Clause of the Fourteenth Amendment; and whatever may be said as to the positive values of avoiding intra-family controversy, the choice in this context may not lawfully be mandated solely on the basis of sex.

—*Reed v. Reed*, 93 Idaho 511, 465 P.2d 635 (1971).

In terms of business transactions, the issue of capacity can arise when minors try to purchase a car. Minors, or persons under the age of majority, can disaffirm or get out of a contract but must do so before they reach the age of majority. For example, suppose that John appears old for his age. He is only 17 years old, but he has a fake ID showing him to be older. John goes to the used-car dealer and purchases a car. The dealer thought John was 20 years old and able to enter into a contract. After he drove the car home, John's parents demand that he return the car. John returns the car, and the dealer is unable to enforce the contract because John is a minor. John is also able to get back the small deposit he paid to the dealership. The person entering into a contract with a minor cannot invalidate the contract—only the minor can. Minors, however, are responsible for necessaries that they purchase while they are underage. Necessaries are food, clothing, and shelter. Minors are also responsible for contracts that they entered into while minors but that were affirmed after they reached their majority. For instance, if John continued to drive the car after his 18th birthday, or made a payment on the car after his 18th birthday, he would then have affirmed the contract and be obligated to the terms he agreed to as a minor.

To determine the mental capacity of parties claiming that they were incapacitated when they made the contract, courts allow psychiatric testimony for both sides to be introduced. This could involve having a psychiatrist examine one of the parties, and then having that doctor testify at trial. Also, a party could submit to tests and those tests could be brought in as evidence. Ultimately, a balancing of competing interests is conducted by the court or the jury.

## CONTRACTUAL INTENT

The concepts of a meeting of the minds, the mirror image rule, and mutual assent all describe the intent of parties to enter into an agreement. If intent is invalid, the contract is also invalid. There are four circumstances that raise a question about the contractual intent of a party. These are **Fraud** and **Misrepresentation, Duress,** and **Mistake**.

Each of these circumstances addresses what the parties were thinking when they exchanged promises. Intent is difficult to prove. Courts look at oral testimony as well as the actions of the parties in order to determine what the parties were thinking when the contract negotiations took place.

## Misrepresentation and Fraud

The law does not like parties entering into bargains in bad faith. For example, securities laws frequently make parties liable for misrepresentations made in order to secure a contract. In the case of *Securities & Exchange Commission v. Texas Gulf Sulphur Co.*, 446 F.2d 1301 (2d Cir. 1971), Texas Gulf Sulphur Company discovered valuable ore near Timmins, Ontario. The company found the deposit by conducting aerial searches for electromagnetic "anomalies." Once they detected an anomaly near Timmons, they bought mineral rights from landowners in the area. The deposit was verified as valuable ore. Company officers began to buy more stock before the public knew of the company's discovery. This amounted to insider trading, and the officers were successfully prosecuted. One of the former landowners sued. The landowner's position was that Texas Gulf Sulphur bought his land without disclosing to him a material fact about the ore on the property—a misrepresentation in bad faith. The court found that the law requires good faith in dealing, and that Texas Gulf Sulphur bought the land in bad faith.

A misrepresentation is a misstatement that must be made with respect to a fact, as opposed to an opinion. Fraud occurs when one party tricks another into entering into a transaction that the latter otherwise would not have entered into. Not all misrepresentations are fraud. There can be innocent misrepresentations. But contract law is most concerned with misrepresentations that amount to fraud. Fraud occurs when a party misrepresents a fact relied upon by a party in entering into a contract. There are five elements that must be shown in order to rescind a contract due to fraud:

1. A misrepresentation;
2. Of a material fact;
3. Made with the intent to deceive;
4. Relied upon by the other party;
5. To their detriment.

A **Material Fact** is a fact that is important to a person in deciding whether to enter into a particular transaction. A material fact is distinguished from a trivial or unimportant detail of a transaction. The

**Fraud:**
A knowing misrepresentation of the truth or concealment of a material fact to trick someone into entering into a transaction that he or she would otherwise not have entered into.

**Misrepresentation:**
A misstatement of fact.

**Duress:**
Improper pressure on another party in order to force the other party to do something against his or her will.

**Mistake:**
A misunderstanding that materially impacts the contract.

**Material Fact:**
A fact that is important to a person in deciding whether to enter into a particular transaction.

material misrepresentation must be made with the **Intent to Deceive** the other party into assenting to the contract. A misrepresentation made by mistake is not a legally actionable misrepresentation that could void a contract.

**Intent to Deceive:**
The intent to obtain a thing of value through misrepresentation.

An example of misrepresentation is shown in the case of *Hollywood Credit Clothing Co. v. Gibson*, 188 A.2d 348 (D.C.1963), where the court considered a contract for the sale of a television. Two days before Christmas Mr. Gibson went to the Hollywood Clothing Store. He found a television for sale. The price of the television was $189.00, and Mr. Gibson agreed to buy it. A conditional sales contract was filled in, and he signed it. Mr. Gibson was not given a copy of the conditional bill of sale. When he got home he looked at his account book and saw that the store had charged him $289.00 for the television, and with additional charges, the bill of sale came to a total of $354.35.

Mr. Gibson returned to the store as soon as it opened after Christmas. He returned the set to the store and said that he had been charged too much. The store salespeople refused to take the television back. Mr. Gibson left the television at the store and did not pay on his account. The store sued to enforce the contract. The store argued that Mr. Gibson could not rescind the contract just because he did not read it. Mr. Gibson argued that his agreement to the contract was achieved by fraud. Evidence was presented at trial convincing the court that the salesperson did represent that the price of the television was $189.00. The court found in favor of Mr. Gibson.

The case of Mr. Gibson can also serve as an example of a party's reliance on a misrepresentation. Mr. Gibson entered into the contract to buy the television because he relied on the stated price of the television as $189.00. **Reliance** occurs when a person understands a situation to be one way and acts upon that understanding. The person relies by reasonably accepting something as fact and then acting as if that fact is true.

**Reliance:**
Depending on a fact to be true when taking some action.

A misrepresentation that acts to a party's **Detriment** means that the misrepresentation leaves the party in a worse position. In the case of Mr. Gibson, after he bought the television, he was worse off. He had the television, but he also had to pay off the $354.35 charged to his account by the store. Even after Mr. Gibson returned the television, he still had the amount charged to his account. He was left without the television, but with the bill. This amounted to detrimental reliance.

**Detriment:**
Loss or harm that comes from a person's acting based on wrong information, thereby placing him or her in a worse position than if no action had been taken (when referring to misrepresentation).

## Duress

A contract will be voidable if a party accepted the terms of the contract while under duress. As noted above, duress occurs when one

## ETHICAL ISSUES

● ● ●

When drafting contracts attorneys enter into negotiations on behalf of their clients. Attorneys are bound by Rules of Professional conduct issued by their state bar. The American Bar Association (ABA) has Model Rules of Professional Conduct that states may adopt.

ABA Model Model Rule of Professional Conduct 4.1 states that a lawyer cannot knowingly make misrepresentations during negotiations such as contract negotiations.

Why is this rule in place?

**Transactions With Persons Other Than Clients Rule 4.1 Truthfulness In Statements To Others***

In the course of representing a client a lawyer shall not knowingly:

(a) make a false statement of material fact or law to a third person; or

(b) fail to disclose a material fact to a third person when disclosure is necessary to avoid assisting a criminal or fraudulent act by a client, unless disclosure is prohibited by Rule 1.6.

*Source: http://www.abanet.org/cpr/mrpc/mrpc_toc.html.

party puts improper pressure on another party to the contract in order to force the other party to do something against his or her will. The improper pressure must force the party into the agreement. Courts will usually only allow duress claims to negate formation of a valid contract if there was improper physical force or the threat of physical harm to another person. In order for duress to be an acceptable defense to contract formation, no alternative must have been available to the party claiming duress. Some courts have been known to accept "economic duress" or "business compulsion" as duress.

### Mistake

A party may attempt to rescind a contract by claiming that there was a mistake. To be effective in eroding contractual intent, the mistake must materially affect the agreed exchange of performances. Mistakes can be mutual or unilateral. **Mutual Mistakes** occur where both parties to the contract act on a mistaken belief. A **Unilateral Mistake** is one in which only one party has a mistaken belief.

**Mutual Mistake:**
A mistake on which both parties to the contract act.

**Unilateral Mistake:**
A mistake by only one party to the contract.

## CHAPTER SUMMARY

A contract is a legally enforceable promise. Contract law specifies the requirements for contract formation. Those requirements include the existence of an offer, acceptance that is a mirror image of the offer, and valid consideration. The subject matter of the contract must be legal, and the parties must have the capacity to enter into the contract. There are circumstances that will negate contractual intent. Among them are fraud and misrepresentation, duress, and mistake. In these situations the underlying contract will not be valid, and courts will not enforce it.

## Relevant Web Sites

http://www.law.cornell.edu/ucc/ucc.table.html
http://smallbusiness.findlaw.com/business-forms-contracts/business-forms-contracts-overview/
http://www.law.cornell.edu/topics/contracts.html

## Exercises

1. Describe in one paragraph a situation that is an invitation to deal and not an offer.
2. Search online for the case *Carlill v. Carbolic Smoke Ball Co.* [1893] 1 Q.B. 256. Read it and describe in several paragraphs the contract principle it represents.
3. Review your state's laws on incapacity. What conditions are evidence of legal incapacity to enter into a contract?
4. Review the course syllabus for your business law course. Draft a contract based on what is contained in the syllabus. Is there mutual assent? Is there consideration?
5. Describe the terms of your mobile phone contract. What consideration supports the agreement?

## Questions

1. What is mutual assent?
2. What is misrepresentation?
3. What is legal detriment?
4. Why does the law require consideration?
5. What must an offer have to be valid?
6. How can an offer be terminated?
7. What is duress?
8. What is acceptance?
9. What is a possible illegal purpose for a contract?
10. Can a statement of opinion lead to a claim of fraud, thereby eroding contractual intent? Why or why not?

## Hypotheticals

1. Sam offers to sell his laptop to James for a fair price. Is this a valid offer?
2. Carol offers to sell her personal computer to Bob for $200. Bob says that he will buy the PC for $200 if Carol will include the monitor and keyboard. Is this a valid acceptance?
3. Roger offers to sell his motorcycle to Roxanne for $1,000. On Monday, Roger mails Roxanne a letter revoking the offer. The letter arrives on Wednesday. When is the revocation effective?
4. Widget Corp. wants to dispose of a pollutant without the authorities knowing. Widget enters into a contract with a private removal company to haul away the pollutant. Widget stops paying the removal company under the contract. Can the removal company sue for breach of contract?
5. Ken has lost his pet gecko, Oscar. He posted Missing Gecko flyers all over town offering a reward of $50. What kind of offer is this?

## Sample Cases

1. William McVicker believed he was unlawfully terminated from his job with the Borough of Jefferson Hills. He filed a claim with the Equal Employment Opportunity Commission (EEOC). In an attempt to contradict testimony given under deposition, McVicker argued that certain anonymous blog posts made on "YourSouthhills.com," a Web site with an interactive discussion board owned by Trib Total Media, Inc., contradicted, in his favor, previous deposition testimony. McVicker filed a Motion to Compel Response to a Subpoena to get the company to reveal the identities of users who posted in the discussion forum. The Web site had a privacy policy. Users of the discussion board had an expectation of privacy and anonymity under the

terms of service of the Web site, but the terms were boilerplate. Could users rely on that anonymity as part of their contract for using the service?

*McVicker v. King*, 266 F.R.D. 92 (W.D. Pa. 2010).

2. American Prairie Construction was formerly known as North Central Construction (NCC). NCC built an ethanol plant and retained an equity interest in it after Tri-State Ethanol (TSE) purchased the property. TSE failed to pay NCC, and foreclosure proceedings were initiated. Ultimately, TSE filed a Chapter 11 bankruptcy petition. A group of investors, in an effort to save the ethanol plant and TSE, provided funding through a shell corporation called Tri-State Financial (TSF). TSF's representative was John Hoich. Hoich began negotiations with NCC regarding payments and claims that would work toward assisting TSE through bankruptcy and make the ethanol plant profitable. These discussions regarding the settlement agreement were recorded in notes but never formalized, and there was considerable confusion regarding the terms of the agreement. NCC sued to enforce the agreement. Was there a meeting of the minds?

*American Prairie Constr. Co. v. Hoich*, 594 F.3d 1015 (8th Cir. 2010).

## Key Terms

**Acceptance:** Manifestation of assent to the offer proposed.

**Assumpsit:** A historical cause of action for recovery for breach of contract. It is based in tort law.

**Benefit:** Something received as a part of a contract.

**Bilateral Contract:** A contract in which both parties make promises.

**Consideration:** The bargain of the contract—a benefit conferred by or detriment incurred at the request of the other party.

**Contract:** An agreement or exchange of promises that is legally enforceable.

**Contractual Capacity:** The legal ability of a person to enter into a contractual relationship.

**Contractual Intent:** The purposefulness of forming a contractual relationship.

**Counteroffer:** A rejection of an offer and the creation of a new offer.

**Course of Dealing:** How the parties have done business together in the past.

**Detriment:** Something given up as a part of a contract (when referring to consideration); loss or harm that comes from a person's acting based on wrong information, thereby placing him or her in a worse position than if no action had been taken (when referring to misrepresentation).

**Duress:** Improper pressure on another party in order to force the other party to do something against his or her will. Duress may be mental or physical.

**Executory Promises:** Promises to be performed in the future.

**Fraud:** A knowing misrepresentation of the truth or concealment of a material fact to trick someone into entering into a transaction that he or she would otherwise not have entered into.

**Illusory Promise:** A promise that is based on the whim of the promisor but without the intention to really perform.

**Implied-in-Law Contract:** A contract implied by a court of law. It is the same as a quasi-contract. The court will conclude that a contract exists based on what has transpired between the parties.

**Intent to Deceive:** The intent to obtain a thing of value through misrepresentation.

**Invitation to Deal:** An act that looks like an offer but is simply an invitation to start the negotiation process or to come in and buy.

**Legal Subject Matter:** One of the requirements of a valid contract, meaning that a contract can only be formed for a legal purpose.

**Material Fact:** A fact that is important to a person in deciding whether to enter into a particular transaction.

**Mirror Image Rule:** The common law concept providing that no terms of the offer can be changed in the acceptance. If the acceptance looks different from the offer, it will be considered a counteroffer.

**Misrepresentation:**  A misstatement of fact.

**Mistake:**  A misunderstanding that materially impacts the contract.

**Mutual Assent:**  A valid offer by the offeror and a valid acceptance by the offeree.

**Mutual Mistake:**  A mistake on which both parties to the contract act.

**Offer:**  A proposal by one party to another showing an intent to enter into a valid contract.

**Offeree:**  The party to whom an offer is made.

**Offeror:**  The party making an offer.

**Oral Contract:**  A contract created by verbal discussion but not memorialized in writing.

**Past Consideration:**  Something that was done previously without expectation of payment or receipt of something in return.

**Quasi-Contract:**  A contract implied by a court of law.

**Reliance:**  Depending on a fact to be true when taking an action.

**Revocation:**  The timely withdrawal of an offer.

**Tort Law:**  A civil wrongful act (other than breach of contract) causing harm or injury, for which relief may be obtained, usually in the form of damages.

**Unilateral Contract:**  A contract in which one party makes a promise and the other party performs in some way.

**Unilateral Mistake:**  A mistake by only one party to the contract.

## CHAPTER 4

# Contracts in Action

**LEARNING OBJECTIVES**

You will be able to answer the following questions after reading this chapter:

1. What is a condition?
2. What is the parol evidence rule?
3. What is the Statute of Frauds?
4. What is frustration of purpose?
5. Who are third-party beneficiaries?
6. What are remedies?

## INTRODUCTION

Learning the requirements for creating a valid contract provides a starting point for understanding contract law, but digging deeper to see how contracts work in the real world gives a much broader view of this important area of law. This chapter covers a range of issues pertaining to the contract in action in the real world—how the contract works, how to prove that a contract exists, and what remedies the law allows when contracts are breached.

Each contract contains provisions called clauses, which expressly state the terms of each agreement. Some clauses describe conditions of the contract. Such conditions protect the parties by allowing a party to stop his or her own performance under a contract if the other party fails to perform.

Frequently, in contract negotiations, discussions take place about topics that do not become part of the contract. Sometimes things are left out of the contract inadvertently that are crucial to a full understanding of the party's agreement. When disputes arise in these cases, courts use rules of construction to guide them in deciding whether a contract accurately expresses the agreement of the parties. These rules provide a step-by-step process that guides all the individuals involved in a contract dispute. In conducting their analysis, courts must hear evidence presented by the parties at trial. Permissible evidence is limited by the parol evidence rule, a substantive rule of law that goes to the law of contracts rather than the law of evidence.

Also important to how contracts work in action is the Statute of Frauds. The Statute of Frauds lists the types of contracts that must be in writing to be enforceable.

When a contract is breached, the injured party may be entitled to damages. The law allows various remedies when contracts are breached. This chapter describes some of those remedies. Finally, the chapter covers the general concepts involved in alternative dispute resolution, which is increasingly how contract disputes are resolved.

## CONDITIONS

A condition is one type of provision in a contract, which allows the parties to agree that certain performances under the contract are not due unless a stated event has occurred. An example of a conditional statement in daily life declares, "I will take out the garbage when you clean up the living room." There is an important timing element to conditional statements and conditions in contracts. Conditions are often recognized because they include the words "on condition that" or "provided that" and include the word "if."

Conditions can be express or constructive. An **Express Condition** is one on which the parties have agreed during the negotiation offer-acceptance phase. A **Constructive Condition** is not agreed upon by the parties but rather is supplied by the court in the interest of fairness to all parties to the contract.

**Express Condition:** A condition that the parties have agreed upon and that is explicitly stated in the contract.

**Constructive Condition:** A condition that is not agreed upon by the parties or mentioned in the contract but rather is supplied by the court in the interest of fairness.

### Express Condition

Parties to a contract must comply with express conditions because they are an integral part of the contract. They represent the substance of the agreement between the parties.

For example, suppose that John and Sam entered into a contract to merge their corporate holdings into a single new company. They agree that the merger will not be effective unless the parties raise $650,000 in additional capital. The raising of the additional capital is an express condition of the duties of both men. The raising of the capital is also a **Condition Precedent**. This condition must be met before a party's promise becomes absolute. If the money is not raised, neither John nor Sam is required to perform any of his duties under the contract.

**Condition Precedent:** A condition that must be met before a party's promise under a contract becomes absolute.

## Constructive Condition

Constructive conditions are imposed by the court during a contract dispute. Generally, when two parties exchange promises, performance of those promises is a constructive condition. The court will impose a duty on each party to a contract to perform its respective side of the bargain. If a party does not perform, the other party is relieved of the obligation to perform.

If a condition in the contract is not met, which means it was not performed, then the parties have several options. They need to know if the condition has been excused or not. If the condition has been excused, the party does not need to perform its obligation or keep its promise. What a court may do in the event a condition is not met really depends on the importance of that condition to the essence of the contract. If the condition is not important, the party complaining about nonperformance may not be able to recover much in court.

For example, suppose that Axel Company is under contract to deliver 400 steel rods to Bice Incorporated on January 5. The delivery is specified to be in the morning since the workers on the loading dock at Bice prefer to avoid traffic by ending their day at 4:30. If delivery does not happen until 5 p.m., a morning delivery condition is not essential to the contract—loading dock workers will be inconvenienced, but their convenience is not an important part of the essence of the contract.

On the other hand, if an unmet condition concerns a material provision in the contract, it may result in a judgment against the nonperforming party. For example, in the situation above, if delivery in the morning was because the loading dock was shared with other companies taking deliveries and Bice was permitted to receive goods only in the morning, then early delivery would be a material provision. Late delivery would be the failure of a condition because delivery of the 400 steel rods—the basic point to the contract—could not occur.

## RULES OF CONTRACT CONSTRUCTION

When parties come to court with a dispute over the provisions of their contract, courts look at many factors in interpreting the contract. Often, people involved in the dispute have been dealing with one another for years. So one factor the courts can look at is the parties' course of dealing or course of performance. But sometimes the parties really do not know one another. So the courts have developed general rules of construction to guide them when they interpret contracts and to promote uniformity in the interpretation of contracts.

This uniformity also helps parties when they draft their contracts. Knowledge of the rules avoids problems because parties have an idea of how a court will interpret the contract should a dispute arise.

## General Rules of Construction

Following are the general rules on contract construction used in most states:

1. *Lengthy communications are viewed as a whole, and any inconsistent words are discarded.* The contract's general intent will need to be determined and all clauses will be subordinated to that intent.
2. *Contracts are to be interpreted according to business custom and usage.* When a contract dispute arises in a particular industry, to resolve the matter, courts will look at how business is customarily conducted in that industry.
3. *Ordinary meaning of words.* Courts will construe words in the contract in such a way that is consistent with their ordinary meaning.
4. *Inconsistency between provisions.* If some provisions of the contract are typed and some are handwritten, the handwritten provisions will prevail over any typed provisions.

Read together, these rules underscore the courts' intention to understand what the parties tried to agree to during their negotiations. In general, these rules of construction create a road map so that when disputes inevitably arise, there is a consistent way to interpret the contract provisions.

## Parol Evidence Rule

Another rule of contract construction is the parol evidence rule. The **Parol Evidence Rule** provides that a written agreement, purportedly the full and final expression of the parties' intentions, may not be altered or contradicted by oral or written agreements made prior to the written agreement. This rule also excludes evidence of contemporaneous negotiations that occurred while the agreement was being written. This rule preserves the integrity of the party's final written agreement by not allowing outside evidence that contradicts or supplements that agreement. The rule never prevents the admission of subsequent agreements. Additionally, written additions to the contract that may have been created at the same time as the final agreement was created are considered part of the final agreement.

**Parol Evidence Rule:**
A rule of contract construction that says a written agreement purporting to be the full and final expression of the parties' intentions may not be altered or contradicted by evidence that adds to, varies, or contradicts the agreement or by oral or written agreements made prior to the writing.

Usually, when parties draft contractual agreements, there have been some discussions, perhaps e-mail exchanged or draft contracts circulated, before the final draft of the agreement is created, or even while the final draft of the agreement was being signed. These exchanges, whether oral or written, are not the final contract. Neither are they individual contracts in and of themselves. Often, when final contracts are signed, they are missing some important provisions that were the subject of previous telephone conversations or e-mail. These inadvertent omissions leave one party trying to show a court that the provision is missing from the contract but was considered in the negotiations as part of the contract. The parol evidence rule comes in at this point to determine whether such missing provisions should be excluded.

Following is the parol evidence rule found in the California Code of Civil Procedure. It is representative of the parol evidence rule in most states.

**§1856 California Code of Civil Procedure:**

(a) Terms set forth in a writing intended by the parties as a final expression of their agreement with respect to such terms as are included therein may not be contradicted by evidence of any prior agreement or of a contemporaneous oral agreement.

(b) The terms set forth in a writing described in subdivision (a) may be explained or supplemented by evidence of consistent additional terms unless the writing is intended also as a complete and exclusive statement of the terms of the agreement.

(c) The terms set forth in a writing described in subdivision (a) may be explained or supplemented by course of dealing or usage of trade or by course of performance.

What needs to be determined is whether the contract was the full expression of the parties' agreement or a partial expression of a larger agreement. The parol evidence rule only applies if the written agreement is the final expression of the agreement. If the document is the final expression of the agreement, it is an integration of all the terms of the agreement.

Documents can reflect a partial integration or a full integration of the agreement. If the document was not intended by the parties to include all the details of the agreement, there is a **Partial Integration**. In this circumstance, under the parol evidence rule no evidence may be admitted that will contradict the written document. If the document was intended by the parties to be a complete description of their agreement, there is a **Total Integration**. If this is the case, the

**Partial Integration:**
Discussing the parties' agreement but not purporting to be a full expression of the agreement.

**Total Integration:**
Full expression of the parties' agreement.

parol evidence rule provides that no evidence may be admitted to be considered by a court in interpreting the contract that would either contradict or add to the agreement.

There are four circumstances in which oral testimony may be permitted to interpret and change some meaning of the contract (but not to vary the terms). Courts will hear oral testimony about a written contract showing:

1. The failure of consideration;
2. That the contract was induced by fraud, duress, or mistake;
3. The existence of a collateral oral agreement; or
4. Ambiguities in a written contract and providing an explanation of them.

## STATUTE OF FRAUDS

The English **Statute of Frauds** was enacted in 1677. Its primary purpose was to avoid fraudulent claims. The statute required a party to produce a writing to prove a claim's existence. The writing has to be the agreement of the parties. All states have a variation of the Statute of Frauds in their contract law today.

**Statute of Frauds:**
A set of state laws and UCC provisions that list contracts that must be in writing in order to be enforceable.

The Statute of Frauds lists six types of contracts that must in writing and signed by the parties in order to be enforceable:

1. Contracts for an interest in real estate;
2. Contracts in consideration of marriage;
3. Contracts that are not performable within one year;
4. Guarantees or suretyship agreements;
5. Contracts for the sale of goods valued over a specified amount; and
6. Executor's promise to pay a decedent's debts.

### Contracts for an Interest in Real Property

A promise to transfer or buy any type of interest in land must be in writing. There are many kinds of interests in land other than selling it outright to someone. There are leases, mortgages, easements, and contracts to buy crops. These all relate to land and must be in writing.

### Contracts in Consideration of Marriage

A contract that has marriage or the promise of marriage as the consideration must be written. Examples of these types of contracts are prenuptial agreements and dowry agreements.

## Contracts Not Performable Within One Year

If a contract is incapable of being performed within one year, then the contract must be written. Time is measured starting from the date the contract is executed rather than how long it will take the parties to perform their duties under the contract. Also, performance within one year must be completely impossible rather than unlikely. Suppose, for example, that Gary agrees in January to have Hannah paint his house summer after next, 18 months in the future. By definition this contract cannot be completed within a year. Therefore, it must be in writing.

## Suretyship

Promises to pay for another's debts must be in writing under the Statute of Frauds. A common example applying this principle is that of the cosigner. Suppose that Darla agrees to guarantee a loan from the bank for her young son, who has poor credit. Darla must agree in writing (cosign) to cover the loan if her son cannot make the payments. Otherwise, the bank cannot enforce the agreement with Darla.

## Contracts for the Sale of Goods Valued at More Than a Specified Amount

This provision of the Statute of Frauds requires that contracts worth more than a certain amount ($500 to $1,000 in most states) be in writing. The provision still applies to most contracts in most states. However, today contracts between merchants are governed by the Uniform Commercial Code (UCC). The UCC is a set of provisions that govern the sale of goods between merchants but not between individuals. The requirements under the UCC are slightly different from those of the Statute of Frauds. In general U.C.C. §2-201 provides that "a contract for the sale of goods for the price of $500 or more" cannot be enforced unless it is in writing. The writing, however, does not have to be as detailed as required under the common law Statute of Frauds.

## Executor's Promise

An executor's promise to pay the debt of a deceased person is similar to a surety arrangement. Normally executors are not obligated to pay the debts of a dead person out of their own funds but rather only by using the funds of the deceased. If the administrator or executor of an estate makes a promise to pay off the debts of that estate using his or her personal funds instead, then the promise must be in writing.

## DISCHARGE OF OBLIGATION

There exist some circumstances that excuse a party from performing under a contract. If these circumstances occur, then the party's obligations under the contract are discharged. This means that the party is not liable under the contract and therefore does not need to perform. There are eight situations that discharge a party's duties under a contract:

1. Excuse of conditions;
2. Performance;
3. Breach of contract;
4. Agreement of the parties;
5. Impossibility of performance;
6. Supervening illegality;
7. Death or destruction of the subject matter or parties; and
8. Frustration of purpose.

### Excuse of Conditions

Often, contractual conditions have a timing element to them. In a contract situation, parties to the contract can agree that some things must happen first before other things can happen. This creates an order in which performance under the contract must take place. If that order is disturbed, the law allows a party to be discharged from his or her obligations. In this case, the law excuses the party for nonperformance. Thus, Marcus and Sheila can agree that Marcus will sell his car to Sheila after she secures a car loan. Until Sheila obtains the car loan, Marcus has no obligation to transfer the car to Sheila. If Sheila does not obtain the car loan, Marcus will never have to transfer the car to her.

### Performance

If a party to a contract has substantially performed under the contract, that performance can discharge the party's obligation. There does not need to be complete and full performance for there to be discharge. Even if performance is not absolutely complete, it can be considered complete in order to facilitate the party's agreement. For example, if David agrees to put a new roof on Shantae's home, his performance is substantially discharged when the roof is essentially complete. If a single nail in the roof is missing, David has done essentially all of the work, discharging his obligations, and Shantae must pay him despite the missing piece.

## Breach of Contract

If one party breaches the agreement, then the non-breaching party is no longer obligated to perform under the contract. This is common sense. Once someone breaks his or her promise to someone else, the latter no longer has to keep any promises made in exchange. If in the example above David stops his roofing job halfway through, leaving Shantae with a leaking roof, Shantae has no obligation to continue to pay him.

## Agreement of the Parties

Under special circumstances, the parties can agree to a discharge of obligations. Parties can make a subsequent agreement that relieves them of the obligation to perform under the contract. This is called **Mutual Rescission**. Both sides are making a new agreement. They agree to not perform under the contract. This rescission is itself a contract that is valid and binding on the parties.

**Mutual Rescission:**
An agreement by both parties to relieve one another of the obligation to perform.

Parties can also agree to an **Accord and Satisfaction**. An accord and satisfaction describes what happens when a party owes money and satisfies this debt through a payment of less than the total amount. The accord and satisfaction acts to satisfy the debt. For instance, if Ivan and Abdul had a contract under which in return for services Ivan would pay Abdul $5,000, and for whatever reason Abdul does not pay the full amount, Ivan and Abdul could agree to settle the contractual debt of $5,000 for a lesser amount. That agreement is an accord and satisfaction.

**Accord and Satisfaction:**
An agreement by one party to accept as full payment the other party's payment of less than the full sum of a debt owed.

Another way that parties can discharge their obligations through agreement is by **Novation.** A novation occurs when someone else substitutes for a party to a contract. A third person has stepped into the shoes of the original party. The old contract is discharged and a new contract is formed between the new parties. If Sarah hires Michelle to clean her home weekly for a set rate for one year, and Michelle for whatever reason can no longer do the cleaning, if Sarah is agreeable Sarah and Michelle can agree with Thomas that Thomas will do the cleaning instead of Michelle and receive the payments that otherwise would be due to Michelle. Michelle is released from the contract and has no right to payments from Sarah or any obligations to clean Sarah's house.

**Novation:**
The act of substituting someone else for a party to a contract.

## Impossibility of Performance

The courts recognize that some things are beyond a person's control. Hence, a party may have her or his obligations under a contract discharged because performance is impossible. For example, if Jon agrees to put a new deck on Suzi's home next week, and during that week there is a 12-foot blizzard, it is impossible for Jon to complete the contract because he cannot get to the home. Lack of access has made performance impossible. Jon's obligation to build the deck that week under the contract will be discharged, and Suzi will not need to pay him until the deck is completed.

## Supervening Illegality

Contracts are only valid if they are legal. In addition, if the subject matter of a contract becomes illegal after the contract has been validly formed, then the contract can no longer continue. All obligations under the contract are discharged. For example, U.S. companies sometimes contract with foreign governments to sell certain products. If the United States breaks off relations with that foreign government and imposes a trade embargo, then contracts obligating a party to transact business with that government are illegal. All obligations under these contracts are discharged.

## Death or Destruction

When the subject matter of a contract is destroyed before performance under the contract can be completed, all obligations under the contract are discharged. Along the same lines, if a person necessary for performance to be completed under a contract dies, then all obligations are discharged. When the person's estate is capable of performing an obligation, however, such as paying money, the estate can be responsible for contracts entered into by the deceased party. Death will discharge obligations under a contract when the performance could only be completed by a specific person. For example, the death of an artist who was under contract to complete a painting or portrait would discharge that duty. And if in the example above Suzi's house had burned down, Jon would not be obligated to build the deck for the destroyed house.

## Frustration of Purpose

**Frustration of Purpose** is similar to impossibility. It is different in that courts allow the discharge of obligation for frustration of purpose when the contract has lost its purpose because of a change in circumstance, although performance is not technically impossible. Obligations under the contract could be performed but aren't.

**Frustration of Purpose:**
Theory used to discharge a contract that has lost its purpose because of a change in circumstance, although performance is not technically impossible.

Take the famous British case of *Krell v. Henry* to illustrate this concept. In *Krell v. Henry*, 2 K.B. 740 (1903), the court had to consider a rental contract. Edward VII's coronation was scheduled for June 1902. The coronation procession was announced ahead of time so that people could line up to watch. Mr. Henry wanted to see the procession from the comfort of apartments overlooking the procession route. He entered into an agreement with Mr. Krell to rent Mr. Krell's chambers during the coronation. The rooms were leased to Mr. Henry for the purpose of watching the coronation parade. A deposit was made.

Unfortunately, the King became seriously ill and the coronation was postponed. Mr. Henry did not pay for the rental of the rooms. Mr. Krell sued. The court found that the purpose of the contractual agreement was to see the coronation procession. Because the coronation was postponed, the purpose of the rental no longer existed. The execution of the contract was not impossible but instead frustrated by another event—the cancellation.

## THIRD-PARTY BENEFICIARIES

Up to this point the discussion of contractual arrangements has included only two parties. Each party has made a promise to the other. However, there are other types of contractual arrangements. For example, if the parties exchange promises, but one of the parties wants a promised performance to benefit someone else, not him- or herself, this is called a **Third-Party Beneficiary** contract. In these contracts, the parties agree that a third party will receive something under the contract. The third party might receive money, a car, or even a service, such as having their lawn mowed.

**Third-Party Beneficiary:** Someone who receives a benefit under a contract that he or she is not a party to.

A beneficiary can either be intended or incidental. An **Intended Beneficiary** is someone who is expressly mentioned in the contract. There are two types of intended beneficiaries, creditor and donee. A creditor beneficiary is someone who will receive payment for a debt under the contract. A donee beneficiary receives a gift or something not owed. An **Incidental Beneficiary** includes all beneficiaries that do not fall into the intended beneficiary category. An incidental beneficiary does not have rights under the contract.

**Intended Beneficiary:** A third-party beneficiary mentioned in the contract.

**Incidental Beneficiary:** A third-party beneficiary not mentioned in the contract.

## ASSIGNMENT

Another arrangement the parties can make is called an **Assignment**. In an assignment, a party decides, after the contract has been formed, to transfer his or her rights under the contract to someone

**Assignment:** The transfer of a party's rights under a contract to someone else.

else. For instance, a party enters into a contract and will receive some money from the arrangement. Months after the contract is drafted, but before performance is due under it, the party assigns his or her right to receive money to a creditor. This transfer is called an assignment.

**Delegation** occurs if a party to the contract appoints another person to help fulfill the duties required under the contract. The person helping to fulfill the duties has no rights under the contract, and the party still must ensure that the contract is performed properly. The party has just made a side arrangement with respect to his or her duties under the contract. For example, a party may promise to pave a driveway for $250. That duty can be delegated to another person. This commonly occurs when contractually bound employers have their employees fulfill obligations made by the employer to third parties.

> **Delegation:**
> A party's appointment of another person to fulfill the duties required of the party under the contract.

## REMEDIES

If a contract is not performed, usually one of the parties will complain. The party will complain because he or she entered into the contract anticipating that it would be performed. The party may have even entered into other agreements in anticipation of the performance of this first contract. Because the contract was not performed, the party is harmed. A party can be harmed by loss of income, by loss of business, or through emotional distress. The law can attempt to restore the harmed party to that party's unharmed former self. This restoration is completed through a remedy.

In contracts, a remedy puts a party in the position he or she would have been in had the contract been fully performed. Contract remedies usually do not consider forcing a party to perform under the contract (which would be a form of slavery). Instead a remedy is designed to restore the non-breaching party in an appropriate way. It is also designed to protect a party's expectations as to the completion of the contract. The non-breaching party can only recover for the foreseeable consequences of a breach. Usually, a court must predict what position a party would have been in had the contract been fully performed.

There are legal and equitable remedies. This is because of the historical division between courts of law and courts of equity. Courts of law handled a limited type of case dealing with the rules propounded by the rulers of England. Courts of equity on the other hand handled cases where fairness and unjust treatment were involved.

Legal remedies are monetary in nature. They are usually referred to as damages. Legal remedies include the following:

1. Compensatory damages;
2. Punitive damages;
3. Consequential damages; and
4. Liquidated damages.

Equitable remedies are nonmonetary. These remedies include the following:

1. Injunctions;
2. Specific performance;
3. Rescission and restitution;
4. Reformation; and
5. Quasi-contract.

## LEGAL REMEDIES

### Compensatory Damages

**Compensatory Damages** compensate a party monetarily for the breach of contract. To recover, damages must be proved to a reasonable certainty. A party cannot speculate what he or she might have earned had the contract been performed. The losses must be known. Also, damages must be foreseeable when the contract was entered into, and the party harmed must mitigate the harm from the breach. **Mitigation** means that the injured party makes some effort to minimize the losses that flow from the breach.

**Compensatory Damages:**
Cash compensation for a breach of contract limited to the provable amount required to make the injured party whole.

**Mitigation:**
Reduction of damages through the efforts of the injured party. This is a self-help requirement.

### Punitive Damages

**Punitive Damages** are monetary, but they are intended to punish the wrongdoer. Sometimes they are called exemplary damages. They are usually so large that they serve to discourage others from acting in a similar manner. Punitive damages are rarer because they are only awarded when the wrongdoer engaged in extreme or outrageous conduct, rather than just a breach of the contract. That standard is very hard to meet.

**Punitive Damages:**
Compensation paid to a party not to make the injured party whole, but rather to punish the wrongdoer for extreme or outrageous conduct.

### Consequential Damages

**Consequential Damages** are awarded for damages sustained by the plaintiff that do not directly flow from the breach of contract but occur as a secondary effect of the breach. Consequential damages are only awarded in special circumstances, where the plaintiff can

**Consequential Damages:**
Damages that do not directly flow from the breach of contract but instead occur as a secondary result of the breach.

prove that the damages were reasonably foreseeable and contemplated by the parties at the time the contract was made, and each party was aware that the circumstances would cause additional losses to a party if the other party breached. These damages are in addition to the compensatory damages  owed to a plaintiff.

## Liquidated Damages

**Liquidated Damages** are agreed to by the parties and are usually mentioned in the contract. The parties stipulate to, or agree ahead of time regarding, what the exact amount damages will be in the event of a breach of contract. Liquidated damages benefit each party because the parties can plan for the consequences if a contract goes badly.

**Liquidated Damages:**
An amount agreed upon at the making of the contract to be recovered by one party if the other party breaches.

## EQUITABLE REMEDIES

### Injunctions

An **Injunction** is a court order that requires a party to stop a particular action. This intervention can prevent a breach of contract if it will result in irreparable injury.

**Injunction:**
A court order requiring a party to a dispute to do or refrain from doing something.

### Specific Performance

**Specific Performance** is a remedy whereby the court orders a breaching party to perform under a contract. Specific performance is only available if money damages are not adequate to make the party whole. One limitation is that specific performance is not available for personal services contracts, as forcing someone to serve someone else is tantamount to slavery.

**Specific Performance:**
A court-ordered requirement that a party perform an obligation under the contract.

### Rescission and Restitution

**Rescission** occurs when the party "takes back" any promise made under the contract. **Restitution** requires that a party be restored to the original position the party was in before entering into the contract. This means that any assets that may have changed hands must be returned. The fair market value of any benefit transferred must also be repaid.

**Rescission:**
A remedy whereby a party "takes back" any promise made under the contract.

**Restitution:**
A remedy whereby a party is made whole under a contract by the return of lost property.

### Reformation

If the remedy sought is **Reformation**, the court will modify or reform the contract to be what the parties originally agreed to. Usually,

**Reformation:**
A remedy under which a court rewrites all or part of a contract.

reformation occurs when the written agreement of the parties does not conform to what the parties agreed to.

## Quasi-Contractual Remedies

When the agreement does not meet all of the requirements to be considered a contract, it still can be considered a quasi-contract under certain circumstances. This situation can arise when the parties never took the time to formalize their agreement. It also can happen when the parties' agreement is unenforceable as a contract because it violates the Statute of Frauds. There are two remedies available for breach of quasi-contracts:

1. Quantum meruit and
2. Quantum valebant.

**Quantum Meruit** means, "as much as he has deserved." When the plaintiff has delivered a service of value to the defendant, then the value of the service should be returned to the plaintiff.

**Quantum Valebant** means, "as much as they are worth." In cases seeking this remedy, the plaintiff should receive the value of the property delivered to the defendant.

## CONTRACT DISPUTES

Increasingly, contracts include a provision called a **Dispute Resolution Clause**. Often, this clause describes how disputes that arise under the contract are to be resolved. The parties can choose which state's laws apply or if arbitration and mediation will be used. **Arbitration** is the resolution of a dispute outside the court system through an agreement of the parties that a third party will decide the dispute. A neutral arbitrator hears all the evidence and issues a judgment that must be enforced by the courts.

If the matter is to be arbitrated, the parties can include in the clause where that arbitration will be held, such as at the offices of the American Arbitration Association (AAA). If the parties select the AAA, it will administer the arbitration for a fee, providing offices and arbitrators to the parties. The AAA also has arbitration rules that will govern the process. This is all perfectly legal.

Recently, however, consumer contracts have included mandatory arbitration clauses. Consumer contracts such as credit card account agreements are typically not negotiated. If a consumer wants a credit card, he or she agrees to the terms of the standard agreement—which includes mandatory arbitration. These manda-

**Quantum Meruit:** Remedy that provides the injured party with the value of the service provided to the other party.

**Quantum Valebant:** Remedy that provides the injured party with the value of the property provided to the other party.

**Dispute Resolution Clause:** A clause in a contract that describes how disputes that arise under the contract are to be resolved.

**Arbitration:** The resolution of a dispute outside the court system through an agreement of the parties that a third party will decide the dispute.

## ETHICAL ISSUES

● ● ●

Contractors entering into contracts with the federal government must comply with the Federal Acquisition Regulation (FAR). FAR encompasses contracting rules, processes, and contract forms and clauses. FAR regulations require a written code of business ethics in many government contracts. These regulations address contract breaches such as fraud, theft, and misappropriation of funds.

Why does the federal government have these rules in place?

Section 52.203-13 of FAR*:

(i) The Contractor's internal control system shall—

A. Facilitate timely discovery of improper conduct in connection with Government contracts; and

B. Ensure corrective measures are promptly instituted and carried out.

(ii) For example, the Contractor's internal control system should provide for—

A. Periodic reviews of company business practices, procedures, policies, and internal controls for compliance with the Contractor's code of business ethics and conduct and the special requirements of Government contracting;

B. An internal reporting mechanism, such as a hotline, by which employees may report suspected instances of improper conduct, and instructions that encourage employees to make such reports;

C. Internal and/or external audits, as appropriate; and

D. Disciplinary action for improper conduct.

*Source: http://www.acquisition.gov/Far/

tory arbitration clauses are also referred to as pre-dispute arbitration agreements. There is no negotiating the mandatory arbitration clause, so consumers completely waive their right to sue in court. This is concerning because frequently those same clauses require disputes to be facilitated at arbitration forums who had a financial interest in resolving disputes in favor of the merchant and not the consumer. In response to this situation, Congress passed the Arbitration Fairness Act of 2009. This Act makes invalid all pre-dispute arbitration agreements mandatory arbitration clauses in consumer and employment contracts—contracts that by their nature are made between parties of greatly disparate economic power. Employees and individuals seeking credit, for example, are not in the position to negotiate the fine print of pre-form agreements.

Many private contract disputes go to arbitration. Because these are disputes between equals, legislation has not interfered with the process. Frequently, arbitration and mediation are faster and cheaper than resolving a dispute in court.

**Mediation** allow a neutral third party, a mediator, to facilitate the parties' negotiations as they attempt to resolve differences on their own, without a decision imposed by a judge, jury, or arbitrator. "Non-binding" arbitration is similar to mediation and can be

**Mediation:**
Process whereby a dispute is resolved outside the court system through an agreement of the parties that a third party will make non-binding recommendations to decide the dispute.

conducted by a mediator or arbitrator. In "'non-binding" arbitration the parties request that a neutral third party make a quantifiable evaluation of the dispute in terms of potential liability and damages payable.

## CHAPTER SUMMARY

Contracts can be as complicated or simple as the parties who draft them want them to be. Contracts can have conditions or benefit third parties. The law provides rules regarding contract construction that guide parties so that they draft valid and enforceable contracts.

If there is a breach of contract, the law allows for recovery of damages through legal and equitable remedies. To know how a particular contractual dispute will be resolved, parties must pay attention to dispute resolution clauses in the contracts they draft and the contracts that they sign.

### Relevant Web Sites

http://www.fairarbitrationnow.org
http://www.adr.org

### Exercises

1. Find a contract with an arbitration clause. Describe whether it is covered by the Arbitration Fairness Act of 2009. If it is not, explain why not.
2. List three types of contracts that must be written to be enforceable.
3. Describe the difference between an assignment and a delegation.
4. Describe the difference between the remedies of rescission, restitution, and reformation.
5. List three ways to discharge a contract obligation.

### Questions

1. What are the limitations of compensatory damages?
2. Why was the Statute of Frauds originally enacted?
3. What is an express condition?
4. What does an injunction do?
5. What is a third-party beneficiary?
6. What is integration?
7. What is a novation?
8. What is an accord and satisfaction?
9. When is quantum meruit available?
10. How can frustration of purpose discharge a contract obligation?

### Hypotheticals

1. Husband claims that Wife agreed to renounce any claim to property that he owned prior to the couple's marriage. Is this agreement within the Statute of Frauds?
2. Eric claims that Sarah hired him in January of 2011 to remove all of the rose bushes on her property by the end of 2012. Is this contract governed by the Statute of Frauds?
3. Mr. and Mrs. George entered into an agreement to buy a house owned by Samantha Jones. The sale will go forward if the Georges obtain financing for the mortgage. What kind of condition is this?
4. Painter has agreed to paint Farmer's barn for $1,500. Painter completes the job, and Farmer refuses to pay because he does not like the color. What quasi-contractual remedy may be available to Painter?

5. Morton contracts with Jenson to refurbish his kitchen. Upon completion Jenson presents Morton a bill for $6,500. Morton believes he has been overcharged for the job. He mails a check for $4,500 and tells Jenson that this amount is satisfaction for what Morton owes. Jenson cashes the check and bills Morton for the remaining balance due. Will Morton be liable for the balance due?

## Sample Cases

1. Thomas Ryan is a flight instructor in Wisconsin. He knew James Sheppard for several decades and had previously given him flight instruction. In 2007, Sheppard and Ryan entered into a two-year agreement for flight instruction services. The agreement specified that Ryan would be paid $35,000 per year plus expenses. Before any flight instruction took place, Sheppard died. Ryan sued the Estate of Sheppard for $105,000, which was the cost of services under the contract. Can Ryan recover from the Estate?

   *Ryan v. Estate of Sheppard*, 2010 Wis. App. 105 (2010).

2. The Hadleys ran a flour mill. The steam engine operating the mill stopped working due to a broken crankshaft. The part needed to be transported to a foundry for repair. The Hadleys contracted with a common carrier, Baxendale. Baxendale promised to deliver the shaft the following day. The shaft was not delivered for several days. The mill remained closed, and the Hadleys suffered losses. The Hadleys sued Baxendale to recover those losses. Baxendale argued that the damages were too remote and not recoverable. Can the Hadleys recover for their losses?

   *Hadley v. Baxendale*, 156 Eng. Rep. 145 (Ct. of the Exchequer 1854).

## Key Terms

**Accord and Satisfaction:** An agreement by one party to accept as full payment the other party's payment of less than the full sum of a debt owed.

**Arbitration:** The resolution of a dispute outside the court system through an agreement of the parties that a third party will decide the dispute.

**Assignment:** The transfer of a party's rights under a contract to someone else.

**Compensatory Damages:** Cash compensation for a breach of contract limited to the provable amount required to make the injured party whole.

**Condition Precedent:** A condition that must be met before a party's promise under a contract becomes absolute.

**Consequential Damages:** Damages that do not directly flow from the breach of contract but rather occur as a secondary result of the breach.

**Constructive Condition:** A condition that is not agreed upon by the parties or mentioned in the contract but rather is supplied by the court in the interest of fairness.

**Delegation:** A party's appointment of another person to fulfill the duties required of the party under the contract.

**Dispute Resolution Clause:** A clause in a contract that describes how disputes that arise under the contract are to be resolved.

**Express Condition:** A condition that the parties have agreed upon and that is explicitly stated in the contract.

**Frustration of Purpose:** Theory used to discharge a contract that has lost its purpose because of a change in circumstance, although performance is not technically impossible.

**Incidental Beneficiary:** A third-party beneficiary not mentioned in the contract.

**Injunction:** A court order requiring a party to a dispute to do or refrain from doing something.

**Intended Beneficiary:** A third-party beneficiary mentioned in the contract.

**Liquidated Damages:** An amount agreed upon at the making of the contract to be recovered by one party if the other party breaches.

**Mediation:** Process whereby a dispute is resolved outside the court system through an agreement of the parties that a third party will make non-binding recommendations to decide the dispute.

**Mitigation:** Reduction of damages through the efforts of the injured party. This is a self-help requirement.

**Mutual Rescission:** Agreement by both parties to relieve one another of the obligation to perform.

**Novation:** The act of substituting someone else for a party to a contract.

**Parol Evidence Rule:** A rule of contract construction that says a written agreement purporting to be the full and final expression of the parties' intentions may not be altered or contradicted by evidence that adds to, varies, or contradicts the agreement or by oral or written agreements made prior to the writing.

**Partial Integration:** Discussing the parties' agreement but not purporting to be a full expression of the agreement.

**Punitive Damages:** Compensation paid to a party not to make the injured party whole but rather to punish the wrongdoer for extreme or outrageous conduct.

**Quantum Meruit:** Remedy that provides the injured party with the value of the service provided to the other party.

**Quantum Valebant:** Remedy that provides the injured party with the value of the property provided to the other party.

**Reformation:** A remedy under which a court rewrites all or part of a contract.

**Rescission:** A remedy whereby a party "takes back" any promise made under the contract.

**Restitution:** A remedy whereby a party is made whole under a contract by the return of lost property.

**Specific Performance:** A court-ordered requirement that a party perform an obligation under the contract.

**Statute of Frauds:** A set of state laws and UCC provisions that list contracts that must be in writing in order to be enforceable.

**Third-Party Beneficiary:** Someone who receives a benefit under a contract that he or she is not a party to.

**Total Integration:** Full expression of the parties' agreement.

# UCC, Commercial Paper, and Electronic Commerce

## INTRODUCTION

The **Uniform Commercial Code (UCC)** was developed through collaboration between the National Conference of Commissioners on Uniform State Laws (NCCUSL) and the American Law Institute (ALI). The UCC was created to make the law of sales and commercial transactions uniform across the different states. The UCC is not a federal statute. Instead, it is a model law that was adopted separately by each state. Some states made changes to the original UCC model code, so although the UCC as a whole applies across the United States, there are minor differences among the laws of the individual states.

This chapter discusses the UCC generally. It considers UCC Articles 1, 2, and 3 in order to illustrate broadly the circumstances under which the UCC might apply. The UCC regulates much more than contract law. It covers a wide range of commercial transactions. For example, the UCC regulates the lease of goods, funds transfers, letters of credit, and negotiable instruments.

The UCC was drafted with the idea that people should be free to enter into contracts without the worry that a contract may fail because not every detail was worked out in the negotiation phase. The UCC provides missing provisions when the contract does not

**Uniform Commercial Code (UCC):**
A model law that has been adopted separately by each state to facilitate making the law of sales and commercial transactions generally uniform across the different states so that these transactions would be easier to complete.

mention them. In this way courts can apply the UCC to "fill in the blanks" and uphold contracts that otherwise would fail for a lack of terms. Parties therefore can better plan and anticipate how their contracts will be interpreted by other parties and by the courts as well.

Article 1 of the UCC provides definitions and rules of interpretation for the other UCC provisions. Article 2 of the UCC regulates sales contracts between merchants. Negotiable instruments are governed by Article 3 of the UCC. This chapter discusses both of those articles' provisions and also briefly discusses the different types of negotiable instruments, their requirements, and the responsibilities of parties to these instruments.

## BACKGROUND OF THE UCC

The NCCUSL met for the first time in Saratoga Springs, New York, in 1892. The NCCUSL has drafted more than 200 uniform laws on numerous subjects such as probate law, child custody, partnership, and family support. The commission is made up of representatives from every state and some territories. The members are practitioners, judges, and professors who work without pay on the drafting of uniform laws.

Work began on the UCC in 1942, and it was not completed until the early 1950s. The UCC was first amended in 1958. There was a strong desire to move away from the common law when the idea of the UCC first arose. Experts in the field of contract law felt strongly that commercial transactions, transactions between merchants, needed to be modernized. Below is the relevant portion of the model UCC that explains what the purpose of the UCC is:

> **Uniform Commercial Code §1-102. Purposes; Rules of Construction; Variation by Agreement.**
>     (1)  This Act shall be liberally construed and applied to promote its underlying purposes and policies.
>     (2)  Underlying purposes and polices of this Act are...
>         (b)  to permit the continued expansion of commercial practices through custom, usage and agreement of the parties.

Liberal (meaning "flexible") construction is a mainstay of UCC application. Section 1-102(2)(b) promotes the flexibility that the drafters hoped the law would allow. Parties who frequently deal with one another develop a custom of dealing. The drafters of the UCC felt that this custom should not be prescribed by law. Instead, commercial actors should be free to act to encourage commerce.

## ELECTRONIC COMMERCE

Electronic commerce describes the sale of goods and services by computer and on the World Wide Web. Buyers and sellers do not enter into their agreements by phone or face to face. They complete the sale online. These transactions occur on Web sites with domain names. Those domain names are registered through various registrars, all governed by the Internet Corporation for Assigned Names and Numbers (ICANN). ICANN was created in 1998 with the purpose of coordinating the Internet's naming system.

Soon after the creation of ICANN, the United States Congress passed the Anticybersquatting Consumer Protection Act (ACPA). This legislation was aimed at preventing the registration of domain names of well-known companies with the intent to extract payment from those companies for use of the domain name, a practice known as cybersquatting. Today this activity can be inadvertent as companies with similar names operate online and register versions of those names with various registrars. ACPA continues to be interpreted in various ways by courts in an effort to protect the interests of legitimately registered domain name holders.

## UCC-Related Electronic Commerce

In 2003 the NCCUSL provided amendments to the UCC to update it to include provisions for electronic commerce (e-commerce). New definitions are included to make the UCC consistent with the **Uniform Electronic Transactions Act (UETA)** and the federal **Electronic Signatures in Global and National Commerce Act (E-SIGN Act)** of 2000. We briefly discuss those laws here.

UETA was created in an attempt to make state governing of e-signatures more uniform. Contracts, for the most part, must be signed by the parties against whom enforcement is sought. Contracts entered into electronically—**E-Contracts**—are signed electronically through technologies that allow digital signatures. State law governs what is an acceptable digital signature so that contracts are respected and enforced. The purpose of UETA is to facilitate **E-Commerce**, which is commerce in electronic form, by giving legal effect to electronic records and signatures. About 48 states have adopted UETA.

The E-SIGN Act provides that all contracts, records, or signatures that are in electronic form are legally valid to the extent they would be legally valid if they were in printed form on paper. An e-signature is valid if the parties agree that it is. An electronic document is valid if it is in a form that can be retained and accurately reproduced. Certain documents are excluded from E-SIGN, including the following:

**Uniform Electronic Transactions Act (UETA):** A model law that was created in an attempt to make state governing of e-signatures more uniform. Under the UETA most contracts must be signed by the parties against whom enforcement is sought.

**Electronic Signatures in Global and National Commerce Act (E-SIGN Act):** A federal law that provides that all contracts, records, or signatures that are in electronic form are legally valid to the extent they would be legally valid if they were in printed form on paper.

**E-Contract:** A contract entered into electronically.

**E-Commerce:** Any commerce in electronic form.

court papers, health insurance termination, prenuptial agreements, and wills. Additionally, the Act provides that states may pass their own regulations regarding electronic signatures.

## UNIFORM COMPUTER INFORMATION TRANSACTIONS ACT

**The Uniform Computer Information Transactions Act (UCITA)** was originally going to be Article 2B of the UCC. It had to be withdrawn because the NCCUSL and the ALI could not agree on how it should read. The NCCUSL sponsored the Act alone and named it UCITA.

UCITA is designed to take certain kinds of contracts out from the purview of the UCC and to govern them separately under the rules of UCITA. The contracts at issue are "pure software" and "software embedded in goods" contracts.

The impetus for the creation of UCITA was the perceived need for uniformity in rules governing transactions involving computer information. Specifically, there is an increasing need for rules that are applicable in the growing global markets. As U.S. companies continue to draft contracts with foreign buyers and sellers of computer information, the UCC and common law contract rules fall short of providing clear and consistent rules for this new marketplace. Very few states supported UCITA. As of 2003, the NCCUSL no longer supported UCITA.

**UCITA:**
Uniform Computer Information Transactions Act, which governs contracts for pure software or software embedded in goods.

## OVERVIEW OF THE UCC

The UCC has nine Articles. They are:

1. General Provisions
2. Sales of Goods
   2A. Leases of Goods
3. Negotiable Instruments
4. Bank Deposits
   4A. Funds Transfer
5. Letters of Credit
6. Bulk Transfers
7. Bills of Lading, Warehouse Receipts
8. Investment Securities
9. Secured Transactions.

The UCC covers a broad spectrum of commercial activities. Article 1 has three parts, which cover the general provisions of the Code as well as definitions. Section 1-303 defines course of performance, course of dealing, and usage of trade.

**Course of Performance, Course of Dealing,** and **Usage of Trade** are key concepts in the UCC. Course of performance (within one contract) and course of dealing (across multiple contracts) recognize that parties develop contractual habits after dealing with one another over the years. Courts will respect these "habits" if a dispute arises. The habits provide evidence of the parties' understanding of their agreement. A court will interpret the pattern of business conduct between two parties over time as an indication of what the parties meant for the written words of the contract to mean. For additional guidance in interpretation of what a contract means, a court will also look at usage of trade, which is the standard practice or set of practices in a particular type of business or trade in a certain region.

One example of how these concepts work is illustrated by the case of *Eastern Airlines, Inc. v. Gulf Oil Corp.*, 415 F. Supp. 429 (S.D. Fla.1975). In that case there existed a contract between two companies for the purchase of oil. It was a requirements contract. A **Requirements Contract** is one in which a buyer agrees to buy from a seller all that the buyer requires of a certain item or items.

Eastern Airlines would refuel at various airports while purchasing the needed fuel from Gulf Oil. Gulf Oil began to complain that Eastern was "fuel freighting." This occurs when an airline refuels only at destinations with the least expensive fuel.

In order to decide the matter, the court considered the course of dealing between the two parties. That is the way the parties have transacted business with one another over time. The court heard witnesses from Gulf and Eastern describe how the fuel was bought under the contract over their 30-year contractual relationship. There was evidence that Eastern would often buy a great deal of fuel in one location and none at all at other locations. This was attributed to various pressures that the airline had to consider, such as weather, schedule changes, economy, passenger convenience, and flight captain judgment.

The court held that Gulf had not previously complained of the fuel freighting that had been going on for years. In fact, the evidence showed that fuel freighting was an airline industry standard.

The court concluded:

> The case here is one where the established courses of performance and dealing between the parties, the established usages of the trade, and the basic contract itself all show that the matters complained of for the first time by Gulf after commencement of this litigation are the fundamental given ingredients of the aviation fuel

**Course of Performance:**
A legal concept embodied in the UCC that recognizes that parties develop contractual habits after dealing with one another over the years. A court will interpret the pattern of business conduct between two parties over time within one contract as an indication of what the parties meant for the written words of the contract to mean.

**Course of Dealing:**
A legal concept embodied in the UCC that recognizes that parties develop contractual habits after dealing with one another over the years. A court will interpret the pattern of business conduct between two parties over time across several contracts as an indication of what the parties meant for the written words of the present contract to mean.

**Usage of Trade:**
A legal concept embodied in the UCC that recognizes that the standard practice or set of practices in a particular type of business or trade in a certain region should guide the interpretation of what a contract means.

**Requirements Contract:**
A contract under which a buyer agrees to buy from a seller all that the buyer requires of a certain item or items.

trade to which the parties have accommodated themselves successfully and without dispute over the years.

—*Eastern Air Lines, Inc. v. Gulf Oil Corp.,*
415 F. Supp. 429 (S.D. Fla.1975)

## UCC ARTICLE 2: SALES OF GOODS

Article 2 of the UCC regulates **Sales Contracts**. Sales contracts concern the sale of goods between merchants. Of course, the common law still applies to the sale of goods. A valid contract still needs an offer, acceptance, and consideration. But if a conflict does arise between the caselaw-based common law and the statutory UCC, the UCC governs.

A sale is "the passing of title from the seller to the buyer for a price" according to UCC §2-106(1). A **Good** is movable. Some transactions may involve a hybrid of a good and a service—and in some states a service is excluded from the provisions of the UCC. For example, when technology services are provided, sometimes software is involved and sometimes there is technical expertise. This can be a hybrid—both a good and a service. Finally, the determination of who is a **Merchant** "may be based upon [their] specialized knowledge as to the goods, specialized knowledge as to business practices, or specialized knowledge as to both."

The definition of a merchant under the UCC §2-104(1) provides that a merchant is someone "who deals in goods of the kind or otherwise by his occupation holds himself out as having knowledge or skill peculiar to the practices or goods involved in the transaction...."

For some of the six requirements for a valid contract there is an applicable UCC provision.

| | |
|---|---|
| Offer: | §2-206(1)(a)—Offer and Acceptance in Formation of Contract |
| Acceptance: | §2-206(1)(b)—Offer and Acceptance in Formation of Contract |
| Consideration: | §1-304 Obligation of Good Faith |
| Legal subject matter: | No express requirement; implied |
| Contractual intent: | No express requirement; implied |
| Contractual capacity: | No express requirement; implied |

Therefore, there are many contract requirements that have no corresponding UCC section. This is primarily due to the fact that the UCC applies to merchants such as corporations or small businesses that enter into contracts on a daily basis. It is assumed that they have

**Sales Contract:**
A contract concerning the sale of goods and not services.

**Good:**
A movable item as defined by the UCC.

**Merchant:**
A buyer or seller of goods with specialized knowledge about that good. This includes any commercial sellers of a product in the ordinary course of business.

the capacity and intent to enter into contracts and that the contracts concern only legal matters, and not illegal agreements. The UCC will allow the terms of the contract, such as price, to be less definite than tolerated under the common law. If a dispute should arise, the court will determine a *reasonable price*. If one of the parties is meant to determine price under the contract, the determination will be made in *good faith*. These concepts of reasonableness and good faith are fundamental and pervasive in the UCC.

Often, the question of whether the contract is for the sale of goods is ambiguous. This was the issue facing the court in the case *Bonebrake v. Cox*, 499 F.2d 951 (8th Cir. 1974). Donald and Claude Cox were brothers and the owners of the Tamarack Bowl in Missouri Valley, Iowa. This bowling alley was extremely active, with league bowling most nights of the week. On February 5, 1968, a fire gutted the bowling alley. It was essential that the repairs and renovation of the building be done quickly before the brothers lost all of their income from the league bowlers.

The Cox brothers entered into a contract for the sale of equipment and installation of that equipment by Mr. Woodrow B. Simek. Mr. Simek owned a bowling alley in Ashland, Nebraska. He also dealt in new and used bowling equipment. A contract was entered into for the purchase by the Cox brothers of various pieces of used equipment, such as ten bowling lane beds, one ball-cleaning machine, and ball storage racks, for the total price of $20,000. Additionally, there was a separate contract made for the purchase and installation of pinspotters for $35,000. The work commenced over the summer. It became clear that the equipment installed required a great deal of repair and that the pinspotters were completely inoperable. Most bowling leagues began in late August and early September. By the beginning of September the Tamarack Bowl was still in disarray. Around the same time, Mr. Simek fell ill. By early September, he was dead.

The Cox brothers had already paid more than $20,000 on their contract. And yet much of the equipment they had ordered and presumably paid for had yet to be delivered. What had been delivered was in disrepair. The Cox brothers visited Mr. Simek before he died and also visited his sister, Frances Bonebrake, several times after Mr. Simek passed. Ms. Bonebrake directed the Cox brothers to search Mr. Simek's warehouse to see if the equipment that had yet to be delivered was anywhere to be found. It was not. Additionally, they were forced to hire new contractors to finish the repair and installation of the equipment they already had.

The Cox brothers hired a lawyer and sent the letter shown in Figure 5-1 on the next page.

September 17, 1968

Mrs. Frances Bonebrake
Ashland, Nebraska

Dear Madam:

We represent Claude and Donald Cox, owners of the Tamarack Bowl in Missouri Valley who entered into a contract with your brother, Woodrow Simek, for the purchase and installation of ten alleys complete and ten automatic pinsetters installed and complete.

At the time of Mr. Simek's death he was engaged in the installation of said items and had the installation over half completed. Following his death the employees which were assisting in the installation left the job, and it was necessary for the Cox brothers to look elsewhere for the additional parts and supplies which had not been delivered, and to commence work on completing the installation of the alleys and pinsetters with such other help as they were able to obtain.

They are gradually locating and obtaining the necessary parts for repairing the pinsetters and are getting them installed, although this is going to result in a considerable delay beyond the date of completion, and which will, of course delay the commencing of the bowling season. It may result in requiring them to have shorter league seasons which will result in a substantial loss of income.

Mr. Donald Cox has recently talked with you about this and he told us that an Administrator has or will be appointed for his estate in Ashland, Nebraska.

The Cox brothers had paid Mr. Simek $27,500.00 at the time of his death on a total contract price of $55,000.00 covering the cost of the alleys and pinsetting equipment and the installation which included a guarantee as to the quality and performance of the equipment.

They hope to be able to complete the installation at a cost not greater than the contract price, but they will nevertheless no doubt sustain substantial loss caused by the delay and lateness in starting the bowling season.

The Cox brothers are greatly concerned about this, and among other things they are concerned about whether or not all of the equipment which has been delivered and partially installed had been paid for by Mr. Simek prior to his death.

**Figure 5-1**
Letter from *Bonebrake v. Cox*

Our clients are keeping an accurate record of all payments which have been made by them, or which are now being made by them in paying the cost of completing the installation, so that they can substantiate a claim for any loss which may be sustained. We wish to be advised as to what action has been taken concerning the probate of the estate of Mr. Simek, and the name of the attorney who will be taking care of this matter for you, and we would suggest that this letter be handed to such attorney so that he will be aware of the position of our clients.

Very truly yours,

ACREA & PEARSON

K. C. Acrea
KCA/mas

**Figure 5-1** cont.

Ms. Bonebrake, as the administratrix of Mr. Simek's estate, then sued the brothers on behalf of the estate to recover the balance due on the contract.

The court found that the contract was first for the sale of goods and for the installation of those goods. Because the UCC only applies to the sale of goods, it was possible that it did not apply to this contract at all. The court applied a **Predominant Factor Test** to determine whether the UCC applied when the contract contains a sales and a service element. The court then looked to see which element was the predominant factor in the contract. The court described the test by asking, "Is the rendition of service with goods incidentally involved (e.g., contract with artist for painting) or is a transaction of sale, with labor incidentally involved? (e.g., installation of a water heater in a bathroom)."

The court held that the UCC did apply because the service of installing the bowling equipment was *incidental* to the sale of the equipment. If the UCC did not apply, the parties would be subject to the common law, with the court considering breach of contract issues under Iowa common law. It is not possible to say if that would have been better or worse for either party. It is only important here that we consider the initial analysis the court has to go through to determine if the UCC applies to any one contract.

**Predominant Factor Test:** Test applied by the court to determine whether the UCC applies when a contract contains both a sales element and a service element, with which the court identifies which of the two elements is the predominant factor in the contract.

The court also held that the Cox brothers were correct in hiring another contractor and buying equipment to finish the renovation of their business. This is allowed under the theory of **Anticipatory Repudiation**.

UCC §2-610. Anticipatory Repudiation.

When either party repudiates the contract with respect to a performance not yet due the loss of which will substantially impair the value of the contract to the other, the aggrieved party may

(a) for a commercially reasonable time await performance by the repudiating party; or

(b) resort to any remedy for breach (Section 2-703 or Section 2-711), even though he has notified the repudiating party that he would await the latter's performance and has urged retraction; and

(c) in either case suspend his own performance or proceed in accordance with the provisions of this Article on the seller's right to identify goods to the contract notwithstanding breach or to salvage unfinished goods (Section 2-704).

In short, if a party to a UCC contract finds that the other party to the contract is not going to perform his or her obligations, the first party doesn't need to continue to harm him- or herself by performing while getting nothing in return. That first party can stop performing under the contract to prevent further harm.

## NEGOTIABLE INSTRUMENTS

**Negotiable Instruments** were once known as **Commercial Paper**. Negotiable instruments are how merchants pay for their products. These instruments are superior to cash because they can be followed, tracked, and identified through records in a manner that cash cannot be. UCC Article 3 governs negotiable instruments.

Drafts and notes are examples of negotiable instruments. A **Draft** (what many people call a check) is an order that payment be made from the account of the person making the draft to the person named in the draft, or to the bearer of the draft. A **Note** is a promise for payment in the future.

Examples of notes include **Certificates of Deposit** and **Promissory Notes**. A certificate of deposit is a negotiable instrument entitling the bearer to receive a fixed sum of interest and principal from a bank on a deposit at the maturity date. A promissory note is a con-

**Anticipatory Repudiation:** Repudiation of a contractual duty by one party to a contract before performance is due when the other party to the contract makes clear statements or conducts himself in such a way as to indicate that he will not be performing under the contract. In such event, the former party may treat the latter's conduct as a breach of contract, stop performance under the contract, and immediately sue for breach of contract.

**Negotiable Instrument:** A written instrument of commerce that includes a promise to pay or order for payment to be made.

**Commercial Paper:** In this context, an alternative name for negotiable instruments; a short-term promissory note.

**Draft:** An order that payment be made, such as a check.

**Note:** A promise for payment in the future, such as a certificate of deposit.

**Certificate of Deposit:** A negotiable instrument entitling the bearer to receive a fixed sum of interest and principal from a bank on a deposit at the maturity date.

**Promissory Note:** A contract in which one party promises to pay or repay a specific amount on a given date or on demand by the holder of the note.

tract in which one party promises to pay or repay a specific amount on a given date or on demand by the holder of the note.

Negotiability, that key characteristic of a negotiable instrument, is the characteristic that makes a document much like cash—it can be transferred from one party to another by endorsement (signing) and delivering the appropriate documentation to the new owner.

The Ohio Revised Code (as a representative example) adopted U.C.C. §3-104 and provides the detailed elements of negotiability:

**1303.03 Negotiable instrument—UCC 3-104.**

(A) Except as provided in divisions (C) and (D) of this section, "negotiable instrument" means an unconditional promise or order to pay a fixed amount of money, with or without interest or other charges described in the promise or order, if it meets all of the following requirements:

(1) It is payable to bearer or to order at the time it is issued or first comes into possession of a holder.

(2) It is payable on demand or at a definite time.

(3) It does not state any other undertaking or instruction by the person promising or ordering payment to do any act in addition to the payment of money, but the promise or order may contain any of the following:

(a) An undertaking or power to give, maintain, or protect collateral to secure payment;

(b) An authorization or power to the holder to confess judgment or realize on or dispose of collateral;

(c) A waiver of the benefit of any law intended for the advantage or protection of an obligor.

(B) "Instrument" means a negotiable instrument.

(C) An order that meets all of the requirements of divisions (A)(2) and (3) of this section and otherwise falls within the definition of "check" is a negotiable instrument and a check.

(D) A promise or order other than a check is not an instrument if, at the time it is issued or first comes into possession of a holder, it contains a conspicuous statement, however expressed, to the effect that the promise or order is not negotiable or is not an instrument governed by this chapter.

(E) (1) "Note" means an instrument that is a promise.

(2) "Draft" means an instrument that is an order.

(3) If an instrument is both a "note" and a "draft," a person entitled to enforce the instrument may treat it as either.

(F) "Check" means either of the following:

(1) A draft, other than a documentary draft, payable on demand and drawn on a bank;

(2) A cashier's check or teller's check.

An instrument may be a "check" even though it is described on its face as a "money order" or by another term.

(G) "Cashier's check" means a draft with respect to which the drawer and drawee are the same bank or branches of the same bank.

(H) "Teller's check" means a draft drawn by a bank on another bank or payable at or through a bank.

(I) "Traveler's check" means an instrument that meets all of the following conditions:

(1) It is payable on demand.

(2) It is drawn on or payable at or through a bank.

(3) It is designated by the term "traveler's check" or by a substantially similar term.

(4) It requires, as a condition to payment, a countersignature by a person whose specimen signature appears on the instrument.

(J) "Certificate of deposit" means an instrument containing an acknowledgment by a bank that a sum of money has been received by the bank and a promise by the bank to repay the sum of money. A "certificate of deposit" is a note of the bank.

In short, a written document is negotiable when it is signed, contains an **Unconditional Promise** to pay a fixed amount of money, and is payable to a bearer or on demand. Negotiability is destroyed if the promise of payment is based on a condition. The fixed amount of money payable must be expressly stated. Also, under subsection (d) the instrument is negotiable if it is payable at a definite time or on demand. A check, for example, is payable when it is presented for payment, such as upon deposit in an account.

**Unconditional Promise:** A promise to pay with no conditions and no reference to other agreements.

## CHAPTER SUMMARY

The UCC codifies some of the common law of contract and limits it to transactions between merchants. The UCC is adopted by the states in an effort in increase uniformity of the law so as to promote interstate commerce. The UCC fills in the blanks in certain contracts in order to save a contract that otherwise would have failed because of missing or contradictory terms.

Negotiable instruments are such legal documents as bank checks and promissory notes. They facilitate commerce by creating a record of payments and act as a substitute for cash.

## ETHICAL ISSUES

●●●

Consider the efforts our legislators go to in order to govern through regulation the use of technology to facilitate business on the Internet. Laws are passed to make electronic signatures valid and enforceable. Laws are also passed to prevent people from using software without paying the licensing fee.

Contrast those efforts with the revelations during the recent foreclosure crisis that many banks were automatically signing ("robo-signing") foreclosure documents without checking their accuracy. Given the centuries of common law concerning contracts, signing a contract without verifying its accuracy can have ethical implications. Add to that the possible end result of the signature, the loss of a home, and it points to a potential serious lapse in business ethics.

What ethical issues are raised by robo-signing?

## Relevant Web Sites

http://www.law.cornell.edu/ucc
http://www.icann.org/
http://codes.ohio.gov/orc/1303.03

## Exercises

1. In two paragraphs describe how the UCC does or does not make a party free to contract.
2. Determine if the sale of computer information is covered under the UCC Article 2, or if it calls for separate legislation.
3. In *Bonebrake v. Cox*, describe why the contract was governed by the UCC.
4. Describe the predominant factor test.
5. Explain course of dealing and give an example.

## Questions

1. What article of the UCC governs negotiable instruments?
2. What is a good under the UCC?
3. What is a sale under the UCC?
4. In *Eastern Airlines, Inc. v. Gulf Oil Corp.*, what did Gulf accuse Eastern of doing?
5. What is the E-SIGN Act?
6. What is UETA?
7. Which UCC provision governs consideration?
8. Which UCC provision governs legality of subject matter?
9. What is UCITA?
10. What is e-commerce?

## Hypotheticals

1. Farley sought investors to help him expand his bakery. Farley had some trouble getting loans from the bank due to some outstanding tax debts. At a local investment seminar that Farley attended to network with wealthy individuals, an attendee named Anne agreed to finance the bakery expansion. Anne gave several documents to Farley that looked like financial instruments. They had *Certified Bankers Check* and *Comptroller Warrant* written on them, and they amount to enough money for Farley to expand his bakery. How can he tell if the notes are valid?
2. Foto Shoppe is a small business located in Ohio. The owner, Oscar, photographs people and digitally alters photos for cards, anniversary announcements, and various other products. Oscar has been hit hard by the recession. To save some money he places an online order for digital photo software from iPhoto, Co. The order form asks for his name, address, e-mail address, and credit card information. The fee for use of the software is $150 per month for

one year. Oscar downloads the software and then refuses to pay the fee after the third month. iPhoto sues Oscar. Can it recover against Oscar?

3. Sam is surfing the Internet and sees that his favorite local skateboard company, Smoothride, Inc., does not own the domain name, Smoothride.com. Sam registers the name at www.godaddy.com, a domain name registrar. Soon after, Smoothride, Inc., desires to sell its skateboards online. The company contacts Sam to acquire the domain name. Sam is willing to sell the domain name for $10,000. Smoothride sues Sam under ACPA. Who will prevail?

4. HK Shrubs and Dirty Thumb nursery enter into a contract whereby HK agrees to sell shrubs to Dirty Thumb. The price, to be set by HK, is to be based upon "the average price for which shrubs of a similar kind are sold in the state." All the relevant information for the contract was expressly agreed to. Is the contract binding as to price?

## Sample Cases

1. Denny grows a grain called millet. Scoular buys and resells millet. Denny and Scoular discuss a contract to buy 15,000 bushels of millet. Denny asked for $5 per hundredweight. Scoular was not sure that the grain could be resold at that price. Several days later Scoular sells the millet to a third party for $5. Scoular attempts to reach Denny by phone to inform him of the sale but is unsuccessful. Eventually, Scoular mails Denny a written and signed purchase contract. Denny does not check his mail and never signed or returned the contract. By harvest the price of millet has tripled. Denny sells the grain to someone else. Can Scoular recover damages?

*Scoular Co. v. Denney*, 151 P.3d 615 (Colo. Ct. App. 2006).

2. The Smiths ran Keystone Tool & Supply Company. They borrowed money from the Zogarts. Promissory notes were executed with the agreement that the monies would be repaid out of the profits of the business. The business was not successful and after less than a year was undercapitalized and operating at a loss each month. The Smiths closed up shop and liquidated the assets. There are monies left over after liquidation. Must the Smiths repay the debt to the Zogarts even though the proceeds would come from liquidation rather than profits of the business?

*Zogarts v. Smith*, 86 Cal. App. 2d 165 (1948).

## Key Terms

**Anticipatory Repudiation:** Repudiation of a contractual duty by one party to a contract before performance is due when the other party to the contract makes clear statements or conducts himself in such a way as to indicate that he will not be performing under the contract. In such event, the former party may treat the latter conduct as a breach of contract, stop performance under the contract, and immediately sue for breach of contract.

**Certificate of Deposit:** A negotiable instrument entitling the bearer to receive a fixed sum of interest and principal from a bank on a deposit at the maturity date.

**Commercial Paper:** In this context, an alternative name for negotiable instruments.

**Course of Dealing:** A legal concept embodied in the UCC that recognizes that parties develop contractual habits after dealing with one another over the years. A court will interpret the pattern of business conduct between two parties over time across several contracts as an indication of what the parties meant for the written words of the present contract to mean.

**Course of Performance:** A legal concept embodied in the UCC that recognizes that parties develop contractual habits after dealing with one another over the years. A court will interpret the pattern of business conduct between two parties over time within one contract as an indication of what the parties meant for the written words of the contract to mean.

**Draft:** An order that payment be made, such as a check.

**E-Commerce:** Any commerce in electronic form.

**E-Contract:** A contract entered into electronically.

**Electronic Signatures in Global and National Commerce Act (E-SIGN Act):** A federal law that provides that all contracts, records, or signatures that are in electronic form are legally valid to the extent they would be legally valid if they were in printed form on paper.

**Good:** A movable item as defined by the UCC.

**Merchant:** A buyer or seller of goods with specialized knowledge about that good. This includes any commercial sellers of a product in the ordinary course of business.

**Negotiable Instrument:** A written instrument of commerce that includes a promise to pay or order for payment to be made.

**Note:** A promise for payment in the future, such as a certificate of deposit.

**Predominant Factor Test:** Test applied by the court to determine whether the UCC applies when a contract contains both a sales and a service element, with which the court identifies which of the two elements is the predominant factor in the contract.

**Promissory Note:** A contract in which one party promises to pay or repay a specific amount on a given date or on demand by the holder of the note.

**Requirements Contract:** A contract under which a buyer agrees to buy from a seller all that the buyer requires of a certain item or items.

**Sales Contract:** A contract concerning the sale of goods and not services.

**UCITA:** Uniform Computer Information Transactions Act, which governs contracts for pure software or software embedded in goods.

**Unconditional Promise:** A promise to pay with no conditions and no reference to other agreements.

**Uniform Commercial Code (UCC):** A model law that has been adopted separately by each state to facilitate making the law of sales and commercial transactions generally uniform across the different states so that these transactions would be easier to complete.

**Uniform Electronic Transactions Act (UETA):** A model law that was created in an attempt to make state governing of e-signatures more uniform. Under the UETA most contracts must be signed by the parties against whom enforcement is sought.

**Usage of Trade:** A legal concept embodied in the UCC that recognizes that the standard practice or set of practices in a particular type of business or trade in a certain region should guide the interpretation of what a contract means.

## CHAPTER 6

# Agency Law

**LEARNING OBJECTIVES**

You will be able to answer the following questions after reading this chapter:

1. What is an agent?
2. What is an independent contractor?
3. What is a principal?
4. What is employment at will?
5. What duties and liabilities are created under an agency relationship?
6. What are e-agents?

## INTRODUCTION

Agency describes a relationship between parties in which one of the parties asks the other to act on his or her behalf. The principal does the asking, and the agent carries out a task. This is a legal relationship that allows a principal to conduct business transactions through the agent. For example, typically all employees act as agents for their employer (the principal). A tax attorney (the agent) who has a signed power of attorney from a client (the principal) may negotiate directly with the IRS on behalf of that client. Agency also allows the principal to conduct business in multiple locations. For example, owners of a corporation (the principal) may ask a corporate officer (the agent) to enter into various contracts, such as leases, inventory arrangements, and employee hiring agreements, on behalf of the corporation at various corporate worksites.

Agency law is integral to the operation of a corporation because a corporation always needs an agent to conduct corporate business. Agency law is a part of the common law. This chapter describes how an agency relationship is created, identifies the rights and duties of all parties, and describes how an agency is terminated.

## CREATION OF AGENCY

**Agency** is a fiduciary relationship that arises when a **Principal** authorizes another person (the **Agent**) to act on the principal's behalf, subject to the principal's control, as if the other person were the principal. The agent, of course, must agree to act in this capacity for the principal. Agents owe a fiduciary duty to the principal. A **Fiduciary Duty** arises when one person acts on behalf of another person in a particular matter and is obligated to put the other person's interests first. For example, a banker is a fiduciary for depositors at the bank. The banker owes depositors the duty to safeguard their deposits.

An agency relationship can be created by a written or oral contract. If created by contract, contract rules apply. For example, parties must have the capacity to enter into a contract, and the agency relationship must be established for a legal purpose. The agency relationship can also be created through the parties' conduct. If because of the way people are acting, a third party reasonably believes that an agency relationship exists, one may be implied. This **Implied Agency Relationship** contains all the rights and duties that an express relationship has.

## INDEPENDENT CONTRACTORS

**Independent Contractors** are not employees. That is because by definition the person who hires an independent contractor cannot control the day-to-day details of the independent contractor's work. The independent contractor is hired to perform a specific service, but how the goal is achieved or task is completed is beyond the control of the person who hires the independent contractor.

In some situations, a person can be both an independent contractor and an agent. This occurs when the independent contractor represents the principal—for example, when the independent contractor is a real estate agent or an insurance agent. In these cases, agency law will apply.

Employers often try to classify workers as independent contractors rather than employees because employers are responsible for withholding taxes on employees' paychecks, social security contributions and other taxes, and benefits for their employees—but are not responsible for those items for independent contractors.

If there is an issue regarding whether or not a worker is an independent contractor or an employee, courts look to the amount of control and independence in the relationship. There are three main tests that are applied by the government in order to make

**Agency:**
A fiduciary relationship in which a principal authorizes an agent to act on the principal's behalf, subject to the principal's control, as if the agent were the principal.

**Principal:**
The party in an agency relationship who permits an agent to act on the principal's behalf.

**Agent:**
The party in an agency relationship who acts on a principal's behalf.

**Fiduciary Duty:**
An obligation to act in another's best interest when one person acts on behalf of another person in a particular matter.

**Implied Agency Relationship:**
Relationship created by the observed conduct of the principal that shows an intention to create an agency.

**Independent Contractor:**
A person who works independently to accomplish a specific goal or set of goals on behalf of a principal. The independent contractor cannot be controlled in the day-to-day execution of the task by the person who hires him or her.

the independent contractor or employee determination. These three tests simplify an older 20-factor test formerly used by the Internal Revenue Service.

First, the Internal Revenue Service will examine behavior factors to see if the possible employer has either control or the right to control what the worker does and how the worker does his or her job. It will examine if the possible employer has specified:

1. When and where to do the work;
2. What tools or equipment to use;
3. What workers to hire or to assist with the work;
4. Where to purchase supplies and services;
5. What work must be performed by a specified individual; and
6. What order or sequence to follow.

Second, the Internal Revenue Service will examine financial factors like payment arrangements, who supplies tools to complete the job, and reimbursement arrangements in order to determine how much of these expenses are paid by the possible employer. Specifically, it will review:

1. The extent to which the worker has unreimbursed business expenses;
2. The extent of the worker's investment;
3. The extent to which the worker makes services available to the relevant market;
4. How the business pays the worker; and
5. The extent to which the worker can realize a profit or loss.

Third, it will look to the relationship itself to see if there are factors that point to an employer-employee relationship, like written contracts for employment, insurance, vacation pay, pensions, and continuity of employment. The Internal Revenue Service will examine:

1. Written contracts describing the relationship the parties intended to create;
2. Whether the business provides the worker with employee-type benefits, such as insurance, a pension plan, vacation pay, or sick pay;
3. The permanency of the relationship; and
4. The extent to which services performed by the worker are a key aspect of the regular business of the company.

The court will look at the totality of the relationship and use all of these factors to determine if an employer-employee relationship exists, or if the relationship is an independent-contractor-based principal-agent relationship. If an employer-employee relationship does exist, there are rights and responsibilities on each side that spring into action. For that reason, many potential employers attempt to classify their workers as independent contractors, instead of as employees.

## DUTIES

In the agency relationship the principal and agent owe each other duties.

The agent, who is performing the tasks, owes a **Duty of Loyalty** and above all the **Duty to Perform** that task that he or she was hired or authorized to perform. These duties are included within the fiduciary duty requirement discussed above but are worth discussing separately.

"An agent has a fiduciary duty to act loyally for the principal's benefit in all matters connected with the agency relationship," according to the *Restatement (Third) of Agency* §8.01. Often the agent is entrusted with money or goods for delivery and must handle those goods loyally. For example, assume that Brad is a personal assistant for Carol, who owns and runs a boutique bakery named *Marvellieux Pain*. Occasionally, Carol will ask Brad to deliver orders to very special clients such as celebrities or politicians. Brad is expected to make delivery (his duty to perform) and then take payment for the orders. He is then required to return that payment to the bakery. It would be a breach of Brad's duty of loyalty if he were to keep some of the money or commingle it with his own. Also, because Brad is an excellent baker as well as a personal assistant, it would be a breach of his duty of loyalty to try to enter into some separate bakery agreement with a customer.

The principal has a duty to interact with the agent in good faith. The principal must compensate the agent for the agent's work. Also, if a principal is aware or should be aware of any harms or dangers the agent might encounter, the principal has a duty to inform the agent.

**Duty of Loyalty:**
The duty of an agent to act in the principal's interest, and not in the agent's own interest.

**Duty to Perform:**
The duty of an agent to perform his or her duties under an agency agreement.

## LIABILITIES TO THIRD PARTIES

The agency relationship is between the principal and the agent. All the business transacted during the operation of the agency relationship is with third parties. For example, the agent might be entering

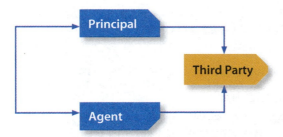

**Figure 6-1**
Liabilities to Third Parties

into commercial lease arrangements for the principal or delivering goods for the principal. Each of these business transactions has the potential to create liability for the principal and agent in terms of contract or tort.

When a principal uses an agent to complete a task, it is as if the principal were the one completing the task. The agent has authority to act on behalf of the principal, so the principal is bound by the contracts that the agent enters into. The principal is bound under contract law if the agent had either actual or apparent authority to make the contract.

**Actual Authority** is authority either given to the agent expressly or inferred from words or conduct of the principal. The latter gives the agent implied authority to make contracts. The communication is to the agent. For example, assume that an agent is sent to buy commercial real estate. The principal sends a letter of introduction that the agent uses to perform his task. The agent has actual authority to enter into these lease agreements.

A **Power of Attorney** creates written actual authority for the agent to act for specific purposes on behalf of the principal. The power of attorney is often a form or a written document that is typically notarized by a notary public and signed by witnesses. The **Notary** is an individual who is authorized by the state to authenticate signatures on documents. The notary stamps the document with a seal that gives assurances to anyone who sees the document that the signatures are authentic.

Below is a standard power of attorney for California that allows an agent to act on behalf of a principal for a variety of different matters, including business-related issues. The principal can give the agent almost unlimited power or limit the agent's authorization to very specific issues, times, and places. A power of attorney does not need to be in a standardized format like this one, but this form provides a good, comprehensive example.

In contrast to actual authority, **Apparent Authority** is created through communication directly to the third party by the principal. This authority is communicated through the actions or conduct of

**Actual Authority:**
Authority that is given to the agent to act, either expressly given by the principal or inferred from words or conduct of the principal.

**Power of Attorney:**
A document that creates written actual authority for the agent to act for specific purposes on behalf of the principal.

**Notary:**
An individual who is authorized by the state to authenticate signatures on documents.

**Apparent Authority:**
The authority of the agent, as reasonably perceived by a third party, to act on behalf of the principal.

## UNIFORM STATUTORY FORM POWER OF ATTORNEY

(California Probate Code Sec. 4401)

NOTICE: THE POWERS GRANTED BY THIS DOCUMENT ARE BROAD AND SWEEPING. THEY ARE EXPLAINED IN THE UNIFORM STATUTORY FORM POWER OF ATTORNEY ACT (CALIFORNIA CIVIL CODE SECTIONS 4400-4465, INCLUSIVE).

IF YOU HAVE ANY QUESTIONS ABOUT THESE POWERS, OBTAIN COMPETENT LEGAL ADVICE. THIS DOCUMENT DOES NOT AUTHORIZE ANYONE TO MAKE MEDICAL AND OTHER HEALTH-CARE DECISIONS FOR YOU. YOU MAY REVOKE THIS POWER OF ATTORNEY IF YOU LATER WISH TO DO SO.

I, _____

(your name and address)

appoint _____

(name and address of the person appointed)

as my agent (attorney-in-fact) to act for me in any lawful way with respect to the following initialed subjects:

TO GRANT ALL OF THE FOLLOWING POWERS, INITIAL THE LINE IN FRONT OF (N) AND IGNORE THE LINES IN FRONT OF THE OTHER POWERS.

TO GRANT ONE OR MORE, BUT FEWER THAN ALL, OF THE FOLLOWING POWERS, INITIAL THE LINE IN FRONT OF EACH POWER YOU ARE GRANTING.

TO WITHHOLD A POWER, DO NOT INITIAL THE LINE IN FRONT OF IT. YOU MAY, BUT NEED NOT, CROSS OUT EACH POWER WITHHELD.

INITIAL

_____ (A) Real property transactions.

_____ (B) Tangible personal property transactions.

_____ (C) Stock and bond transactions.

_____ (D) Commodity and option transactions.

_____ (E) Banking and other financial institution transactions.

_____ (F) Business operating transactions.

_____ (G) Insurance and annuity transactions.

_____ (H) Estate, trust, and other beneficiary transactions.

INITIAL

_____ (I) Claims and litigation.

_____ (J) Personal and family maintenance.

_____ (K) Benefits from social security, medicare, medicaid, or other governmental programs, or civil or military service.

_____ (L) Retirement plan transactions.

_____ (M) Tax matters.

_____ (N) ALL OF THE POWERS LISTED ABOVE.

YOU NEED NOT INITIAL ANY OTHER LINES IF YOU INITIAL LINE (N).

SPECIAL INSTRUCTIONS:

ON THE FOLLOWING LINES YOU MAY GIVE SPECIAL INSTRUCTIONS LIMITING OR EXTENDING THE POWERS GRANTED TO YOUR AGENT.

_____

**Figure 6-2**
Uniform Statutory Form Power of Attorney

UNLESS YOU DIRECT OTHERWISE ABOVE, THIS POWER OF ATTORNEY IS EFFECTIVE IMMEDIATELY AND WILL CONTINUE UNTIL IT IS REVOKED.

This power of attorney will continue to be effective even though I become incapacitated.

STRIKE THE PRECEDING SENTENCE IF YOU DO NOT WANT THIS POWER OF ATTORNEY TO CONTINUE IF YOU BECOME INCAPACITATED.

EXERCISE OF POWER OF ATTORNEY WHERE MORE THAN ONE AGENT DESIGNATED

If I have designated more than one agent, the agents are to act _____ _____ .

IF YOU APPOINTED MORE THAN ONE AGENT AND YOU WANT EACH AGENT TO BE ABLE TO ACT ALONE WITHOUT THE OTHER AGENT JOINING, WRITE THE WORD "SEPARATELY" IN THE BLANK SPACE ABOVE. IF YOU DO NOT INSERT ANY WORD IN THE BLANK SPACE, OR IF YOU INSERT THE WORD "JOINTLY", THEN ALL OF YOUR AGENTS MUST ACT OR SIGN TOGETHER.

I agree that any third party who receives a copy of this document may act under it. Revocation of the power of attorney is not effective as to a third party until the third party has actual knowledge of the revocation. I agree to indemnify the third party for any claims that arise against the third party because of reliance on this power of attorney.

Signed this _____ day of _____ , 20_____

_____
Your Signature

_____
Your Social Security Number


CERTIFICATE OF ACKNOWLEDGMENT OF NOTARY PUBLIC

State of California
County of _____

On _____ before me, (here insert name and title of the officer), personally appeared _____, who proved to me on the basis of satisfactory evidence to be the person(s) whose name(s) is/are subscribed to the within instrument and acknowledged to me that he/she/they executed the same in his/her/their authorized capacity(ies), and that by his/her/their signature(s) on the instrument the person(s), or the entity upon behalf of which the person(s) acted, executed the instrument.
I certify under PENALTY OF PERJURY under the laws of the State of California that the foregoing paragraph is true and correct.

WITNESS my hand and official seal.
                                                        (Seal)
Signature _____

**Figure 6-2** cont.

the principal directly to the third party. For example, if a principal has set an agent up in an office with staff and third parties go in to this location to transact business, the third party could reasonably assume that the agent has the authority to represent and bind the principal. This will be true even if the agent has received express instructions NOT to enter into any contracts. Whatever has been communicated to the third party is what is important.

## Contractual Liability

The authority of the agent is important when determining the liability of a principal for contracts entered into by an agent. If the agent is acting within his or her authority and enters into a contract, the principal is liable under that contract negotiated by the agent on the principal's behalf. However, the agent may also be liable under the contract depending on the third party's knowledge of the principal. The legal issue in this situation is whether the principal was disclosed, partially disclosed, or undisclosed.

A **Disclosed Principal** is one who is known to the third party when the contract is made by the agent. A third party may have been told who the principal is, or if the agent is a salesperson, perhaps a logo was on a business card or on a company car. In such a case, the third party knows the agent is acting for another party.

A **Partially Disclosed Principal** is exactly what it sounds like. The third party knows that the agent is acting for someone but does not know exactly who that person is.

An **Undisclosed Principal** is completely unknown to the third party. In this situation the third party thinks that the agent is acting alone and on his or her own behalf, and not on behalf of anyone else.

The more that the principal is known to the third party, the less liability the agent has to that third party. After all, the agent is a servant of the principal, and the law is not designed to "shoot the messenger." However, the more the agent looks and acts like the principal—to the third party—the more the liability the agent is exposed to.

Hence, when signing a contract on behalf of a disclosed principal, the agent must use disclosure through words of agency, such as *John Smith, signing as agent for Widget Company*. This prevents John Smith as the agent from exposure to personal contract liability. Instead, only the principal, Widget Company, is bound under the contract. But the failure to identify Widget Company as the principal as well as include words of agency exposes the agent to potential liability under the contract.

**Disclosed Principal:**
A principal who is known and identified to the third party when the contract is made by the agent.

**Partially Disclosed Principal:**
A principal who is known to exist by the third party, but is not identified, when the contract is made by the agent.

**Undisclosed Principal:**
A principal who is unknown to the third party when the contract is made by the agent.

## Tort Liability

An agent who commits a tort is liable for the tort. If that agent committed the tort while in the employment of a principal, the principal may be liable as well. When there is **Joint and Several Liability**, the victim of the tort will sue either the agent or the principal, or both. An attorney will often sue both agent and principal in these cases in order to maximize the chance of recovery. The entire amount of damages recovered can be obtained from either the agent or the principal. Often, the agent will **Indemnify**, which means to reimburse, the principal for damages recovered by the victim due to the agent's tort.

For example, assume that Elmer Klutzy has parked his delivery truck for Wahzoo Lighting Co. next to a busy sidewalk. Elmer is offloading boxes of lightbulbs he has delivered on behalf of Wahzoo to a local merchant. He negligently bumps into and injures a pedestrian on the sidewalk. The principal, Wahzoo Lighting Co., and the agent, Elmer Klutzy, are both liable to the pedestrian for injury in tort because Elmer caused the injury while working on behalf of Wahzoo. Elmer is liable to Wahzoo for whatever portion of the recovery Wahzoo pays.

**Joint and Several Liability:** Liability that is apportioned among two or more parties or borne by only one or a few select members of the group. Under this legal principle, the plaintiff sues more than one defendant both together and separately and can recover the entire amount of damages from either one, both, or all of the multiple defendants.

**Indemnify:** To reimburse or promise to reimburse a party for a payment made.

## E-AGENTS

With the advent of e-commerce, computer programs have been developed that perform specific tasks on behalf of a principal. These programs are considered to be an **E-Agent**. The task performed by the software could be data retrieval or order intake for online shopping. Agency principles apply in these situations, and the automated act by the computer program is deemed to be on behalf of and authorized by the principal.

The **Uniform Electronic Transactions Act (UETA)** has specific provisions for a principal's liability for the actions of e-agents. In the states that have adopted UETA, e-agents can bind the principal in contract.

**E-Agent:** A computer program that works on behalf of a principal to execute instructions based on parameters ordered by the principal.

**Uniform Electronic Transactions Act (UETA):** A model law that was created in an attempt to make state governing of e-signatures more uniform. Under the UETA most contracts must be signed by the parties against whom enforcement is sought.

## TERMINATION OF AGENCY

An agency relationship is terminated in much the same way a contract is, by the parties' actions or through operation of law. The agency may have been created by an agreement that stated specifically when the agent's tasks have been completed. For example,

## ETHICAL ISSUES

● ● ●

This chapter has discussed the duty of agents to the principal. The agent has a duty to act in the best interests of the principal. Sometimes this duty can also be fiduciary duty. Some principals may pay agents for their service. But what are the ethical and moral duties of the principal to the agent? What protections does the agent have when principals ask them to perform unethical tasks?

assume that Jones & Co. owns a strip mall and wants to lease two open spaces. The company enters into a contract with Samuel Realtor for him to act as the company's agent until the two spaces are rented. This agency terminates when the last space is rented. This is similar to a contract termination when both parties have fully performed their obligations under the contract.

In the same commercial realty scenario, both Sam Realtor and Jones & Co. could later mutually decide to terminate the agency after only one open space at the strip mall was leased. This is termination by mutual agreement.

If an agent or principal dies or becomes incapacitated, the agency relationship is terminated by operation of law. These events make it impossible for either the agent or the principal to perform, and therefore agency authority is terminated. For example, should the principal die, regardless of whether the agent knows or not, any transaction that is entered into after the principal's death is outside the agency agreement. The death terminates the agent's power, and the principal's estate is not liable for the agent's transactions.

## CHAPTER SUMMARY

Agency describes a relationship between parties in which a principal asks an agent to carry out a task. This is a legal relationship that allows the principal to conduct business transactions through the agent. Agency is a fiduciary relationship, in which the agent owes the duty of loyalty to the principal. The authority of the agent is important when determining the liability of a principal for contracts formed by an agent. An agent acting within his or her authority will make the principal liable under that contract. An e-agent is a computer program that acts as an agent. An agency relationship is terminated very much like a contract is terminated.

## Relevant Web Sites

http://www.irs.gov/businesses/small/article/
   0,,id = 99921,00.html
http://www.taxes.ca.gov/iCorE.bus.shtml

## Exercises

1. Explain why an independent contractor is not generally considered an agent.
2. Describe the differences between a disclosed, partially disclosed, and fully disclosed principal.
3. List three instances that terminate an agency.
4. Find an example on the Internet or in the library of one party acting as an agent for another party. Explain how you can identify the agency relationship
5. Draft your own power of attorney using your state's statutory format.

## Questions

1. What is the duty of loyalty?
2. What is the duty to perform?
3. What is a fiduciary duty?
4. What functions do notaries serve?
5. Does an agency need to be created by a formal written document?
6. What is a power of attorney?
7. What are e-agents?
8. What is indemnification?
9. What is joint and several liability?
10. Why is agency necessary to the smooth functioning of business?

## Hypotheticals

1. Kevin worked for IRC Corp to help the company identify potential properties to buy and develop. IRC gave Kevin a laptop in order to store data and information relevant to his efforts on behalf of the company. Kevin quits IRC to work for a competitor. Before he quits he installs a special program that permanently deletes all the data on the company laptop before he re-

turns it. Some of the information deleted would reveal improper conduct of Kevin. Installing the software was in violation of the understanding between Kevin and IRC regarding the use of the laptop. Did the installation of the software terminate the agency?

2. Allison was a loan officer at a local bank. During her lunch hour she drove to deliver food to the elderly for Meals-on-Wheels, a charity that provides hot food for those unable to leave the home. On her way back to work, Allison's car collides with another vehicle driven by Tom. Tom is slightly injured and a passenger in Tom's car is killed. The passenger's family sues Allison and the bank for wrongful death. Can they recover?

3. Oliver is a cab driver for Diamond Cab Company. After working all day, Oliver reports "off-duty" on his radio to dispatch. While driving home in the cab, Oliver speeds on the freeway. A police officer attempts to pull him over, but Oliver evades the officer by speeding away. Upon exiting the freeway, Oliver rear-ends Mosley. Mosley sues Oliver and Diamond Cab Company for negligence. Who will Mosley recover from?

## Sample Cases

1. Southern Equipment hired Quality Metal Roof (QMR) to install a new metal roof on a building. QMR provided the roofing materials to another firm, Royalty Builders (RB), who did the installation work. RB hired an underage worker, Robert France, to help with roofing work while on break from high school. France was working on the installation of the new roof when he fell and suffered head injuries. France sued QMR for failing to provide a safe work environment, vicarious liability for exposing him to an inherently dangerous job, and negligence for hiring a minor, which violated state and federal law. He recovered $875,000 from QMR. Can France also recover from Southern Equipment?

*France v. Southern Equip. Co.*, 689 S.E.2d 1 (W. Va. 2010).

2. Star of India is a clothing designer. It designed dresses for the manufacturer Sewa International. Star of India orally agreed to deliver dress samples and swatches to an apparel vendor, Performance Commercial LTDA (Performance). The samples and swatches were never delivered. Performance sues Star of India for breach of contract. In the complaint, Performance admits that it understood that Star of India was an agent for Sewa International. Can Performance recover from Star of India?

*Performance Comercial Importadora E Exportadora Ltda v. SEWA Int'l Fashions Pvt. Ltd.*, 79 A.D.3d 673, 915 N.Y.S.2d 44 (1st Dep't 2010).

## Key Terms

**Actual Authority:** Authority that is given to the agent to act, either expressly given by the principal or inferred from words or conduct of the principal.

**Agency:** A fiduciary relationship in which a principal authorizes an agent to act on the principal's behalf, subject to the principal's control, as if the agent were the principal.

**Agent:** The party in an agency relationship who acts on a principal's behalf.

**Apparent Authority:** The authority of the agent, as reasonably perceived by a third party, to act of behalf of the principal.

**Disclosed Principal:** A principal who is known by and identified to the third party when the contract is made by the agent.

**Duty of Loyalty:** The duty of the agent to act in the principal's interest, and not in the agent's own interest.

**Duty to Perform:** The duty of an agent to perform his or her duties under an agency agreement.

**E-Agent:** A computer program that works on behalf of a principal to execute instructions based on parameters ordered by the principal.

**Fiduciary Duty:** An obligation to act in another's best interest when one person acts on behalf of another person in a particular matter.

**Implied Agency Relationship:** Relationship created by the observed conduct of the principal that shows an intention to create an agency.

**Indemnify:** To reimburse or promise to reimburse a party for a payment made.

**Independent Contractor:** A person who works independently to accomplish a specific goal or set of goals on behalf of a principal. The independent contractor cannot be controlled in the day-to-day execution of the task by the person who hires him or her.

**Joint and Several Liability:** Liability that is apportioned among two or more parties or borne by only one or a few select members of the group. Under this legal principle, the plaintiff sues more than one defendant both together and separately and can recover the entire amount of damages from either one, both, or all of the multiple defendants.

**Notary:** An individual who is authorized by the state to authenticate signatures on documents.

**Partially Disclosed Principal:** A principal who is known to exist by the third party, but is not identified, when the contract is made by the agent.

**Power of Attorney:** A document that creates written actual authority for the agent to act for specific purposes on behalf of the principal.

**Principal:** The party in an agency relationship who permits an agent to act on the principal's behalf.

**Undisclosed Principal:** A principal who is unknown to the third party when the contract is made by the agent.

**Uniform Electronic Transactions Act (UETA):** A model law that was created in an attempt to make state governing of e-signatures more uniform. Under the UETA most contracts must be signed by the parties against whom enforcement is sought.

# Employment Law

## INTRODUCTION

Employment law governs the relationship between employers and their employees. Sometimes employees are hurt on the job, are discriminated against for improper reasons, or are terminated illegally. Federal and state employment laws define the rights and obligations of employer and employee to one another on the job. This chapter discusses what employment law is and how it works in practice.

Employment relationships have traditionally been governed by the common law. Rules under common law contract, tort, and agency also apply in the employment context. Those topics are covered elsewhere in this book. The common law interpretation of the employer-employee relationship was in place without much modification until the early twentieth century. The unmodified common law was more favorable to the employer and generally left the employee with few rights or protections. It is because of this that specific federal and state statutes were drafted to provide protection for employees without overburdening the employer. This chapter covers that legislation along with general employment law concepts.

## EMPLOYEE OR INDEPENDENT CONTRACTOR

A fundamental concern (discussed in Chapter 6) is to determine if an employer-employee relationship exists. From that relationship spring many rights and obligations on the part of the employer and employee.

**Employers** hire workers in exchange for work. **Employees** are those hired by an employer to perform work for the employer. The employer then controls the day-to-day details of how and when an employee does that work. In contrast, **Independent Contractors** by definition are not controlled in the day-to-day details of their work by the person who hires them. They are hired to perform a specific job or service, but how they complete the task is beyond the control of the person who hires them.

Another difference between employees and independent contractors is that employers are responsible for withholding taxes on employees' paychecks, paying social security contributions and other taxes, and providing benefits for their employees. They are not responsible for those items for independent contractors. Therefore, there is a strong incentive for those hiring people to do work to classify those workers as independent contractors rather than employees.

As discussed in Chapter 6, the amount of control exercised by the possible employer is at the core of the discussion of the employee–independent contractor divide. The Internal Revenue Service looks at three factors in this analysis in the cases involving these classifications. Most courts use similar factors. First, the IRS examines examine behavioral factors to see if the possible employer has either control or the right to control what the worker does and how the worker does it. Second, the IRS examines financial factors like payment arrangements, who supplies tools to complete the job, and reimbursement arrangements in order to determine how much the possible employer pays toward the worker's job. Third, the IRS will look to the relationship itself to see if there are factors that point to an employer-employee relationship—for example, written contracts for employment, insurance, vacation pay, pensions, and continuity of employment.

The government reviews the totality of the relationship between all of the parties and then uses all of these factors to determine if an employer-employee relationship exists, or if the relationship is between hirer and independent contractor (that is, principal and agent) instead.

For instance, assume that Carol is hired by Cyndi to put a roof on Cyndi's home. The agreement is that Cyndi will pay Carol $5,000,

**Employer:**
The party to the employment relationship who hires workers and pays their wages or salary in exchange for the workers' performance of work.

**Employee:**
The party to the employment relationship who is hired by an employer to perform work.

**Independent Contractor:**
A party hired to perform a specific service. How the independent contractor completes the task is beyond the control of the person who hires him or her.

and Carol will have the new roof meeting certain specifications installed by July 31. Here, Carol is an independent contractor because she has complete control of when and how she will install the roof. She hires the subcontractors, supplies the materials, sets the work schedule, and so forth.

Consider the following, however: Max hired Ivy to install a roof on Max's home. Max agrees to pay Ivy at a rate of $20 per hour, and Max further agrees to provide all the materials, permits, helpers, insurance, and the like. Ivy also is required to work from 9 a.m. to 5 p.m. and is allowed a certain number of vacation days. Here, because there is so much more control over Ivy by Max, a court would likely find that an employer-employee relationship exists.

## EMPLOYMENT AT WILL

A fundamental legal concept in employment law is the idea of employment at will. **Employment at Will** means that either party has the power to terminate the employment contract at any time and for any reason. The courts have developed some exceptions to this default hard-and-fast rule. The assumption, though, is that absent an exception any employment relationship is at will.

An exception to employment at will is the creation of an implied contract. In this situation, an implied contract may be created between the employer and employee based on provisions in an employee manual or oral promises made by the employer that create the understanding that dismissal will only happen for good cause. This implied understanding can give rise to a breach of contract claim if the employee is dismissed.

Another exception is when an employee claims wrongful discharge. This can arise when abusive discharge procedures cause the employee distress, or if an employer violates a statute during the discharge. The various statutory limits on employment at will are discussed below.

A final exception occurs if the employee relationship is governed by a **Collective Bargaining Agreement,** a contract between an employer and a **Union** that regulates employees' working conditions and other job-related issues. Its terms are negotiated by the employer and representatives of an employee **Bargaining Unit**. The union is an organization composed of employees who have joined together to negotiate with the employer on behalf of workers collectively regarding working conditions and other job-related issues. The bargaining unit is a group of employees who have been authorized to engage in collective bargaining on behalf of other employees. They

**Employment at Will:**
A doctrine providing that either party has the power to terminate the employment relationship at any time and for any reason.

**Collective Bargaining Agreement:**
A contract between an employer and a union that regulates employees' working conditions. Its terms are negotiated by the employer and representatives of the bargaining unit.

**Union:**
An organization composed of workers who have joined together to negotiate with an employer on behalf of its members' interests regarding working conditions and other job-related issues.

**Bargaining Unit:**
A group of employees who have been authorized to engage in collective bargaining on behalf of other employees.

are certified by the federal government through the **National Labor Relations Board** to be represented by a union. The collective bargaining agreement's provisions on hiring and firing of employees will apply rather than default employment at will standards in these circumstances.

Public policy also protects employees from discharge. An employee can sue if he or she feels that the discharge was in retaliation for refusing to perform an illegal task asked of the employee by the employer or if the discharge was in connection with an employee's whistleblowing. **Whistleblowing** occurs when an employee reports illegal activities of the employer to authorities, which can lead to an employee's discharge. There is now some protection for whistleblowing under certain federal laws.

## COMMON LAW CLAIMS

Historically, under common law tort law, employees had a difficult time bringing a claim for injury on the job. Concepts such as **Contributory Negligence**—meaning that the employee's contribution to the injury made the employer not liable for the damage—and **Assumption of the Risk**—meaning that the employee assumed any risk of injury by taking the job—provided defenses for the employer against claims. Even if an employee recovered in court, that recovery of lost wages, medical bills, and other damages could come many years down the road. Success was not guaranteed, and the employee needed to hire and pay an attorney to advocate on behalf of the employee's cause. In the meantime, the employee might not have a source of income or security—and in the end the employee may very well lose the case.

## WORKERS' COMPENSATION

State **Workers' Compensation** laws require that injury-related disputes between employees and employers be managed by an administrative agency or board. These laws replaced the common law in every state in the early twentieth century as part of a grand bargain between employers and employees. In this bargain, so long as they are injured during the course of their employment, employees are able to file claims for specific damages for specific injuries without going through the regular court system and its attendant costs and delays. In exchange, employers are not exposed to endless lawsuits from employees in the courts, and the unpredictable costs that go with litigation. Instead, employers purchase insurance at a pre-

**National Labor Relations Board:**
A federal agency that monitors employer-union relations.

**Whistleblowing:**
Reporting of illegal activities of the employer to authorities by an employee.

**Contributory Negligence:**
A defense to unintentional torts that provides that if the plaintiff was negligent at all, she would not be able to recover for any of the injuries caused by the defendant.

**Assumption of the Risk:**
Under the law of torts, the act of assuming the risk of loss or injury by taking a dangerous job or engaging in a dangerous activity.

**Workers' Compensation Statutes:**
State statutes in every state that provide that so long as an employee is injured during the course of employment, the employee is able to file a claim for specific damages for specific injuries without a lawsuit or proof of the employer's fault.

dictable cost in order to cover the cost of workers' compensation claims.

Under workers' compensation systems, the employee files a claim for compensation for a work-related injury. Employees are not able to sue the employer in the courts for the same injury. The state statute governing workers' compensation specifies which employees are covered by the law. Not every line of work is included.

Employers can no longer raise defenses to injury claims that would serve as a complete bar to recovery.

For instance, assume that Ed employs Marie as a mailroom clerk. Marie slips and falls on some loose envelopes on a slick floor and breaks her leg while at work. Marie is hurt during the course of her employment. Worker's compensation laws apply and Marie is entitled to workers' compensation funds according to a preset schedule. These funds come very quickly, with minimal court intervention, if any at all. Marie cannot sue Ed for the slip and fall. Ed cannot claim that Marie was contributorily negligent and deserves nothing because she wasn't watching where she was going when she slipped. Note, however, that Marie may be able to sue third parties besides her employer (like the floor polishing company) for their possible negligence.

## OCCUPATIONAL SAFETY AND HEALTH ACT OF 1970

The **Occupational Safety and Health Act of 1970** was passed to protect employees' safety and health while on the job. This legislation mandates that employers keep a safe workplace for all employees.

There are several agencies that work together to develop and enforce the standards of the Act. The primary one is the **Occupational Safety and Health Administration (OSHA)**. OSHA is part of the Department of Labor and sets standards and regulations, enforces the relevant legislation, and makes workplace inspections. Another agency is the **Occupational Safety and Health Review Commission**. It functions as a review board, hearing appeals from measures taken by OSHA. Finally, the **National Institute for Occupational Safety and Health**, which is part of the Department of Health and Human Services, conducts research in the area and makes recommendations to OSHA.

## FAMILY AND MEDICAL LEAVE ACT OF 1993

The **Family and Medical Leave Act of 1993 (FMLA)** provides that most employers (including the federal government) that employ 50

**Occupational Safety and Health Act of 1970:**
A federal statute that is meant to protect employees' safety and health while on the job through workplace safety standards.

**Occupational Safety and Health Administration (OSHA):**
A federal agency that sets standards and regulations, enforces the relevant legislation, and makes workplace inspections.

**Occupational Safety and Health Review Commission:**
A federal agency that acts as a review board to hear appeals from measures taken by OSHA.

**National Institute for Occupational Safety and Health:**
A federal agency that conducts research on workplace safety and makes recommendations to OSHA.

**Family and Medical Leave Act of 1993 (FMLA):**
A federal statute mandating that certain employers must provide an eligible employee up to a total of 12 weeks of unpaid leave during any 12-month period.

or more employees must provide an eligible employee up to a total of 12 weeks of unpaid leave during any 12-month period.

The unpaid leave can be for one or more of the following life events:

1.  For the birth and care of the newborn child of the employee;
2.  For placement with the employee of a son or daughter for adoption or foster care;
3.  To care for an immediate family member (spouse, child, same-sex partner, or parent) with a serious health condition; or
4.  To take medical leave when the employee is unable to work because of a serious health condition.

The employer is not required to pay the employee during leave. However, the employee may use personal leave, sick time, and vacation time to maintain his or her income during the leave. Employees who take FMLA leave are entitled to maintain health benefits coverage, but they are responsible for their employee copays of any coverage and must pay that cost of coverage during the leave or when they return to work.

The law was modified in 2008 to allow the spouses, children, parents, or other next of kin who provide care for an injured service member to take as many as 26 weeks of unpaid leave in a 12-month period. The law was modified in 2010 to include same-sex partners within the definition of "immediate family member."

An employee is not guaranteed the same position when he or she returns to her job from leave. The FMLA requires that an employee be returned to the same position that he or she held prior to leave, or to an equivalent position with equivalent benefits, pay, status, and other terms and conditions of employment.

Employees must tell their employer that they intend to take FMLA leave at least 30 days beforehand. In emergencies, the employee must notify the employer as soon as reasonably possible. The employer can request proof that a leave is for an FMLA-eligible reason. The employer can ask the employee to provide medical documentation for FMLA leave.

## DISCRIMINATION

There are several federal statutes that prohibit **Employment Discrimination**. What these laws do is limit the employment at will doctrine by carving out special groups of people and prohibiting the employer from firing them just because of their status as a member of the protected group. These laws do not prohibit all types of discrimination. Remember that all hiring, promotion, demotion, pay,

**Employment Discrimination Laws:**
A set of laws that prohibits an employer from treating certain employees or applicants differently because of their status as a member of a protected group.

and firing decisions involve discrimination in favor of one employee to the detriment of another. Rather these laws only prohibit *illegal* discrimination based on someone's protected status.

There are several pieces of significant legislation in this area. The most important statute is **Title VII of the Civil Rights Act of 1964**. Title VII prohibits discrimination against employees in hiring, firing, promotion, compensation, or any other aspect of employment based on race, color, religion, national origin, and gender.

Related legislation, the **Equal Employment Opportunity Act of 1972**, along with amendments, created the **Equal Employment Opportunity Commission (EEOC)**. The EEOC enforces the provisions of Title VII as well as other statutes such as the **Age Discrimination in Employment Act (ADEA)**, the **Equal Pay Act**, and the **Americans with Disabilities Act (ADA)**. The EEOC enforces the statutes through investigation and by litigating claims of discrimination by employers on behalf of employees, itself, or state fair employment commissions.

The ADEA makes it illegal to discriminate against an employee or job applicant because of his or her age. It applies to employees and applicants who are over age 40. Employers may make age an employment requirement only if age is demonstrably a **Bona Fide Occupational Qualification (BFOQ)** reasonably necessary to the normal operation of the business. Thus, Crazy Inc. cannot refuse to hire Russ as a manager just because he is 55 years old. Crazy may be worried that a 55-year-old has a shorter working life than a 25-year-old, or that a 55-year-old will demand more pay and benefits going forward, but it cannot take that speculation into consideration in its hiring decision.

A relatively recent case illustrates the point: In *Reeves v. Sanderson Plumbing Products, Inc.*, 530 U.S. 133 (2000), Mr. Reeves was 57 years old and working as a supervisor at Sanderson Plumbing Products in a department called the "Hinges Room." The manager of the department felt that employees were absent and leaving early, so he ordered an audit of the department. At the conclusion of the audit, Reeves and another employee were fired. Reeves filed suit claiming that he was fired because of his age.

At trial the plumbing company argued that Reeves had kept inaccurate records and that he was fired for that reason. Reeves provided evidence that he accurately recorded the attendance and hours of the employees that he supervised. The case went to a jury trial, and based on the evidence the jury decided in favor of Reeves. The case eventually went to the Supreme Court of the United States. The Court held that Reeves provided proof that he kept good records and that these records completely refuted the employer's stated reason for firing him, leaving his age as the only possible reason for his

**Title VII of the Civil Rights Act of 1964:**
A federal statute that prohibits discrimination in hiring, firing, promotion, compensation, or any other aspect of employment based on race, color, religion, national origin, and gender.

**Equal Employment Opportunity Act of 1972:**
A federal statute that created the EEOC.

**Equal Employment Opportunity Commission (EEOC):**
A federal agency that administers and enforces the provisions of Title VII and other employment discrimination laws.

**Age Discrimination in Employment Act (ADEA):**
A federal statute that makes it illegal to discriminate against an employee or job applicant over 40 years of age because of his or her age.

**Equal Pay Act:**
A federal statute requiring that men and women be paid the same for work that requires equal levels of skill, effort, and responsibility, performed under similar conditions.

**Americans with Disabilities Act (ADA):**
A federal statute that prevents employers from discriminating against qualified individuals with disabilities and that requires employers to make reasonable accommodations to applicants and employees with disabilities unless doing so would cause the employer undue hardship.

**Bona Fide Occupational Qualification (BFOQ):**
A job requirement that is reasonably necessary to the normal operation of the business.

firing. Thus, Reeves was discriminated against due to his age and won the case.

The Equal Pay Act requires that men and women be paid the same for equal work. Equal work is defined as work that requires equal levels of skill, effort, and responsibility, performed under similar conditions. Any pay difference between men and women is permissible only if it was based on a seniority system, a merit system, a system that pays for the quantity or quality of work produced, or another factor other than sex. Thus, assume that Pat and Alex are both senior project engineers, working the same hours, and with the same responsibilities. Pat and Alex should be paid the same, unless one or the other has seniority, better performance, more experience, or the like. Pay disparities may not be based on gender.

The ADA is a federal statute that applies to employers with 15 or more employees. It prohibits discrimination in recruitment, hiring, promotions, training, pay, social activities, and other privileges of employment against qualified disabled individuals. The ADA prevents the employer from asking questions about a job applicant's disabilities before a job offer is made. It applies to individuals subject to an adverse employment action because of a disability covered by the ADA that is not transitory and minor. It also requires that employers provide **Reasonable Accommodation** to the known disabilities of employees unless that accommodation results in **Undue Hardship**.

The definition of conditions that qualify for protection as disabilities under the ADA was substantially changed in 2009. The Americans with Disabilities Act Amendments Act of 2008 (ADAAA) became effective law on January 1, 2009. The ADAAA changed the law to make it easier for individuals to qualify as disabled for the purposes of the ADA. A disability under the ADAAA requires a physical or mental impairment that results in a substantial limitation of one or more major life activities.

The statute is helpful in that it provides two comprehensive definitions of "major life activities" by including two lists of conditions and diseases that qualify. The law also specifies that the use of "ordinary eyeglasses or contact lenses" is not a disability, but other mitigating measures that help an individual address his or her condition are not to be considered to solve the disability issue (thus disqualifying them from the ADA's protection). The law explicitly notes that a condition that is episodic (such as epilepsy) or in remission (such as cancer) is a disability if it would substantially limit a major life activity when the condition is active.

Moreover, the ADA requires employment agencies, labor organizations, and joint labor-management committees to provide

**Reasonable Accommodation:**
An accommodation made by an employer to the known disabilities of an employee, done in such a way that the accommodation does not impose an undue hardship on the employer.

**Undue Hardship:**
The result when an accommodation by an employer to an employee's disability in the workplace in order to allow the employee to perform the essential functions of his or her position is unreasonable to the employer in terms of the time or money required.

reasonable accommodations. A reasonable accommodation is a modification or adjustment that is made to allow the disabled person equal access to facilities or the ability to continue working without difficulty. Under the ADA, there are three categories of "reasonable accommodations":

> (i) Modifications or adjustments to a job application process that enable a qualified applicant with a disability to be considered for the position such qualified applicant desires; or
>
> (ii) Modifications or adjustments to the work environment, or to the manner or circumstances under which the position held or desired is customarily performed, that enable a qualified individual with a disability to perform the essential functions of that position; or
>
> (iii) Modifications or adjustments that enable a covered entity's employee with a disability to enjoy equal benefits and privileges of employment as are enjoyed by its other similarly situated employees without disabilities.
>
> —29 C.F.R. §1630.2(o).

For example, Uva works for Sparkle Co, which is covered by the ADA. Uva is an administrative assistant and she uses her computer all day long writing letters, sending e-mail, and preparing reports as part of her job. Uva develops carpal tunnel syndrome, a condition that makes it very, very painful for her to type. She is disabled and covered by the ADA. Uva can, however, work if Sparkle Co. provides her with a desk extension and wrist guards that cost a total of $500. These provisions are reasonable accommodations under the ADA, and Sparkle must supply Uva with these accommodations so that she may continue work. The cost compared to the benefit of Uva's continued work is minimal. If, however, the accommodation required a significant change, such as a new wing on a building for one employee, the employer would likely not be required to make changes to accommodate the employee's disability as the changes would be unreasonable.

Most states also prohibit discrimination based on these factors, and some expand protection to include factors such as sexual orientation.

## INTENTIONAL VERSUS UNINTENTIONAL DISCRIMINATION

### Disparate Treatment

Under Title VII of the Civil Rights Act of 1964, both intentional and unintentional discrimination are prohibited. When the discrimination is intentional, it is known as **Disparate Treatment Discrimination**.

**Disparate Treatment Discrimination:**
A type of illegal discrimination that is intentional and discriminatory on its face.

The employee must show that the treatment he or she received was discriminatory on its face. Although disparate treatment was common in hiring decisions prior to the 1960s, these types of facial discrimination claims are rare today. They do still occur though.

Customer preference is not a valid reason for an employer to practice disparate treatment. Regardless of what an employer's customer base may demand, the employer cannot accommodate its customer's preferences for employees of a certain race, color, religion, national origin, or gender unless it can demonstrate that one of those qualities is a BFOQ of the job, which is extremely unlikely.

## Disparate Impact

The other type of discrimination claim is unintentional (or appears to be unintentional) and is thus far more common. There does not need to be intentional discrimination under disparate impact theory. **Disparate Impact** allows plaintiffs to show that nondiscriminatory actions, neutral on their face (not mentioning or based on the protected classes of age, gender, religion, race, color, national origin, disability, etc.), can have a discriminatory impact on certain groups of people. An employer can defend against this claim by showing that the action was a Bona Fide Occupational Requirement—a "business necessity"—and not for the purpose of discrimination.

**Disparate Impact Discrimination:** A type of illegal discrimination in which nondiscriminatory actions, neutral on their face, can have a discriminatory impact on protected groups of people.

For instance, assume that Garbage Inc. hires 20 new sanitation engineers, and its human resources department posts as a job requirement that the engineers have four-year college degrees. The job posting mentions nothing about a protected class. However, statistically the pool of applicants for that posting is going to be skewed away from some minority applicants and toward Caucasian and Asian applicants because a greater percentage of the populations of those two groups have college degrees. Here, an applicant could challenge the job posting as discriminatory because a college degree requirement is not reasonably a BFOQ for the position of sanitation engineer. Although the posting is not discriminatory on its face, a disparate impact on minority groups occurs here.

## AFFIRMATIVE ACTION

**Affirmative Action** is a policy put in place by executive order after the passage of Title VII of the Civil Rights Act of 1964 that gives preference to protected individuals based on their race, color,

**Affirmative Action:** A policy that gives preference to protected individuals based on their race, color, religion, national origin, and gender, if the protected individuals are otherwise qualified for the position.

religion, national origin, and gender, if the protected individuals are otherwise qualified. Strict quota systems are unconstitutional, but employers and educational institutions may consider membership in a protected class based on race, color, religion, national origin, and gender as a factor in employment and admissions decisions. It permits actions appropriate to overcome the effects of past or present practices, policies, or other barriers to equal employment opportunity.

## INCOME SECURITY

There are various laws in place that provide income to workers who have been laid off, who are disabled, or who are retired. States have developed an insurance system designed to compensate unemployed workers. This system was created by the **Federal Unemployment Tax Act of 1935**. Employers pay into a fund under the system, and eligible individuals are paid **Unemployment Compensation**.

For the retired or disabled worker the significant federal statutes are the **Social Security Act of 1935 (SSA)** and the **Employee Retirement Income Security Act of 1974 (ERISA)**.

The Social Security Administration administers the SSA. It provides compensation to individuals when their employment is terminated due to death, disability, or retirement. It also can provide income when employment is reduced.

**Medicare** is administered by the Social Security Administration. Medicare provides health insurance for people who are 65 years old and older as well as for disabled persons under age 65. Both the employer and employee contribute to Medicare.

The **Federal Insurance Contribution Act (FICA)** mandates that the employer and employee contribute to the fund of monies providing compensation to retired and disabled workers eligible to receive payments on a monthly basis. In 2010 both employer and employee paid 6.2 percent of the employee's gross wages as a tax to the federal government up to a limit of $106,800 for Social Security. The employer and employee both pay an additional 1.45 percent of gross wages to fund Medicare. Self-employed individuals (who are both employer and employee) pay both halves of the tax.

Social Security benefits are supplemented by ERISA. This legislation regulates employee retirement plans that are established by employers. Employers are not required to have a pension plan, but if they do have one, then ERISA applies. ERISA sets out specific regulations that require employers offering these retirement plans to provide employee participants with basic information about plan

**Federal Unemployment Tax Act of 1935:**
A federal statute that provides unemployment compensation to the involuntarily unemployed.

**Unemployment Compensation:**
Payments made to involuntarily unemployed individuals.

**Social Security Act of 1935 (SSA):**
A federal statute that provides for Social Security payments for the aged and disabled.

**Employee Retirement Income Security Act of 1974 (ERISA):**
A federal statute that provides standards and controls for pension and retirement plans.

**Medicare:**
A federal statute that provides health insurance for persons 65 years old and older and for disabled persons under age 65.

**Federal Insurance Contribution Act (FICA):**
A federal statute that requires the employer and the employee to contribute tax dollars to Social Security and Medicare.

features and funding. It designates specific fiduciary responsibilities for plan managers. It also requires plans to establish processes for employee participants to challenge decisions made about their plans. Finally, it gives employee participants the right to sue for unpaid or missing benefits and breaches of fiduciary duty by the plan managers.

## SEXUAL HARASSMENT

It is a violation of Title VII of the Civil Rights Act of 1964 to commit sexual harassment in the workplace. **Sexual Harassment** is defined as unwelcome sexual advances, requests for sexual favors, and other forms of unwelcome conduct. There are two forms of sexual harassment under Title VII: quid pro quo sexual harassment and hostile work environment harassment.

**Sexual Harassment:** Unwelcome sexual advances, requests for sexual favors, and other forms of unwelcome conduct in the workplace.

**Quid pro quo** sexual harassment—something for something else—describes harassment that occurs when any condition of employment (like promotions, hiring, firing, or salary increases) is provided by one party to another in return for sexual activity. This type of sexual harassment is relatively easy to recognize. The sexual activity (or advances toward that goal) must be unwelcome. This does not mean that interoffice dating cannot occur. However, it does mean that one party cannot use his or her power within the workplace to coerce another to engage in sexual activities.

**Quid Pro Quo Harassment:** A type of sexual harassment that occurs when an employment decision is conditioned on sexual activity or the basis for the decision is the satisfaction of a sexual demand.

**Hostile Work Environment Harassment** occurs when there is a work environment pervasive with sexual advances, or unwelcome sex-related humor or comments. This environment must so pervasive that it creates what a reasonable person would consider to be an abusive work environment. The environment must be so hostile that there is a constructive firing.

**Hostile Work Environment Harassment:** A type of sexual harassment that occurs when there is a work environment pervasive with sexual advances, or unwelcome sex-related humor or comments.

The determination of what makes a work environment hostile has been clarified by the United States Supreme Court. In *Harris v. Forklift Systems, Inc.*, 510 U.S. 17 (1993), the Court held that a workplace must be an objectively hostile or abusive environment and one that the reasonable person, as well as the victim, would find hostile and abusive. In that case Ms. Harris worked at Forklift Systems and claimed that the president of the company created a hostile work environment. The Supreme Court decided that in hostile workplace claims, the courts must look at all of the circumstances surrounding the claim, including the frequency of the discriminatory conduct and its severity. The determination can include the emotional or psychological impact on the victim—but that alone is not conclusive of a hostile environment.

## ETHICAL ISSUES

● ● ●

Pay disparity still exists based on recent Census data. See the Table below.

Even with the numerous laws that have been enacted, what explains the persistence of this disparity? What are the moral and ethical implications of the pay gap? Can you think of any non-legal actions that can be taken to remedy the discrepancy?

| Race and Ethnicity | Male | Female | Women's Earnings as a percent of White Male Earnings* |
|---|---|---|---|
| All Races | 47,127 | 36,278 | 77% |
| White Alone | 51,405 | 38,533 | 75% |
| Black or African-American only | 37,496 | 31.824 | 61.9% |
| Asian only | 51,760 | 42,331 | 82.3% |
| Hispanic or Latino (any race) | 31,393 | 27,181 | 52.9% |

*Source:* Institute for Women's Policy Research Compilation of Current Population Survey Labor Force Statistics, 2009
http://www.census.gov/hhes/www/cpstables/032010/perinc/new05_001.htm  (retrieved Sept. 16, 2010)
*The ratio for All Races is for Males and Females of All Races

## EMPLOYEE PRIVACY

A more recent issue in employment law is the concept of employee privacy. Employers have a right to be concerned about employee productivity with the advent of the Internet, e-mail, and social networking sites such as Facebook. Along the same lines, employees do expect some privacy in the workplace. Employers increasingly monitor employees' Internet and e-mail use at work through special software. Employees have brought suits claiming that this is an invasion of their privacy.

Many laws provide for privacy rights. The United States Constitution, according to the Supreme Court, grants a personal right to privacy under the First, Third, Fourth, Fifth, and Ninth Amendments. Also tort law and state constitutions provide a right to privacy. In terms of electronic communications and privacy, the major statute is the **Electronic Communications Privacy Act of 1986**. This Act provides that employers can monitor employee business-related electronic communications but not personal ones. Employers can avoid

**Electronic Communications Privacy Act of 1986:**
A federal statute that permits employers to monitor employee business-related electronic communications but not personal ones, unless by employee consent.

liability under the Act for monitoring personal communications by acquiring employee consent. Employee consent can be required as a condition of employment.

## CHAPTER SUMMARY

The employer-employee relationship is governed by many federal and state laws. Many of these laws were developed to protect the employee from the common law defenses available to employers when employees brought claims in tort. This chapter described the most significant laws in this arena.

### Relevant Web Sites

http://www.law.cornell.edu/topics/agency.html
http://www.irs.gov/pub/irs-pdf/f2848.pdf
http://www.dol.gov
http://www.eeoc.gov/policy/docs/accommodation.html

### Exercises

1. Explain two exceptions to employment at will.
2. Explain the difference between legal and illegal discrimination.
3. Find and describe a real-world example of a reasonable accommodation in the workplace.
4. Describe what the Equal Employment Opportunity Commission does.
5. Explain how a court determines whether a workplace has a hostile work environment.

### Questions

1. Which federal commission oversees the payment of Social Security benefits?
2. What is the difference between disparate impact and disparate treatment illegal discrimination?
3. What is quid pro quo sexual harassment?
4. What is hostile work environment sexual harassment?
5. What is the role of FICA taxes, and who pays them?
6. What is a collective bargaining agreement?
7. What is a whistleblower, and what protections exist for them?
8. What does OSHA do?
9. What is the role of a bona fide occupational qualification in workplace hiring?
10. Does the Equal Pay Act require that all men and women be paid the same?

### Hypotheticals

1. Johnson Power Company historically discriminated against Hispanics. At the Company, the lowest paying jobs were held by Hispanics. The Company had employees take a broad aptitude (IQ) test, on which Hispanics performed poorly. The Company also required certain jobs to be held by those with a high school diploma. Where Johnson Power is located, most Hispanic workers do not have a high school diploma. If challenged on this policy, what will the Company need to show?
2. Siobhan loves the stock market and decides to take a job working as equity trader. The investment bank where she works had an all-male trading desk prior to Siobhan's joining. There was a good deal of gender-based humor, vulgar language, and even calendars with skimpily clad female bathing suit models around. Siobhan complained to her boss after several months of working in this environment. The boss does nothing. Can Siobhan file a claim? If so, what kind?

3. Joseph works at a grocery store. He has worked there for three years. He would like to begin to move into a management position. He discusses his chances for promotion with his boss, Eileen. Eileen explains to Joseph that she will be more than happy to consider him for a promotion as long as he starts to clean her apartment monthly. Joseph does not like those terms for promotion. What should Joseph do now?

4. A local coffee shop prefers to hire veterans before non-veterans. Silvia is not a veteran, and she applied for a job opening as a cashier at the shop. She did not get the job, but another applicant who was a veteran did. Silvia sues for gender discrimination. Will she prevail?

## Sample Cases

1. Peconic Asset Managers, LLC (Peconic), is an institutional investment manager and registered investment adviser. William Harnisch is the President. Peconic is regulated by federal securities laws. Joseph Sullivan was Peconic's Chief Compliance Officer (CCO). Peconic has a Code of Ethics (Code), which requires the CCO, "on pains of termination," to determine whether an employee has violated the Code. It is a violation of the Code for employees to make trades in their personal brokerage accounts without prior authorization from the CCO. On one occasion, Harnisch sold large quantities of a stock in his personal brokerage account without advising Sullivan. Sullivan questioned Harnisch regarding the sale of stock and Code violation. Harnisch refused to answer, and shortly thereafter Sullivan was terminated. Sullivan sues, claiming that his situation was an exception to the employment-at-will doctrine. What is the result?

*Sullivan v. Harnisch*, 915 N.Y.S.2d 514 (App. Div. 1st Dep't 2010).

2. Barbara Conley was hired by the Delaware Division of the State Police (DSP) in 1983. In 2001, she was promoted to the rank of Captain and assumed the position of Director of the Traffic Control Section. Conley supervised John Campanella, who was the Deputy Director in her department. Other female employees in Conley's department complained about Campanella's inappropriate behavior. He told off-color jokes and talked about his experiences with prostitutes. Conley overlooked these complaints at first but eventually requested that Campanella be transferred. Internal Affairs opened an investigation into Campanella's behavior and concluded that he be transferred. During the investigation, however, concerns were raised about Conley's inappropriate behavior. She had made derogatory and sexual comments about her co-workers. The investigation concluded that Conley had engaged in unprofessional conduct and charged her with sexual harassment. DSP suspended Conley, and she voluntarily retired in 2007. Conley sued the DSP for employment discrimination. What is the result?

*Conley v. State*, No. 08-C-09-026 (RBY) (Del. Super. Ct. Jan. 6, 2011).

## Key Terms

**Affirmative Action:** A policy that gives preference to protected individuals based on their race, color, religion, national origin, and gender, if the protected individuals are otherwise qualified for the position.

**Age Discrimination in Employment Act (ADEA):** A federal statute that makes it illegal to discriminate against an employee or job applicant over 40 years of age because of his or her age.

**Americans with Disabilities Act (ADA):** A federal statute that prevents employers from discriminating against qualified individuals with disabilities and that requires employers to make reasonable accommodations to applicants and employees with disabilities unless doing so would cause the employer undue hardship.

**Assumption of the Risk:** Under the law of torts, the act of assuming the risk of loss or injury by taking a dangerous job or engaging in a dangerous activity.

**Bargaining Unit:** A group of employees who have been authorized to engage in collective bargaining on behalf of other employees.

**Bona Fide Occupational Qualification (BFOQ):** A job requirement that is reasonably necessary to the normal operation of the business.

**Collective Bargaining Agreement:** A contract between an employer and a union that regulates employees' working conditions. Its terms are negotiated by the employer and representatives of the bargaining unit.

**Contributory Negligence:** A defense to unintentional torts that provides that if the plaintiff was negligent at all, she would not be able to recover for any of the injuries caused by the defendant.

**Disparate Impact Discrimination:** A type of illegal discrimination in which nondiscriminatory actions, neutral on their face, can have a discriminatory impact on protected groups of people.

**Disparate Treatment Discrimination:** A type of illegal discrimination that is intentional and discriminatory on its face.

**Electronic Communications Privacy Act of 1986:** A federal statute that permits employers to monitor employee business-related electronic communications but not personal ones, unless by employee consent.

**Employee:** The party to the employment relationship who is hired by an employer to perform work.

**Employee Retirement Income Security Act of 1974 (ERISA):** A federal statute that provides standards and controls for pension and retirement plans.

**Employer:** The party to the employment relationship who hires workers and pays their wages or salary in exchange for the workers' performance of work.

**Employment at Will:** A doctrine providing that either the employer or the employee has the power to terminate the employment relationship at any time and for any reason.

**Employment Discrimination Laws:** A set of laws that prohibits an employer from treating certain employees or applicants differently because of their status as a member of a protected group.

**Equal Employment Opportunity Act of 1972:** A federal statute that created the EEOC.

**Equal Employment Opportunity Commission (EEOC):** A federal agency that administers and enforces the provisions of Title VII and other employment discrimination laws.

**Equal Pay Act:** A federal statute requiring that men and women be paid the same for work that requires equal levels of skill, effort, and responsibility, performed under similar conditions.

**Family and Medical Leave Act of 1993 (FMLA):** A federal statute mandating that certain employers must provide an eligible employee up to a total of 12 weeks of unpaid leave during any 12-month period.

**Federal Insurance Contribution Act (FICA):** A federal statute that requires the employer and the employee to contribute tax dollars to Social Security and Medicare.

**Federal Unemployment Tax Act of 1935:** A federal statute that provides unemployment compensation to the involuntarily unemployed.

**Hostile Work Environment Harassment:** A type of sexual harassment that occurs when there is a work environment pervasive with sexual advances, or unwelcome sex-related humor or comments.

**Independent Contractor:** A party hired to perform a specific service. How the independent contractor completes the task is beyond the control of the person who hires him or her.

**Medicare:** A federal statute that provides health insurance for persons 65 years old and older and for disabled persons under age 65.

**National Institute for Occupational Safety and Health:** A federal agency that conducts research on workplace safety and makes recommendations to OSHA.

**National Labor Relations Board:** A federal agency that monitors employer-union relations.

**Occupational Safety and Health Act of 1970:** A federal statute that is meant to protect employees' safety and health while on the job through workplace safety standards.

**Occupational Safety and Health Administration (OSHA):** A federal agency that sets standards and regulations, enforces the relevant legislation, and makes workplace inspections.

**Occupational Safety and Health Review Commission:** A federal agency that acts as a review board to hear appeals from measures taken by OSHA.

**Quid Pro Quo Harassment:** A type of sexual harassment that occurs when an employment decision is conditioned on sexual activity or the basis for the decision is the satisfaction of a sexual demand.

**Reasonable Accommodation:** An accommodation made by an employer to the known disabilities of an employee, done in such a way that the accommodation does not impose an undue hardship on the employer.

**Sexual Harassment:** Unwelcome sexual advances, requests for sexual favors, and other forms of unwelcome conduct in the workplace.

**Social Security Act of 1935 (SSA):** A federal statute that provides for Social Security payments for the aged and disabled.

**Title VII of the Civil Rights Act of 1964:** A federal statute that prohibits discrimination in hiring, firing, promotion, compensation, or any other aspect of employment based on race, color, religion, national origin, and gender.

**Undue Hardship:** The result when an accommodation by an employer to an employee's disability in the workplace in order to allow the employee to perform the essential functions of his or her position is unreasonable to the employer in terms of the time or money required.

**Unemployment Compensation:** Payments made to involuntarily unemployed individuals.

**Union:** An organization composed of workers who have joined together to negotiate with an employer on behalf of its members' interests regarding working conditions and other job-related issues.

**Whistleblowing:** Reporting of illegal activities of the employer to authorities by an employee.

**Workers' Compensation Statutes:** State statutes in every state that provide that so long as an employee is injured during the course of employment, the employee is able to file a claim for specific damages for specific injuries without a lawsuit or proof of the employer's fault.

## CHAPTER 8

# Property Rights

## LEARNING OBJECTIVES

You will be able to answer the following questions after reading this chapter:

1. What are the basic attributes of property rights?
2. What are the differences between real property, personal property, and intellectual property?
3. What are the four types of concurrent ownership and their individual attributes?
4. What are bailments, leases, and licenses?
5. What is a gift?
6. What are the features of eminent domain, zoning, easements, and covenants?

## INTRODUCTION

The right to own and control private property is a fundamental pillar of the economic system. Without the ability to buy, sell, and control property, there is little incentive to contract, motivation to grow enterprises, drive to trade, or impetus to take commercial and financial risks. In short, there is little reason for businesspeople to do business without some form of private property rights. Property rights take many forms and can be combined, divided, bought, sold, inherited, restricted, or taken away. This chapter discusses the basic attributes of all property. It also addresses the various types of property, the rights of ownership that are part and parcel of private property, and the other possible manifestations of property rights in the legal environment.

## PROPERTY ATTRIBUTES

Anyone who owns property has certain rights inherent in that ownership status. The basic elements of a working system of private property rights are **Universality**, **Exclusivity**, and **Transferability**. Under the principle of universality, every limited resource is owned by some person or entity. All property is either owned by private individuals, by business entities, or by the government, or it is **Abandoned**. Under the principle of exclusivity, any owner has the right to exclude others from her property. Under the principle of transferability, an owner's property rights may be conveyed from one party to another. These basic concepts are illustrated by the **General Incidents of Ownership** of property. The general incidents of ownership are possession, exclusion, alienation, use, benefit, and destruction.

**Possession** of property means the right to have property, to hold it, to handle it, and to keep it, or to live in it without anyone else taking that property or interfering with use of the property. Possession is likely the property attribute that first comes to mind when trying to describe ownership quickly. In fact, the old saying that "possession is nine-tenths of the law," though not literally true, is based on this basic property attribute.

**Exclusion** in this context refers to the property owner's right to keep others from using property that the owner holds. The property owner is able to exclude others from the use, enjoyment, or possession of her property. Think of the farmer saying "get off my land!" The property owner can prevent others from living in her home, using her MP3 player, borrowing her textbook, driving her car, and the like. Those are clear and common illustrations of the exclusionary property right.

**Alienation** is the right of a property owner to dispose of her property in a manner of the owner's choosing. For example, an owner can generally sell, give away, abandon, or will at death all or part of his property. In fact, owners can choose to alienate only part of their rights to a given piece of property and retain other rights for themselves. Landlords commonly alienate their right to possession of a rented property for a specific period of time in exchange for rent, while retaining all the other attributes of ownership. In that way the rights of ownership are temporarily split between the landlord and lessee.

The **Use** incident of ownership is the right to utilize property as the owner wishes. The owner may use (or not use) the property in whatever way he or she wants, so long as that use is not illegal. Property owners may use their laptop computers for surfing the Web, word processing, and e-mail, or as a doorstop or paperweight as they choose. Arson (willful destruction by fire) of the owner's property is prohibited.

**Benefit** refers to any profits gained by a property owner because of a property's use. Examples include recording artists' rights to

**Universality:**
A legal theory that provides that every limited resource is owned by someone.

**Exclusivity:**
A legal theory that provides that a property owner has the right to exclude others from the property.

**Transferability:**
The ability of an owner of property to convey his property rights to another.

**Abandoned Property:**
Property that is not owned by anyone because its former owner no longer exercises any general incident of ownership of the property.

**General Incidents of Ownership:**
The rights of control of property, which are possession, exclusion, alienation, use, benefit, and destruction.

**Possession:**
The property owner's right to have and hold property to the exclusion of others.

**Exclusion:**
The state of being kept from using property that the owner holds. This incident of ownership of property gives the property owner the right to exclude others from using the property.

**Alienation:**
Disposal or transfer of property in a manner of the owner's choosing.

**Use:**
The incident of ownership referring to the property owner's right to utilize property as the owner wishes.

**Benefit:**
The profits gained by a property owner because of a property's use.

royalties from the sale of music that they record and own, or the right of a shopping center owner to the rent generated by leasing possession of a part of the shopping center to a supermarket.

**Destruction** as an incident of ownership gives a property owner the right to destroy her property. For instance, an owner who does not enjoy a music CD purchased at the store might smash it to bits, or an owner may become frustrated with a computer system and break the computer monitor. Most instances of destruction are acceptable under the law, so long as that destruction does not harm or endanger anyone else. A common limitation on the right of destruction is the law against arson, which prevent property owners from burning down their buildings because of the twin dangers of harm to or destruction of life and the possibility of insurance fraud.

**Destruction:**
The ruination of a property owner's property. This incident of ownership gives property owners the right to destroy property they own.

## PROPERTY TYPES

Property can be divided into two basic types. **Real Property** is land, and anything attached to the land. This definition includes buildings, plants, fences, and crops. Real property also includes property that is attached to buildings, such as windows, ceiling fans, lighting fixtures, and similar items. **Personal Property** is all other property that is not real property. Examples of personal property are automobiles, computers, clothes, televisions, and office furniture. **Intellectual Property** is a subset of personal property that includes the "intangible" property of copyrights, trademarks, and patents.

**Real Property:**
Land, and any property attached to the land.

**Personal Property:**
All other property that is not real property.

**Intellectual Property:**
The "intangible" personal property primarily made up of copyrights, trademarks, and patents.

**Copyrights** are the property rights granted by a government to the author or creator of an original work. An original work is a unique expression of an idea (but not the idea itself). Examples of original works are literary, musical, or artistic works in any form, including written, audio, and video formats. These property rights include the right to copy, distribute, or adapt the original work. In the United States copyrights are granted by the U.S. Copyright Office. Generally copyright lasts for the lifetime of the original work's creator plus 70 years. After a copyright expires, the original work becomes part of the **Public Domain** and anyone is allowed to copy, make use of, or adapt the work.

**Copyrights:**
Property rights granted by a government to the author or creator of an original work.

**Public Domain:**
Property that is no longer protected by intellectual property laws. Anyone is allowed to copy, make use of, or adapt the work.

**Trademarks** are also property rights granted by a government to a trademark holder. In the United States trademarks are issued by the U.S. Patent and Trademark Office. Trademarks are rights that protect words, phrases, names, logos, symbols, sounds, or colors that distinguish goods and services from those manufactured or sold by others and to indicate the source of the goods. Trademarks last forever so long as they are continuously used in commerce.

**Trademarks:**
Property rights that protect words, phrases, names, logos, symbols, sounds, or colors that distinguish goods and services from those manufactured or sold by others and to indicate the source of the goods.

**Patents** are property rights held by an inventor. The inventor has the right to prevent and exclude others (a general incident of ownership discussed above) from making, using, offering for sale, or selling the inventor's creation in the United States or importing the invention into the United States. This patent right is granted by the government for a limited time in exchange for the public disclosure of the invention's existence when the patent is granted. Article 1, Section 8, of the United States Constitution establishes patent law rights "to promote the science and useful arts by securing for a limited time to the inventors the exclusive right to their respective rights and discoveries." Examples of patents are **Utility Patents**, **Design Patents**, and **Plant Patents**. According to the U.S. Patent and Trademark Office, utility patents may be granted to anyone who invents or discovers any new and useful process, machine, article of manufacture, or composition of matter, or any new and useful improvement thereof. Design patents may be granted to anyone who invents a new, original, and ornamental design for an article of manufacture. Plant patents may be granted to anyone who invents or discovers a new and distinct variety of asexually reproducing plant (such as prize strains of roses, or new hardier varieties of food crops).

## PROOF OF OWNERSHIP AND TITLE

In order to exercise the general incidents of ownership of property, an owner must be able to prove that he in facts owns the property. All real property ownership is proven by a **Deed**. A deed is a document in writing through which ownership and title to real property is transferred between two parties. **Title** is the right to ownership of property and at the same time the written proof of ownership of property. This means that with rare exceptions, an individual holds title on every item of property that he owns. However, only certain types of property actually commonly have a written title that denotes ownership. Cars, boats, planes, firearms, jewelry, and similar items quite often have written titles associated with them, either by custom or because the government requires it.

In most cases property is held without a deed or title. However, an owner may establish proof of ownership through possession, sales receipts, will records, or other means that show a lawful transfer of ownership from one person to another.

## CONCURRENT OWNERSHIP

Property can be held by multiple parties at one time, and their property interests (the general incidents of ownership) can be divided

**Patent:**
Property right that allows the inventor to prevent others from making, using, offering for sale, or selling the inventor's creation.

**Utility Patents:**
Patents granted to anyone who invents or discovers any new and useful process, machine, article of manufacture, or composition of matter, or any new and useful improvement thereof.

**Design Patents:**
Patents granted to anyone who invents a new, original, and ornamental design for an article of manufacture.

**Plant Patents:**
Patents granted to anyone who invents or discovers a new and distinct variety of asexually reproducing plant.

**Deed:**
A written document through which ownership and title to real property or an interest in real property is conveyed between parties.

**Title:**
The right to ownership of property and at the same time the written proof of ownership of property.

between the multiple owners in a variety of ways. Several important methods of sharing title to property are tenancy in common, joint tenancy, tenancy by the entireties, and community property.

**Tenancy in Common** is the most common form of concurrent ownership, and it is the default ownership form when there is more than one owner of property. The owners all own equal undivided shares in the entire property unless they specify otherwise. Upon the death of one of the owners, her shares will be passed on to her heirs or to whomever the owner has named to receive her share of the property. In general a co-tenant may sell his share without the permission of the other parties, but often a court proceeding is necessary in order to authorize the sale (this is especially common with real estate). However, even though a co-tenant may wish to sell his share of an asset to a third party, finding a third party who would wish to own a part-share in the property is another matter entirely.

**Joint Tenancy** has many of the same attributes as a tenancy in common. However, the major difference between the two forms of ownership is that jointly owned property is passed immediately to the remaining joint owners upon a joint owner's death. This transfer occurs regardless of the deceased owner's wishes or will provisions. Joint owners have equal interests in the property, and the last owner living will eventually own all the property. Because a joint tenancy is not a default form of property ownership, the deed or title that conveys ownership to the joint owners must indicate that they own the property jointly, rather than as tenants in common. In many states when a married couple purchases property together, the default form of property ownership is joint tenancy, so unless the deed or title states otherwise, it is assumed that the property is jointly held.

**Tenancy by the Entirety** is closely related to joint tenancy. Tenancy by the entirety ownership is available in about half the states. In those states, when a married couple gains title to property, they can choose to hold the title not in their individual names or as joint tenants but rather in the name of the marriage. In that way, if either spouse dies, the other spouse will instantly inherit the property. Additionally the property technically held by the marriage cannot be taken to pay the debt of just one of the spouses.

**Community Property** is a form of property ownership found in western states. In those states, any property acquired by either spouse during the course of a marriage (with the exception of property acquired by inheritance or gift to one spouse) is considered community property, and both spouses have an undivided 50 percent interest in the property.

**Tenancy in Common:** Ownership form in which the owners all own equal undivided shares in the entire property unless they specify otherwise. Each owner designates to whom his share should go in the event of his death.

**Joint Tenancy:** Ownership form in which the owners all own equal undivided shares in the entire property. Each owner's share passes to the remaining owners upon her death.

**Tenancy by the Entirety:** Ownership form closely related to joint tenancy but only available to married couples and only in some states. The property is protected from the debts of one spouse.

**Community Property:** Ownership form in western states whereby any property acquired by either spouse during the course of a marriage (with the exception of property acquired by inheritance or gift to one spouse) is considered community property, and both spouses have an undivided 50 percent interest in the property.

## USE AND CONTROL OF OTHER'S PROPERTY

Use and possession as discussed above are two of the general incidents of ownership of property. An owner may transfer those rights on a temporary basis to another party. **Bailments, Leases,** and **Licenses** are common methods for owners to transfer control or possession of property without the owner's giving up complete rights in the property.

Bailments are the willing or unwilling grant of possession and control of personal property by the owner (the **Bailor**) to another party (the **Bailee**). Bailments are completed with the understanding that the bailor will regain possession and control at a later date. The bailee must take reasonable care of the personal property. If an unreasonable time passes, the property might be considered to be abandoned and the conclusion made that the bailor gave up his rights to the property. Common examples of bailments are attended parking garages, dry cleaners, baggage claims at airports, and coat checks at restaurants. In each case the owner of the property does not intend to permanently give away possession and control of his car, dress suit, suitcase, and winter coat, respectively. However, the owner does intend to entrust the possession, use, and care of his property for a reasonable period of time to the bailee garage attendant, dry cleaner operator, airline, or coat check person.

Leases are a common method used by property owners to transfer possession and use of a piece of real property for a temporary time period. Real property **Lessors**—the owners—lease the use and possession of their property for specified periods (say, an apartment for one year), and then reclaim that right of use and possession from the **Lessee**—the renter—at the end of the lease term.

Licenses are granted by a **Licensor** to a **Licensee**. A license gives the licensee the right to use property of a licensor for a specific purpose. For instance, purchasers of commercial music gain a license to play that music for their own use and entertainment. That license does not extend to the right to copy or distribute that music publicly.

## GIFTS

A **Gift** occurs when a **Donor** gives up all dominion over and control of a piece of property to a willing **Donee** without anything of value received in exchange. A gift must have no strings attached to the transfer. After the completed gift, the donor has no rights to the property and cannot control it in any way. The donor must not just intend the gift. She must actually offer the gift to the donee, and the donee must accept it.

---

**Bailments:**
The willing or unwilling grant of possession and control of personal property by the owner to another party.

**Leases:**
Contractual tools used by property owners to transfer the possession and use of a piece of property for a temporary time period.

**License:**
Contractual tool that grants a licensee the right to use the property of a licensor for a specific purpose.

**Bailor:**
Person granting possession and control of personal property to another for a temporary period.

**Bailee:**
Person granted possession and control of personal property by another for a temporary period.

**Lessors:**
Persons granting possession and control of real property to another for a temporary period.

**Lessee:**
Person granted possession and control of real property by another for a temporary period.

**Licensor:**
Person granting another the right to use property for a specific purpose for a specific period of time.

**Licensee:**
Person granted the right to use property of another for a specific purpose for a specific period of time.

**Gift:**
A transfer of property whereby a donor gives up all dominion over and control of a piece of property to a willing donee for no compensation.

**Donor:**
The maker of a gift.

**Donee:**
The recipient of a gift.

## PUBLIC AND EXTERNAL CONTROL

Property rights are not absolute. For instance, real property owners find their rights to use their property as they see fit often constrained by eminent domain, zoning, easements, and covenants.

**Eminent Domain** is a procedure whereby the government may take private property for a public use with just compensation. The Fifth Amendment to the Constitution sets out the requirements for eminent domain. The taking of an owner's property must be for a public use, but the term *public use* has been interpreted very broadly. It is clear that the government may take a landowner's property to build a public work, like a highway, so long as the former property owner is paid a "just"—not necessarily fair market value—price. However, the United States Supreme Court decided in *Kelo v. City of New London*, 545 U.S. 469 (2005), that "public use" can also include taking private property from one private landowner to give it to another private landowner for economic uses that would apparently better benefit the public. Many states, in direct reaction to the *Kelo* decision, have modified their own state constitutions in order to prohibit this type of private owner to private owner eminent domain proceeding.

**Zoning** is a device used to restrict the types of buildings and the uses available to an owner of a given piece of real property. Zoning is generally regulated by local governments. It dictates where certain types of land uses may occur. For instance, one zone may be dedicated to single-family residential housing, while another area may be dedicated to light industrial or commercial uses. Zoning often includes restrictions for property owners on building size, building height, setbacks from property lines, and requirements for parking spaces. Zoning takes away the property owners' right to use her land in any way that she sees fit, in order to make sure that the property is harmonious with and does not unreasonably interfere with her neighbors' land. As an example, this type of zoning commonly prevents a homeowner in a single-family suburban neighborhood from opening a retail store or a restaurant or a factory on her property.

An **Easement** is an interest in real property owned by another that gives its holder the right to do or prevent something from being done on it. Easements are very common. They are often granted to utility companies so that they are able to run sewers, electrical lines, phone lines, cable lines, and similar items across private property. Easements are either granted by the government in a form of eminent domain proceeding over part of a property owner's land, or by builders and planners when they design subdivisions and office parks, or willingly by one private party to another. For instance,

**Eminent Domain:**
A procedure whereby the government may take private property for a public use with just compensation.

**Zoning:**
A device used to restrict the types of buildings and the uses available to an owner of a given piece of real property.

**Easement:**
An interest in real property owned by another person which gives its holder the right to use the land for a specific purpose or prevent something from being done on it.

many suburban home developments have easements written into the deeds of each homeowner that allow the local utilities to enter each property to run gas lines, sewer and water lines, and electricity wiring. Those easements may have provisions that allow representatives of the subdivision to enter the land of an individual property owner in order to mow lawns, mulch planting beds, and the like. Private parties may sell easements to adjoining landowners that allow the other owners to drive over one property to get to another. Today, virtually every developed property in the United States has some sort of easement affecting the use of that property.

**Covenants**, as relevant here, are promises that are attached to real property and are often included in real property contracts. They require no consideration by the property owner to be enforced. Covenants usually are restrictive, in that they prevent a property owner from doing something that the property owner may otherwise have a right to do on or with his real property. These restrictive covenants are contained in the deed to the property. Normally restrictive covenants are implemented by the original developer of a set of properties. The restrictions vary depending on the original developer's intent. Quite commonly, suburban residential subdivisions have restrictive covenants that prevent property owners from building homes outside a certain style or size, or parking unused vehicles on the land, or the like. Covenants are common on most properties, commercial, industrial, and residential, that have been subdivided and developed within the last 70 years.

**Covenants:**
Promises that are attached to real property and contained in deeds.

## CHAPTER SUMMARY

Property rights take many forms and can be combined, divided, bought, sold, inherited, restricted, or taken away. The elements of all property rights are universality, exclusivity, and transferability. The general incidents of ownership of property are possession, exclusion, alienation, use, benefit, and destruction. Real property is land and anything attached to the land. Personal property is all other property, including intellectual property. Intellectual property includes the "intangible" property of copyrights, trademarks, and patents. Bailments, leases, and licenses allow owners to transfer control or possession of property without the owner's giving up all her rights to the property. Title is the right to ownership of property and at the same time the written proof of ownership of property. A gift occurs when a donor gives up all rights in property to a donee. Real property owners' rights to use their property are restricted by eminent domain, zoning, easements, and covenants.

## ETHICAL ISSUES

●●●

The *Kelo v. City of New London* case revolved around the reactivation by the city government of New London, Connecticut, of its "New London Development Corporation," a private enterprise that was still under the control of the city government. The homes of private landowners would be condemned through eminent domain proceedings, and then their properties given to the New London Development Corporation. Those properties were next to land owned by the Pfizer Corporation. The land would be rebuilt according to a comprehensive redevelopment plan that was estimated to produce 3,169 new jobs and $1.2 million a year in new tax revenue as part of a new real estate complex anchored by Pfizer. Is it ethical for the government to take private property when that use is not a purely public use (like a highway or city hall), but when the new use will create many new jobs and revenue?

### Relevant Web Sites

http://www.copyright.gov/

http://www.uspto.gov/

http://www.txfb.org/newsmaager/templates/
eminentdomainaspx?articleid=4236&zone
id=86

http://memory.loc.gov/ammem/awhhtml/aw
law3/property.html

### Exercises

1. Determine whether or not your state recognizes tenancies by the entirety.
2. Research the deed on property that you or a family member or friend owns. Identify any easements or covenants that are attached to the land referenced in the deed.
3. Give five examples of completed gifts and one example of an incomplete gift that you have experienced in your lifetime.
4. Research abandoned property in your state. Determine whether your state has a system whereby it holds abandoned property for a specified period of time so that owners may reclaim it. Describe the types of property that are covered by this system.
5. Conduct Internet research to find at least four examples of intellectual property lawsuits in which one party is suing another for violations of a patent, trademark, or copyright.

### Questions

1. What is a bailment?
2. What are the differences between a license, licensor, and licensee?
3. Under what circumstances may eminent domain be used by the government?
4. How are zoning and restrictive covenants similar?
5. What is the legal status of intellectual property in the public domain?
6. What is the fundamental difference between real and personal property?
7. What is the difference between exclusion and alienation of property?
8. May a property owner destroy her property without limitations?
9. What is the principle of universality?
10. What is the fundamental difference between jointly owned property and property owned as a co-tenancy?

### Hypotheticals

1. Gavin, in a fit of generosity, decides to give his car to his granddaughter, Hannah. Gavin signs the title papers to make the transfer. However, instead of sending the title papers to the state department of motor vehicles or giving the title to Hannah, he files it away in his desk drawer without anyone's knowing about it.

Hannah later finds the title as she is cleaning Gavin's home office as a favor. Has a valid gift occurred?

2. Nicole and Shawn own their home as joint tenants. Nicole states in her will that her share of the home will go to Ronaldo when Nicole dies. When Nicole dies, Ronaldo attempts to claim Nicole's share of the property. Who owns the home after Nicole's death?

3. Jason has the exclusive right to sell, distribute, and reproduce his new cookbook. What type of intellectual property does Jason hold—a patent, a trademark, or a copyright?

4. Declan gives Savannah the right to cross his land in order to get to Savannah's land. Savannah's land is separated from the public road by Declan's property. What is the legal term for the right that Savannah has to cross Declan's property?

5. Marcus decides to copy and publish a new edition of *Moby Dick*. The book was originally published in 1851. Based on these facts, what would be Marcus's best defense to a lawsuit by the family of Herman Melville, the novel's author, for stealing their intellectual property?

## Sample Cases

1. Two parties purchased land. In the deed the title was held by the parties as joint tenants. Both parties contributed to the purchase, but the plaintiff paid five times more of the down payment on the property than the defendant. In the lawsuit, the plaintiff attempted to split title to the property and get full credit for the greater contribution to the purchase price. Does the plaintiff get credit for the greater contribution under the law, or does the title control without reference to the amount each party paid into the purchase?

*D'Arcy v. Buckley*, 71 Bucks Cty. L. Rep. 167 (Bucks Cty., Pa., 1997).

2. In the Florida Panhandle several beachfront landowners objected to a beach replenishment project in front of their properties. The properties were formerly private beachfront, and the owners owned all the land up to the high tide mark on the beach. The beach replenishment project would build a public access beach between the water and the formerly waterfront property. The state owns the land immediately offshore and underwater. Does the state have the right build up its property and in the process convert the private property owners' private beach into a public one?

*Stop the Beach Renourishment, Inc. v. Florida Dep't of Envtl. Prot.*, 130 S. Ct. 2592 (2010).

## Key Terms

**Abandoned Property:** Property that is not owned by anyone because its former owner no longer exercises any general incident of ownership of the property.

**Alienation:** Disposal or transfer of property in a manner of the owner's choosing.

**Bailee:** Person granted possession and control of personal property by another for a temporary period.

**Bailments:** The willing or unwilling grant of possession and control of personal property by the owner to another party.

**Bailor:** Person granting possession and control of personal property to another for a temporary period.

**Benefit:** The profits gained by a property owner because of a property's use.

**Community Property:** Ownership form in western states whereby any property acquired by either spouse during the course of a marriage (with the exception of property acquired by inheritance or gift to one spouse) is considered community property, and both spouses have an undivided 50 percent interest in the property.

**Copyrights:** Property rights granted by a government to the author or creator of an original work.

**Covenants:** Promises that are attached to real property and contained in deeds.

**Deed:** A written document through which ownership and title to real property or an interest in real property is conveyed between parties.

**Design Patents:** Patents granted to anyone who invents a new, original, and ornamental design for an article of manufacture.

**Destruction:** The ruination of a property owner's property. This incident of ownership gives property owners the right to destroy property they own.

**Donee:** The recipient of a gift.

**Donor:** The maker of a gift.

**Easement:** An interest in real property owned by another person which gives its holder the right to use the land for a specific purpose or prevent something from being done on it.

**Eminent Domain:** A procedure whereby the government may take private property for a public use with just compensation.

**Exclusion:** The state of being kept from using property that the owner holds. This incident of ownership of property gives the property owner the right to exclude others from using the property.

**Exclusivity:** A legal theory that provides that a property owner has the right to exclude others from the property.

**General Incidents of Ownership:** The rights of control of property, which are possession, exclusion, alienation, use, benefit, and destruction.

**Gift:** A transfer of property whereby a donor gives up all dominion over and control of a piece of property to a willing donee for no compensation.

**Intellectual Property:** The "intangible" personal property primarily made up of copyrights, trademarks, and patents.

**Joint Tenancy:** Ownership form in which the owners all own equal undivided shares in the entire property. Each owner's share passes to the remaining owners upon her death.

**Leases:** Contractual tools used by property owners to transfer the possession and use of a piece of property for a temporary time period.

**Lessee:** Person granted possession and control of real property by another for a temporary period.

**Lessors:** Persons granting possession and control of real property to another for a temporary period.

**License:** Contractual tool that grants a licensee the right to use the property of a licensor for a specific purpose.

**Licensee:** Person granted the right to use property of another for a specific purpose for a specific period of time.

**Licensor:** Person granting another the right to use property for a specific purpose for a specific period of time.

**Patent:** Property right that allows the inventor to prevent others from making, using, offering for sale, or selling the inventor's creation.

**Personal Property:** All other property that is not real property.

**Plant Patents:** Patents granted to anyone who invents or discovers a new and distinct variety of asexually reproducing plant.

**Possession:** The property owner's right to have and hold property to the exclusion of others.

**Public Domain:** Property that is no longer protected by intellectual property laws. Anyone is allowed to copy, make use of, or adapt the work.

**Real Property:** Land, and any property attached to the land.

**Tenancy by the Entirety:** Ownership form closely related to joint tenancy but only available to married couples and only in some states. The property is protected from the debts of one spouse.

**Tenancy in Common:** Ownership form in which the owners all own equal undivided shares in the entire property unless they specify otherwise. Each owner designates to whom his share should go in the event of his death.

**Title:** The right to ownership of property and at the same time the written proof of ownership of property.

**Trademarks:** Property rights that protect words, phrases, names, logos, symbols, sounds, or colors that distinguish goods and services from those manufactured or sold by others and to indicate the source of the goods.

**Transferability:** The ability of an owner of property to convey his property rights to another.

**Universality:** A legal theory that provides that every limited resource is owned by someone.

**Use:** The incident of ownership referring to the property owner's right to utilize property as the owner wishes.

**Utility Patents:** Patents granted to anyone who invents or discovers any new and useful process, machine, article of manufacture, or composition of matter, or any new and useful improvement thereof.

**Zoning:** A device used to restrict the types of buildings and the uses available to an owner of a given piece of real property.

## CHAPTER 9

# Torts and Civil Wrongs

**LEARNING OBJECTIVES**

You will be able to answer the following questions after reading this chapter:

1. What is reasonable foreseeability?
2. What is considered trespass?
3. What is an unintentional tort?
4. What are the elements of negligence?
5. What is res ipsa loquitur?
6. What is an abnormally dangerous activity?
7. What are cyber torts?

## INTRODUCTION

"Tort" is the French word for "wrong." Tort law is concerned with compensating victims for civil wrongs that have been committed against them. When conducting business on a daily basis, companies face the risk of causing harm to individuals and other businesses. These torts can subject businesses to potential lawsuits and possible money damages based on one or more tort theory.

For example, Sarah is injured when she slips on a wet floor in Store-Mart, twisting her ankle as she falls to the ground. After her fall, Sarah visited the emergency room, where she was treated for a broken ankle. All of this medical attention was costly. Sarah therefore sued Store-Mart, seeking compensation to cover the costs. The cause of action for the lawsuit (negligence) is a tort law concept that provides Sarah with a tool to recover.

This chapter covers the various causes of action in tort, with specific attention to the torts that pertain to businesses.

## BASIC TORT LAW

Tort law developed under the common law as a civil wrong. That means that the suit is brought by private parties for compensation for wrongs committed against them. Some torts can also be criminal acts punished by the criminal justice system, but criminal acts are beyond the scope of this discussion. Most states have adopted the **Restatement of Torts**, which provides a common codification of the common law developed by the states on their own.

There are two main types of torts. The first is **Intentional Torts**, whereby a person acts with intention and as a result harms another person. The intention is to act, but not necessarily to harm. The second is **Unintentional Torts,** whereby a person unintentionally acts in a way that causes harm to another. An example of an unintentional tort is negligence.

Regardless of the type of tort, the law generally requires not only that a defendant actually caused damages to a plaintiff but also that the damages could be predicted by a reasonable person. The general test is that if it was **Reasonably Foreseeable** that the harm would occur as a result of the intentional act, then the actor is responsible for the consequences of that action. Reasonably foreseeable means that a reasonable person could foresee that harm would result from the act or behavior.

**Restatement of Torts:**
An important treatise on tort law that provides a measure of uniformity among most of the states.

**Intentional Torts:**
Torts in which a person acts with intention and as a result harms another person.

**Unintentional Torts:**
Torts in which a person unintentionally acts in a way that causes harm to another.

**Reasonably Foreseeable:**
A legal standard that asks whether a reasonable person could foresee that there would be harm from the act or behavior.

## INTENTIONAL TORTS

### Trespass

Many businesses have a **Bricks and Mortar** location—a physical location—where customers come to buy goods or consult with professionals. At these locations businesses can control who has permission to enter their property. Lack of permission from the owner of the business to enter the property can result in a trespass and a claim for damages from the property owner against the trespasser.

The tort of **Trespass to Land** occurs when a tortfeasor invades the real property of another, such as a business or an individual, without permission. A **Tortfeasor** is the party who commits a tort. The owner of the property is not required to have a "no trespassing" sign posted anywhere.

In most states, a party is liable for trespass to land if she:

1. Intentionally
2. Enters another's land, or
3. Causes someone or something to enter the land, or
4. Remains on the land, or

**Bricks and Mortar:**
A physical location of a business where customers come to buy goods or consult with professionals.

**Trespass to Land:**
The tort that results when a defendant invades the real property of another, such as a business or an individual, without permission.

**Tortfeasor:**
A party who commits a tort.

5. Leaves on the land something that she is legally obligated to remove
6. Without permission of the landowner or a legal right of entry,
7. Regardless of whether any harm occurs.

So, for instance, if Mara crosses land owned by Woodwork, Inc., without permission in order to save time, she has then entered another's land without permission and is liable for trespass to land. Woodwork, Inc., could sue her to recover damages—even if they are very slight—and to prevent her from doing it again.

## Assault

An **Assault** is an intentional, unexcused act that creates in another person a reasonable apprehension that he is about to suffer an immediate harmful or offensive physical contact.

For an assault to occur there must be an action. Words alone are not enough to create an apprehension (fear) in someone. Threatening to hit another person by words while standing completely still and making no physical movement indicating that the person is going to be hit is not sufficient to create reasonable apprehension of an immediate harm in that person.

Additionally, the apprehension must be of immediate harmful contact. The apprehension cannot be for some harmful contact occurring in the near future. Apprehension about future harm will not create an assault—only immediate harm will. So if Hannah tells Max that she will "beat you up if you don't get here on time next week," there is no reasonable threat of immediate harm. The threat is in the future—next week. However, Hannah may be guilty of a *criminal* act, even if she is not liable for civil damages to Max for the threat.

**Assault:**
An intentional, unexcused act that creates in another person a reasonable apprehension that he is about to suffer an immediate harmful or offensive physical contact.

## Battery

**Battery** is an extension of Assault. If there is a *completed* act of harmful or offensive contact, then a battery has occurred. The contact can also be to or by something connected to a person, such as a hat or a cane. A battery can occur when an individual causes something else to make harmful contact such as shooting a bullet that strikes an individual.

The harmful or offensive contact must be one that a reasonable person would consider to be so. Therefore, shaking hands with an individual who abhors personal contact would not be reasonably offensive. But touching someone in a private area when first meeting her would be seen as reasonably offensive.

**Battery:**
An intentional tort in which there is a completed act of harmful or offensive contact.

So, for example, if Hannah actually does beat Max with a baseball bat (or the palm of her hand), she has completed contact with Max that a reasonable person would consider to be a harmful or offensive contact.

## UNINTENTIONAL TORTS

Unlike intentional torts where a tortfeasor intends to act, the unintentional tort occurs without the tortfeasor's wishing or even believing harm will occur. The actor takes an action that has a risk of adverse consequences. Those consequences must be reasonably foreseeable when the action takes place. Negligence is the primary unintentional tort.

### Negligence

A party is liable for **Negligence** if he unintentionally breaches a duty that he owes to another. Negligence has the following four elements. These elements must be proved to exist by a plaintiff in order to recover from a defendant:

1. Duty of care owed by the defendant;
2. Breach of that duty by the defendant;
3. Breach of that duty caused harm to the plaintiff; and
4. Actual damages (harm) to the plaintiff.

**Negligence:**
An unintentional tort in which a defendant breaches a duty that he owes to another, causing damages.

For example, Kevin is riding the train to work one morning. He has commuted on this train for years from his home in the suburbs to the big city nearby. He has his coffee and is reading his paper, comfortably seated on the train. As more passengers board the train, the seats next to Kevin become full of fellow riders. Kevin takes the lid off his coffee to allow it to cool faster. He simultaneously begins to turn the pages of his paper with the same hand that is holding his very hot coffee. Kevin loses his grip on his coffee and spills the contents of the cup on Shawnee, who is sitting next to him. Shawnee suffers burns from the coffee spill and sues Kevin for negligence.

In this case Shawnee must prove all of the elements of negligence against Kevin in order to recover damages for the burns. Below is an analysis of how the elements of negligence—duty, breach, causation, and damages—relate to the facts of the coffee spill.

### Duty and Breach

In this situation, Kevin owes the duty of the reasonable person to everyone around him. The **Reasonable Person Standard** is how courts

**Reasonable Person Standard:**
A test used by the courts to determine if a reasonably prudent person in the same circumstances would have acted in the manner that the defendant did.

measure the duty of care owed by people to one another. A duty is breached when a person does not act in the way she should based on the duty of care in a particular situation. Here the court would ask if a reasonably prudent person would take the lid off the cup full of piping hot coffee and then begin to turn pages while holding the cup on a crowded moving train. If the answer is no (likely), then the duty of the reasonable person walking and working in society has been breached. This standard is also used in other circumstances by asking if the person acted like a reasonable doctor, lawyer, driver, or policeman under the circumstances.

Duty also may be imposed by statute, regardless of what a reasonable person might do under the circumstances. For instance, if a statute required train riders to have no food or drink on train cars in order to prevent slips, falls, and spills, then regardless of what a reasonable person might do, Kevin and anyone else on the train with food will have breached that legal duty.

## Causation

Shawnee must not only show that Kevin had a duty and breached it, but that this breach of the duty of care by Kevin to the people around him in fact caused Shawnee's injury. In order to do this, Shawnee must show a two-pronged approach to causation: **Cause-in-Fact** and **Proximate Cause**.

Cause-in-fact means that Shawnee must show that the injuries would not have occurred but for Kevin's negligent handling of the cup on a crowded train. What if the engineer of the train applied the brakes suddenly and unexpectedly just as Kevin was turning a page in his newspaper? In that circumstance, it would not be so easy to show that the coffee spilled because of Kevin's negligence alone. In fact, there are thousands of causes-in-fact for the spilled coffee (or any fact scenario), ranging from the fact that Kevin missed his usual train that morning, to the fact that Shawnee decided to sit where she did. Every single event in both Kevin's and Shawnee's lives are causes that made them sit next to each other and act as they did at that particular time and place. However, not all (or many) of these happenings are enough to attach liability to the people making those decisions. In this scenario there was no sudden application of the train brakes or other possible simultaneous cause—so Kevin was the only and immediate cause of the spill.

The second question to ask in the causation analysis is if Kevin's actions were the proximate cause of the harm or injury. Proximate cause is when the injury could be reasonably anticipated from the negligent act as a consequence of the breach of duty. Here, the burn

**Cause-in-Fact:**
The subset of causation in negligence that holds that an injury would not have occurred but for the defendant's negligence.

**Proximate Cause:**
The subset of causation in negligence that holds that an injury could be reasonably anticipated from the defendant's act.

to a fellow passenger was a reasonably foreseeable consequence of mishandling hot coffee on a crowded train. A reasonable person in similar circumstances would anticipate that a coffee cup with no lid might spill on a fellow passenger in a crowded, moving, train, particularly when it is mishandled.

## Damages

Lastly, Shawnee must show that all of this conduct caused her an injury for which she must be compensated. These injuries are **Damages**. Because burns cause pain and require medical treatment, incurring expenses as a direct result of this injury, she has satisfied the final element of a successful negligence claim and therefore may attempt to recover damages in a lawsuit against Kevin.

**Damages:**
Money to be paid to the plaintiff for injuries or loss caused by the defendant.

## Res Ipsa Loquitur

There is a tort theory that serves as a short-cut for proving negligence. **Res Ipsa Loquitur** is Latin for the phrase "the thing speaks for itself." In some situations, it is patently obvious that a party was negligent. A good example of this is when after a surgery an instrument is left inside the patient by medical staff. Here, the injured individual does not need to go through all the steps of proving negligence. Negligence will be presumed because unless someone was negligent there would be no instrument inside a surgery patient.

**Res Ipsa Loquitur:**
Latin for "the thing speaks for itself," a tort theory that the fact that an accident took place means that the defendant had a duty to the plaintiff and breached it.

Res ipsa loquitur claims are also used in cases like plane crashes or ship sinkings where it is impossible to prove the exact negligence that caused a plane to crash or ship to sink, but it is clear that the plaintiff had a duty and breached it.

## Good-Samaritan Laws

Most states have enacted laws that limit the liability of nurses, doctors, and other medical professionals for services that they render to help victims of accidents. These laws, called good-samaritan laws, shield such professionals and others from lawsuits for ordinary negligence caused during an emergency rescue situation.

## DEFENSES TO TORTS

Defendants sued in tort will defend themselves. The law provides for several valid defenses to tort claims.

## Assumption of Risk

**Assumption of the Risk** is a complete defense to most tort claims. A defendant may successfully argue in a case that the plaintiff knew the risk of harm in a given situation yet still participated in the behavior.

This defense may be applicable when the plaintiff is involved in a very dangerous sport. For instance, an individual "assumes the risk" when willingly entering a boxing ring to fight. Anyone who boxes in that ring engages in civil assaults and batteries against the person of the other boxer. But he would have a defense against any lawsuit brought in court against him for the damages that he caused that other boxer in the ring because the boxer assumed the risk by entering the ring.

**Assumption of the Risk:**
The plaintiff's knowing the risk of harm in a given situation yet still participating in the behavior. It is a defense to certain tort claims.

## Comparative Negligence

**Comparative Negligence** is a legal defense to unintentional torts that provides that if the plaintiff was negligent (as well as the defendant), the plaintiff can only recover a portion of his damages from the defendant because he caused some of his own injuries. The court will reduce the recovery of damages by the plaintiff by some amount equal to the plaintiff's own negligence.

A common scenario where comparative negligence is applied is in car accidents. Assume that Pat is in a car accident that is Jim's fault. Pat, however, was not wearing her seat belt when she was hurt. A jury later decides that 60 percent of Pat's injuries were Jim's fault, and 40 percent were because Pat didn't have her seat belt on. In that case, Pat could only recover 60 percent of her damages from Jim.

**Contributory Negligence** is an older legal defense related to comparative negligence. It is generally not used today. Under contributory negligence if a plaintiff is at all negligent (even just 1 percent), she would not be able to recover for any of the injuries caused by the defendant.

**Comparative Negligence:**
A defense to unintentional torts that provides that if the plaintiff was negligent (as well as the defendant), the plaintiff can only recover a portion of his damages from the defendant because he caused some of his own injuries.

**Contributory Negligence:**
A defense to unintentional torts that provides that if the plaintiff was negligent at all, she would not be able to recover for any of the injuries caused by the defendant.

## STRICT LIABILITY

An area of tort liability of particular concern to businesspeople, manufacturers, and merchants is the theory of **Strict Liability**. Under strict liability, someone who sells a defective product in the regular course of business or engages in certain abnormally dangerous activities is liable for any damages stemming from using that product

**Strict Liability:**
Liability of one who sells a defective product or engages in abnormally hazardous activities for any damages that may occur because of using that product or engaging in that activity even if there was no negligence or intent to harm.

or engaging in that activity even if the person did nothing wrong—no negligence claim is necessary.

## Products Liability

**Products liability** is a tort theory that holds manufacturers and sellers of goods liable for harm that is caused by those goods. In order to prove a claim of products liability a plaintiff must prove:

1. The defendant is a seller of a product in the regular course of his business.
2. The product was sold in a defective condition that is unreasonably dangerous to the user or consumer or to his property.
3. The product is expected to and does reach the end user without substantial change in the condition in which it is sold.

There are three types of defective conditions that can occur in products-liability cases. **Design Defects** occur when the product was poorly designed. **Manufacturing Defects** occur when a product was correctly and safely designed but there was an error in the manufacturing process on one, some, or all of the units. **Failure-to-Warn** claims occur where there are dangers inherent in the products that are not obvious to the user and the defendant did not warn of those dangers.

## Abnormally Dangerous Activities

Some activities such as crop dusting, manufacturing fireworks, and housing wild animals are activities so dangerous that regardless of the safety precautions in place, there is a very strong risk of damages occurring. In those cases of **Abnormally Dangerous Activities**, no matter how careful a potential defendant has been, if something goes wrong, she will be held liable for the harm caused. The general standard for liability for a defendant in an abnormally dangerous activity case is:

1. The defendant engaged in an abnormally dangerous activity;
2. There was harm to the person, land, or property of the plaintiff resulting from that activity;
3. Liability attaches regardless of the precautions and care taken by the defendant to prevent harm to others; and
4. The strict liability is limited to the type of harm that normally would stem from the abnormally dangerous activity.

**Products Liability:**
A tort theory that holds manufacturers and sellers of defective products liable for harm that is caused by those products.

**Design Defects:**
A products-liability defective condition that occurs when the product was poorly designed.

**Manufacturing Defects:**
A products-liability defective condition that occurs when a product was correctly and safely designed but there was an error in the manufacturing process on one, some, or all of the units.

**Failure to Warn:**
A products-liability defective condition that occurs when there are dangers inherent in the products which are not obvious to the user and the defendant did not warn of those dangers.

**Abnormally Dangerous Activity:**
An activity in which a defendant engages that cannot be performed safely and for which a defendant is held strictly liable for the harm caused if something goes wrong regardless of fault or precautions taken.

Assume that Gavin owns a fireworks factory. Making fireworks is considered to be an abnormally dangerous activity. Gavin takes every single precaution ever considered, spending millions of dollars, in order to make sure that the factory is safe and that there are no explosions of the highly volatile chemicals in the plant. Unfortunately, one day the plant explodes through a freak accident that was not Gavin's fault, injuring Tessa, a passing motorist. Because Gavin was engaged in an abnormally dangerous activity and there was harm to Tessa from the explosion, Gavin is liable. The explosion is the type of harm that would potentially stem from fireworks manufacturing. It does not matter that Gavin went above and beyond the call of duty to prevent the accident.

## CLASS ACTION LAWSUITS

Many cases against manufacturers are **Class Action Lawsuits**. Class action lawsuits are cases in which one or more plaintiffs join together in a suit and represent the interests of many other plaintiffs who suffered similar harms. The class action allows plaintiffs to join together in complex litigation in which alone they would not be able to participate because of cost.

In 2005, the **Class Action Fairness Act of 2005 (CAFA)** was passed. CAFA increased federal court jurisdiction over class actions where the amount in controversy was more than $5 million and there are plaintiffs who come from several different states. States only have jurisdiction under CAFA if more than two-thirds of the plaintiffs and at least one defendant are from the state and the injury occurred in the state.

Previous to CAFA, attorneys would engage in **Forum Shopping**, or look for the state with the most favorable laws with regard to the particular claim, and bring a claim there as opposed to someplace else. CAFA puts an end to that issue but may cause other problems. Federal courts are more expensive than state courts. This may prevent some claims from making it to trial. Federal courts are also unfamiliar with consumer products-liability, making those courts less than ideal for hearing tort claims like these.

## BUSINESS TORTS

Certain torts apply solely to the interference with business dealings. The most common are the torts of wrongful interference with

**Class Action Lawsuits:**
Cases in which one or more plaintiffs represent the interests of all the plaintiffs who have similar damages from a similar set of facts.

**Class Action Fairness Act of 2005 (CAFA):**
A federal law that increased federal court jurisdiction over class actions where the amount in controversy was more than $5 million and there are plaintiffs who come from several different states.

**Forum Shopping:**
A tactic used by plaintiffs to look for the state or court with the most favorable laws to bring a claim.

a contractual relationship and wrongful interference with a business relationship.

The tort of **Wrongful Interference with a Contractual Relationship** has three elements:

1. A valid, enforceable contract between two parties;
2. A third party who knows of the contract; and
3. Intentional interference with the contract by the third party, which causes one party to breach the contract.

Here, the third party must know of the valid contract and intentionally induce the breach of contract. This can happen by providing some monetary incentive to breach, such as offering a bribe or a better deal to someone to breach an existing contract.

For instance, assume that Logan and Reese have a valid contract whereby Logan will paint Reese's store for $5,000. Quinn knows of the contract, and goes to Reese and offers to paint the store for $4,000 if Reese breaks the contract with Logan. Reese does break the contract. At that point Logan would have a claim for wrongful interference with a contractual relationship against Quinn.

Similar to that tort is the **Wrongful Interference with a Business Relationship**. This tort has three elements:

1. An established business relationship exists between the plaintiff and a third party;
2. A defendant intentionally interferes with the business relationship, thereby causing the relationship to end; and
3. The plaintiff suffers damage due to the interference.

Assume in this example that Anthony and Luke have an ongoing business relationship. Bella is not very happy with this relationship because Anthony is a competitor. She contacts Luke and tells him that Anthony has a bad reputation in his personal and business life. Luke stops doing business with Anthony because of Bella's statements. Regardless of whether or not what Bella said was true, Anthony would have a claim against her for wrongful interference with a business relationship.

## CYBER TORTS

Actions on the Internet and using modern communications technologies like mobile phones that cause harm to others have come to be called **Cyber Torts**. For example, spam, or unsolicited junk e-mail, can be considered a trespass to personal property. Many states have enacted statutes that regulate its use. The federal act in this area

**Wrongful Interference with a Contractual Relationship:** A business tort in which there is a valid, enforceable contract between two parties; a third party knows of the contract; and the third party intentionally interferes with the contract and causes one party to breach the contract.

**Wrongful Interference with a Business Relationship:** A business tort in which there is an established business relationship between the plaintiff and a third party; a defendant intentionally interferes with the business relationship, thereby causing the relationship to end; and the plaintiff suffers damage due to the interference.

**Cyber Tort:** Use of the Internet and modern communications technologies like mobile phones that causes harm to others.

## ETHICAL ISSUES

•••

In a real-life case, two four-year-olds are riding their bikes on a sidewalk in New York City as their parents supervise them. While riding, one of the children strikes an 87-year-old woman. Three days later the woman dies of her injuries. A judge in New York holds that the four-year-old may be sued for negligence (not the parents). Should a four-year-old be sued? What ethical issue does this raise in terms of our current system for seeking relief under tort law?

is the **Controlling the Assault of Non-Solicited Pornography and Marketing Act (CAN-SPAM)**. This law federalizes claims instead of relying on a patchwork of state laws to combat fraud and abuse on the Internet.

Electronic marketers (mainly bulk e-mailers) are required to adhere to specific guidelines. Penalties for violations of this law include prison time and fines. However, the law does not provide for damages payable directly to a potential private plaintiff. Instead, the plaintiff here is the federal government.

Under CAN-SPAM, marketers must:

1. Require an "opt-in" from e-mail addressees to receive the e-mails;
2. Provide an "unsubscribe" option in every e-mail to "opt-out" of future e-mails;
3. Use accurate subject lines;
4. Include a physical address of the sender; and
5. Include no sexual subject matter in e-mails.

The Act has been only partially successful as mainstream marketers comply with its requirements, but many smaller marketers and marketers based outside the United States do not follow its strictures.

> **Controlling the Assault of Non-Solicited Pornography and Marketing Act (CAN-SPAM):** A federal law that places restrictions on bulk electronic marketing.

## CHAPTER SUMMARY

This chapter outlined the basic concepts of tort law. Torts are civil wrongs. When people harm or injure other people intentionally or unintentionally, the law often provides a mean of recovery for a plaintiff's damages. Defendants to a tort action can raise defenses such as assumption of risk and comparative negligence. Tort law has developed so that consumers can bring claims against manufacturers for harms caused by their products under consumer products-liability theory.

## Relevant Web Sites

http://thomas.loc.gov/cgi-bin/query/z?c108:
 H.R.1115:

http://www.atra.org/

## Exercises

1. Explain the difference between an intentional tort and an unintentional tort.
2. Describe some of the defenses to torts.
3. Describe the two elements of causation necessary to prove negligence.
4. Give an example of wrongful interference with a business relationship.
5. Explain res ipsa loquitur.

## Questions

1. What is CAFA?
2. What is a civil assault?
3. What is a tortfeasor?
4. What is strict liability?
5. What is a class action?
6. What are the three types of defective conditions that can occur in products liability cases?
7. What is a battery?
8. What are the elements of a negligence claim?
9. What is forum shopping?
10. What is a cyber tort?

## Hypotheticals

1. Carol plays golf each Thursday. There are some houses on the left side of the fairway. This week Carol hits her ball and it goes straight but hits a branch of a tree and bounces into Sonia's backyard. Carol climbs the short wall that separates the yard from the gold course to retrieve her ball. Sonia has a persimmon tree in her yard. Carol retrieves her golf ball and takes a few ripe persimmons from Sonia's tree. What torts did Carol commit?
2. Dan and Tom are sitting eating lunch in the teachers' lounge at Northranch High School where they teach. The lounge is crowded as all of the teachers eat lunch. Dan gets up to microwave his food. When he returns to his seat, Tom quickly pulls his chair from under him as he begins to sit down. Dan falls hard, and his food flies from his hand. What tort might Tom have committed?
3. Alex suffered a heart attack and was admitted to the hospital. He must have a heart operation. Dr. Steve performs the operation. During the operation there are complications. Alex dies. The Estate of Alex sues Dr. Steve. Under what tort theory does the Estate sue?
4. Fatima has an involuntary muscle spasm. One day while driving she has a spasm causing her to stop the car suddenly. Hahn is driving behind Fatima. Hahn slams on the brakes and successfully stops. Unknown to Hahn, her taillights are not functioning. Bilal, driving behind Hahn, is changing the station on the radio and collides with the back of Hahn's car without ever braking. Hahn's car then hits Fatima's car. Who is liable?

## Sample Cases

1. Jessica Manosa held a party at a vacant rental property owned by her parents. She and her friends invited many of their friends to the party via text message, word of mouth, and telephone. Many non-friends were invited. Manosa had a friend sit at the entrance of the house during the party and charge between $3 and $5 for non-friends to gain access to the party. Food and alcohol were provided. Andrew Ennabe, aged 19, was a friend of Manosa, and he arrived at the party already intoxicated. Thomas Garcia, aged 20, a non-friend, came to the party and paid admission. Garcia harassed several female partygoers and dropped his pants several times. He was asked to leave and escorted off the property by Ennabe. When driving away, Garcia struck Ennabe, who later died of his injuries. Will the parents and Estate of Ennabe be successful in suing Jessica Manosa and her parents for Wrongful Death?

   *Ennabe v. Manosa*, 190 Cal. App. 4th 707 (2010).

2. Gregory was arrested on outstanding misdemeanor charges. During the arrest Gregory was

violent, kicking at the police officers. While in the police car, Gregory spoke irrationally and shouted for the police to shoot him. At the police station, Gregory was strapped to a chair and placed in a holding cell. Eventually Gregory became calm, and the police put him in a regular cell. No physical or mental exam was administered. Gregory was observed crying in his cell. Ten minutes later, Gregory hung himself with a sheet. The Estate of Gregory sues the police department for negligence. The jury is advised to consider assumption of the risk as a defense at trial. Is that a viable defense?

*Gregoire v. City of Oak Harbor*, 170 Wash. 2d 628 (2010).

## Key Terms

**Abnormally Dangerous Activity:** An activity in which a defendant engages that cannot be performed safely and for which a defendant is held strictly liable for the harm caused if something goes wrong regardless of fault or precautions taken.

**Assault:** An intentional, unexcused act that creates in another person a reasonable apprehension that he is about to suffer an immediate harmful or offensive physical contact.

**Assumption of the Risk:** The plaintiff's knowing the risk of harm in a given situation yet still participating in the behavior. It is a defense to certain tort claims.

**Battery:** An intentional tort in which there is a completed act of harmful or offensive contact.

**Bricks and Mortar:** A physical location of a business where customers come to buy goods or consult with professionals.

**Cause-in-Fact:** The subset of causation in negligence that holds that an injury would not have occurred but for the defendant's negligence.

**Class Action Fairness Act of 2005 (CAFA):** A federal law that increased federal court jurisdiction over class actions where the amount in controversy was more than $5 million and there are plaintiffs who come from several different states.

**Class Action Lawsuits:** Cases in which one or more plaintiffs represent the interests of all the plaintiffs who have similar damages from a similar set of facts.

**Comparative Negligence:** A defense to unintentional torts that provides that if the plaintiff was negligent (as well as the defendant), the plaintiff can only recover a portion of his damages from the defendant because he caused some of his own injuries.

**Contributory Negligence:** A defense to unintentional torts that provides that if the plaintiff was negligent at all, she would not be able to recover for any of the injuries caused by the defendant.

**Controlling the Assault of Non-Solicited Pornography and Marketing Act (CAN-SPAM):** A federal law that places restrictions on bulk electronic marketing.

**Cyber Tort:** Use of the Internet and modern communications technologies like mobile phones that causes harm to others.

**Damages:** Money to be paid to the plaintiff for injuries or loss caused by the defendant.

**Design Defects:** A products-liability defective condition that occurs when the product was poorly designed.

**Failure to Warn:** A products-liability defective condition that occurs when there are dangers inherent in the products which are not obvious to the user and the defendant did not warn of those dangers.

**Forum Shopping:** A tactic used by plaintiffs to look for the state or court with the most favorable laws to bring a claim.

**Intentional Torts:** Torts in which a person acts with intention and as a result harms another person.

**Manufacturing Defects:** A products-liability defective condition that occurs when a product was correctly and safely designed but there was an error in the manufacturing process on one, some, or all of the units.

**Negligence:** An unintentional tort in which a defendant breaches a duty that he owes to another, causing damages.

**Products Liability:** A tort theory that holds manufacturers and sellers of defective products liable for harm that is caused by those products.

**Proximate Cause:** The subset of causation in negligence that holds that an injury could be reasonably anticipated from the defendant's act.

**Reasonable Person Standard:** A test used by the courts to determine if a reasonably prudent person in the same circumstances would have acted in the manner that the defendant did.

**Reasonably Foreseeable:** A legal standard that asks whether a reasonable person could foresee that there would be harm from the act or behavior.

**Res Ipsa Loquitur:** Latin for "the thing speaks for itself," a tort theory holding that the fact that an accident took place means that the defendant had a duty to the plaintiff and breached it.

**Restatement of Torts:** An important treatise on tort law that provides a measure of uniformity among most of the states.

**Strict Liability:** Liability of one who sells a defective product or engages in abnormally hazardous activities for any damages that may occur because of using that product or engaging in that activity even if there was no negligence or intent to harm.

**Tortfeasor:** A party who commits a tort.

**Trespass to Land:** The tort that results when a defendant invades the real property of another, such as a business or an individual, without permission.

**Unintentional Torts:** Torts in which a person unintentionally acts in a way that causes harm to another.

**Wrongful Interference with a Business Relationship:** A business tort in which there is an established business relationship between the plaintiff and a third party; a defendant intentionally interferes with the business relationship, thereby causing the relationship to end; and the plaintiff suffers damage due to the interference.

**Wrongful Interference with a Contractual Relationship:** A business tort in which there is a valid, enforceable contract between two parties; a third party knows of the contract; and the third party intentionally interferes with the contract and causes one party to breach the contract.

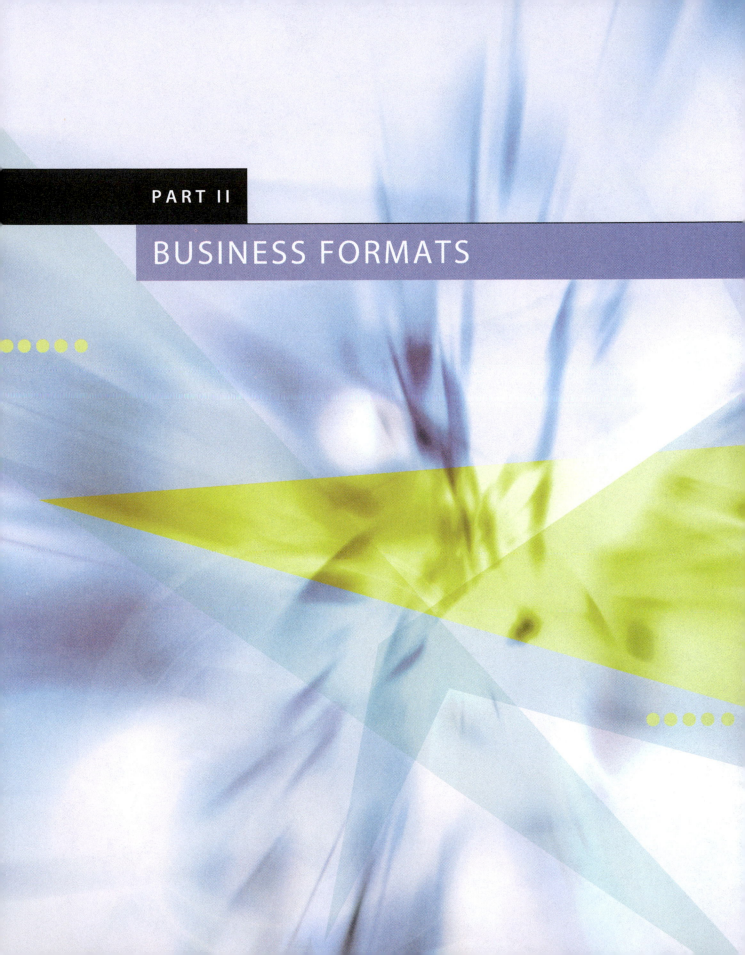

**PART II**

# BUSINESS FORMATS

## CHAPTER 10

# Legal Considerations in Selecting the Business Format

## INTRODUCTION

Every business begins somewhere. It starts with a concept, a business plan, an opportunity, vision, hope, and perseverance. But any business is faced with hard decisions in the background—where should it be located? What should it be named? Will it have employees? How will operations be financed? The list is endless.

Some decisions that every business must face are the legal issues that come with every business type and business format. This chapter covers the basic legal considerations that every business owner must face as he or she begins operations. Even business owners who ignore these considerations are, by default, making legal choices that have very real consequences. This chapter is meant to be introductory. It can even be viewed as a checklist. Each consideration is addressed in detail in later chapters.

## WHERE TO SET UP THE BUSINESS

One of basic legal decisions that needs to be made about any business is where it should be set up—its **Situs**. Of course, the business

**Situs:**
The legal and operating jurisdiction of a business.

owner's home state is an obvious choice, as is anywhere that the business actually does business. But under the choice-of-law options that are available to businesses in the United States, essentially any state is an option. Many businesses choose Delaware for reasons described in a later chapter. Many use their home state, or the state where most of their business activity occurs. Some jurisdictions are friendlier to business generally, or to certain kinds of business, than others. Convenience is a factor, as well as costs and protection from liability. In short, the options are endless, and each option has specific costs and benefits.

## CONTROL

The gut instinct of any business owner is that she is in charge. Period. That, of course, is not always the case. But control of the business is an important consideration that any business owner must evaluate.

For example, total **Control**, which is available in a sole proprietorship, inherently has the benefit that the business owner may do essentially what he or she wants to do, so long as it is legal, with complete options of control. There is a cost to that option, however—with total control comes total liability, tax consequences, and a myriad of other issues.

**Control:**
The mechanisms by which a business is governed.

A business owner who wants tax advantages, outside funding, and protection from liability may choose certain types of business formats, like C corporations (discussed in a later chapter). But the consequence of these advantages is often a profound loss of control to shareholders and equity stakeholders. Therefore, every business owner must use a balancing test to evaluate the advantages and disadvantages of each type of business format.

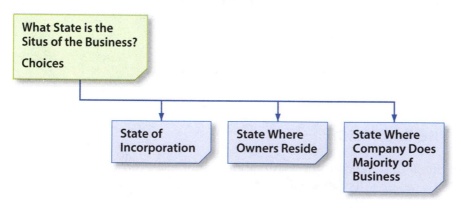

**Figure 10-1**
Situs

## LIABILITY

One of the main reasons that business owners choose certain forms of business entity—for example, a corporation or a limited liability company (LLC)—is that the business owner does not want personal **Liability** for the actions (or inactions) of the business. A sole proprietorship makes the owner (the sole proprietor) fully liable personally for the actions of the business. That means that the owner's personal assets are on the line—the owner's house, car, bank accounts, and so forth. An owner may choose to make compromises of control and flexibility in order to change this. How? An owner may pick a corporate business form that protects the owner's personal assets from the liabilities of the business's operations through some form of **Limited Liability**. Limited liability generally makes the owner of a business not personally liable for any of the debts of the business. The owner can only lose her investment in that business.

## TAX TREATMENT

An old saying assures us that the only things in life that are inevitable are death and taxes. Death can be delayed through medicine, diet, and lifestyle changes. Taxes can be managed (and sometimes eliminated), too, through choice of business entity.

**Tax Planning** is an art. A business owner making the choice of business format needs to review these tax-planning strategies because the choice has an immediate and real impact on the financial bottom line. It can influence the **Tax Rate** that applies to the business, the levels of taxation that apply (that is, how many times the business will be taxed), and the governmental entity to which the business pays those taxes.

For instance, a sole proprietor will pay the business' taxes on the profits of the business as if they were her own. She will also write off as a deduction any losses from the business. There is an advantage to this because the business's profits are taxed just once.

A corporation will in many circumstances pay taxes on its profits at a corporate tax rate. Then the profits it passes on to its **Shareholders** (the owners of a corporation) are taxed personally to the shareholders. The taxation scheme is called **Double Taxation**. Generally business owners want, for obvious reasons, to avoid double taxation. It severely reduces the after-tax **Profit** to the owners. It also reduces the capital available to the business for growing, prospering, and adapting.

**Liability:**
Responsibility for the inappropriate action or the inaction of a person or an entity like a business.

**Limited Liability:**
Liability that is restricted by law or by contract and that prevents the owner of a business from being held personally liable for business debts. The owner can only lose his or her investment in that company.

**Tax Planning:**
The advanced study of the tax consequences of a given business' configuration and operations. Tax planning also includes directing the configuration and operations in such a way so as to minimize or eliminate tax liabilities.

**Tax Rate:**
The percentage of tax paid by an entity on every given dollar of taxable income received.

**Shareholders:**
The owners of a corporation through shares.

**Double Taxation:**
The taxation of a business' profits twice—first, at the level of the business, and second, at the level of the owners.

**Profit:**
The money made for the business and its owners after all expenses, taxes, and costs are paid.

However, larger businesses or businesses that are **Publicly Traded** may opt for, or may be required by law to submit to, double taxation. In cases where the double taxation scheme is optional, business owners have decided that the costs of double taxation are outweighed by the possible benefits (size, public trading, sheltering of profits, and so forth) of using a business form that requires double taxation.

**Publicly Traded:**
Description of shares that are available on public exchanges for the general public to buy and sell.

## CAPITALIZATION

How a business is capitalized matters in this decision-making process. **Capitalization** refers to the long-term, long-held assets of a business. If a business requires large amounts of capitalization (like a factory requiring millions of dollars to build and operate), a sole proprietorship is likely not the best choice.

**Capitalization:**
The long-term, long-held assets of a business.

Why? A sole proprietor who wants to build and maintain a very expensive enterprise like a factory will need large amounts of personal or family funds to begin, or loans backed by credit that few if any banks would be willing to extend to just one person. It is possible, especially in the age of venture capital.

However, if the business owner chose, instead, to create a corporation that would sell shares of the company to the public in exchange for money, or to create an LLC that would allow many groups to own parts of the company in exchange for money, the prospect of a large enterprise like a factory becomes much closer to possible.

## TRANSFERABILITY OF OWNERSHIP

Transferability is an issue for business. One of the values of running a business enterprise is the possibility that the business, or part of it, can be bought or sold to others. That transferability has value.

If Bob's Catering is a sole proprietorship, the business is Bob. Although it is possible for Bob to sell his business, it is harder for him to do so since he would, in the final analysis, need to sell himself. If, however, Bob decided to incorporate Bob's Catering, Inc., as a corporation, the equation changes. Bob is not the business. The business is an entity separate from him. Bob can sell all or part of the shares in the business, and therefore transfer the company to someone else. That prospect of being able to swiftly transfer shares in the corporation from one person to another is an important consideration as he first considers how his business should be run.

## ETHICAL ISSUES

● ● ●

When a businessperson chooses a business format, such as a subchapter S corporation or limited liability company, for their new business, she may be choosing a business format that has both less tax liability and limited liability features built into the format. That is perfectly legal and quite common. In essence the business owner can "get away with" paying less taxes and protect his personal assets from the potential mistakes and harm she may cause through the business. Are there ethical concerns here? Is there a rationale behind policies like limited liability that on balance make them better than the alternative of business owners' always being personally liable for the actions of the business?

Other business forms have different transferability options. Later chapters will focus on this issue in detail.

## CHAPTER SUMMARY

This chapter is meant to be an introductory checklist. The site of a business, how the business is controlled, taxation of the business, capitalization for its operations, and transferability of ownership all are important and necessary considerations for the business owner and her advisers.

### Relevant Web Sites

http://revenue.delaware.gov/services/Business_Tax/Step3.shtml
http://www.doreservices.state.pa.us/BusinessTax/PA100/FormatSelection.htm
http://business.nv.gov/StartABusiness.htm

### Exercises

1. Define three types of business structures that are available in your jurisdiction.
2. Describe why a business may want to site itself in a state other than its home state.
3. Describe a benefit of publicly traded companies to the owners.
4. Describe why transferability of ownership is an important consideration for a business owner.
5. Describe the control available to a sole proprietor of a business.

### Questions

1. What is the importance of liability protection in a business, and why should a business owner consider business forms that provide personal liability protection?
2. What is double taxation?
3. What is tax planning?
4. Why is control an important consideration for a business owner?
5. What is a tax rate?

### Hypotheticals

1. Paul is very successful. He has a very large personal bank account, three beach houses, his regular residence, and four luxury cars. He starts a new business through which he provides a special new type of widget to consumers. He is a sole proprietor. One of those widgets

explodes and severely injures a consumer. The consumer sues. What portion of Paul's property is available to satisfy any judgment against Paul's business for the explosion?

2. Jack is planning on opening a business that will require very large amounts of money to get off the ground. How will this affect his choice of business?

3. Sandy is starting a new business venture. She wants to pay the minimum amount of taxes possible. How will that consideration influence her choice of business format?

4. Mackenzie wants to start a new business that does business in two states. What are some of the issues that Mackenzie must consider as she determines the situs of her business?

5. Yolanda wants to start a new business. She wants to maintain a tight leash on her project. She wants to answer to no one else unless she absolutely has to. How will these questions of control influence her choice of business format?

## Sample Cases

1. If a sole proprietor is doing business under another name, is the sole proprietor liable for the debts of the business?

   *Old Republic Ins. Co. v. EX-IM Servs. Corp.*, 920 S.W.2d 393, 396 (Tex. App (1996).

2. May a business owner transfer her shares to another without taking into consideration the right of first refusal that was granted to the corporation on the back of the stock certificates representing ownership?

   *Giaimo v. EGA Assocs. Inc.*, 68 A.D.3d 523, 891 N.Y.S.2d 49 (1st Dep't 2009).

## Key Terms

**Capitalization:** The long-term, long-held assets of a business.

**Control:** The mechanisms by which a business is governed.

**Double Taxation:** The taxation of a business' profits twice—first, at the level of the business, and second, at the level of the owners.

**Liability:** Responsibility for the inappropriate action or the inaction of a person or an entity like a business.

**Limited Liability:** Liability that is restricted by law or by contract and that prevents the owner of a business from being held personally liable for business debts. The owner can only lose his or her investment in that company.

**Profit:** The money made for the business and its owners after all expenses, taxes, and costs are paid.

**Publicly Traded:** Description given to shares that are available on public exchanges for the general public to buy and sell.

**Shareholders:** The owners of a corporation through shares.

**Situs:** The legal and operating jurisdiction of a business.

**Tax Planning:** The advanced study of the tax consequences of a given business' configuration and operations. Tax planning also includes directing the configuration and operations in such a way so as to minimize or eliminate tax liabilities.

**Tax Rate:** The percentage of tax paid by an entity on every given dollar of taxable income received.

## CHAPTER 11

# Overview of the Variety of Business Formats

**LEARNING OBJECTIVES**

You will be able to answer the following questions after reading this chapter:

1. What are the basic differences between sole proprietorships, partnerships, limited partnerships, corporations, limited liability partnerships, and limited liability companies?
2. Who are the owners of each business type?
3. What are tax attributes of each business type?
4. How is each type of business created?
5. What are the transfer advantages and disadvantages for each business type?
6. What are the liability features of each business type?
7. What are the control mechanisms for each business type?

## INTRODUCTION

Before any business can begin, the business owner must choose a legal format for his or her enterprise. Even to *not* choose is to choose. There are six main types of business formats: sole proprietorships, partnerships, limited partnerships, corporations, limited liability partnerships, and limited liability companies. Each of these business types has different attributes. Each attribute is a cost or a benefit to running the business in that format. The business owners, and their advisers, need to balance all these factors as they make their decisions. This chapter provides an overview of how each business format relates to the others, how each business format is structured, and what each attribute means in this context.

A step-by-step, detailed examination of all of these business forms follows. The reviews given assume a level playing field across legal jurisdictions. They do not account for minor variations in the laws of different jurisdictions and legal technicalities like business licenses required in City X, or restaurant permits in County Y.

## SOLE PROPRIETORSHIPS

A **Sole Proprietorship** is defined by the Internal Revenue Service as an unincorporated business owned by someone him- or herself. In many ways, it really is as simple as that definition. A sole proprietorship is created and ended on the whim of the business owner. It is the oldest and most fundamental form of business entity. It has great advantages because of its simplicity, and great disadvantages, too.

**Sole Proprietorship:**
The oldest form of business, formed by one person, and easily created and ended without interference from the state (excluding licensing and permit issues). It provides no liability protection for the sole proprietor.

### Owners

The owner of a sole proprietorship is the sole proprietor herself. There are no other owners. The sole proprietor is, in essence, the business.

### Ownership

The sole proprietor does not have anything that signifies his ownership of the business. He may have title to a car used in the business, or a deed to property used by the business, because he *is* the business. But he does not (licensing and other local permit requirements aside) hold shares or units, or any other documentation that signifies that he is the business. It is really that informal.

### Liability

Sole proprietors are **Personally Liable** for the actions or inactions of their business. Remember that they are the business. So, when the business owes a party money in a lawsuit, the sole proprietor's personal assets could be at risk.

**Personal Liability:**
Liability for which a person's personal assets are subject to collection to satisfy a debt.

For example, suppose that Mary runs a street corner hot dog stand as a sole proprietor. She is the business. Her business, including all its equipment, is worth $20,000. One day she serves a bad hot dog to a customer. The customer becomes violently ill and then recovers. The customer sues and wins a $50,000 judgment against Mary's business (and the business *is* Mary). The customer would be able to take the $20,000 business from Mary to satisfy the judgment. In addition, the customer would be able to collect the remaining $30,000 from Mary's personal assets. That means that Mary's house, personal car, personal bank accounts and investments, and so forth are all possible targets of the customer collecting damages, and Mary could lose some or all of them.

Clearly, this is not an ideal situation, and it is one area in which a sole proprietorship is at a severe disadvantage in comparison to the other business formats.

## Taxes

Because a sole proprietorship *is* the owner (the sole proprietor), it is also the owner for tax purposes. The sole proprietor uses his Social Security number for the business's taxes. He reports all his taxes on his tax returns each year. The business's taxes are reported on Schedule C of his tax return. He is responsible for all the taxes on business profits, and he can use all the losses of the business (generally) to offset income shown elsewhere on his tax return. He pays tax on the business's profits at his marginal tax rate. He pays those taxes even if the profits are not going directly into his pockets but rather are being used as reinvestments in the business. There is no separation between business and sole proprietor.

## Control

The sole proprietor is the business, and the business is the sole proprietor. Because the two are one and the same, and the sole proprietor by definition is just one person, the sole proprietor has absolute and total control over what the business does. The only real restrictions are outside legal codes, license and permit requirements, and similar requirements. However, in the vacuum, the sole proprietor has complete and absolute authority over her business.

## Transferability of Interest

The sole proprietor may transfer her business at any time to anyone, assuming that no outside licensing requirements, permit regulations, or the like prevent it. The drawback to a sole proprietorship is that although transfer itself is relatively easy, the value of that transfer is often low. Why? Because the sole proprietor, as the business, becomes very closely identified with the business itself. The business, without the owner who is identified with it, may be worth far less than otherwise would be the case. In fact, the transfer really creates a new business run by the purchaser. Often, because licensing and permitting requirements are likely personal to the previous owner, the new owner is required to obtain those permissions once again. This is another disadvantage of a sole proprietorship.

## Creation

A sole proprietorship is created at the whim of the owner. Aside from external licensing and permitting requirements (which could be substantial), all that a sole proprietor needs to do to go into business is literally say or do something that states, "I'm in business!"

That is a major advantage to the sole proprietorship. This flexibility allows the sole proprietor to begin and end business opportunities as the need arises. This can be, however, a false advantage as the inherent lack of planning required to go into business as a sole proprietor may also make the sole proprietor more prone to mistakes, missteps, and misjudgments—and can even result in cases where the sole proprietor is in business without even realizing that he or she is in business.

## Continuity

The sole proprietorship terminates on the death of the sole proprietor. The business is the sole proprietor. So, when the sole proprietor is no longer living, the business itself must terminate. This is a profound disadvantage, as many businesses could otherwise continue after the death of the sole proprietor who created them. This is not to say that the business could not continue in another form. A child of the sole proprietor, another heir, or an outside purchaser could purchase the assets of the business and run it as his own, but technically the business is a new one.

For an example, let's return to Mary's hot dog stand. Mary has run her stand as a sole proprietor for many years. She is the business. She passes away. With her death, her sole proprietorship ends. Bob, an employee who has worked for Mary for many years, now wants to continue the business. In order to do this, he buys the hot dog cart from Mary's estate. He even buys the right to use "Mary's Hot Dogs" as the name under which he does business. When Bob begins to sell his hot dogs, on the outside he seems to be the same business as Mary's old sole proprietorship. But he is not Mary. He has created a new business, as a sole proprietor, that *is* Bob. That new business uses Bob's Social Security number, Bob's tax returns, and Bob's decision-making skills. It is not Mary's old business. Instead, it is a successor business.

## PARTNERSHIPS

### Owners

The owners of a **Partnership** are called partners. There must be at least two partners in any partnership. In most states there is no real limit aside from the practical aspects of administration on the number of partners in the partnership. This type of partnership is also called a general partnership. The Internal Revenue Service defines a partnership in its consumer materials as "the relationship existing

**Partnership:**
A business whereby two or more partners join together with common purpose to accomplish a goal.

between two or more persons who join to carry on a trade or business. Each person contributes money, property, labor, or skill, and expects to share in the profits and losses of the business."

## Ownership

The partners in a partnership have partnership shares. These shares are presumed by the law to be equal among all the partners. However, the partners may agree otherwise, so that, for instance, one partner may hold 90 percent of the partnership, and another partner may hold 10 percent. Partnership shares may be represented by certificates or paperwork designating the appropriate shares for the partners, but the reality is that no such paperwork is needed, especially for an equal partnership.

## Liability

A partnership provides no protection from personal liability for the partners. In that way, a partnership is actually very much like a sole proprietorship. In fact, a partner can be fully personally liable in many cases for the acts of another partner in the furtherance of the partnership's business. **Joint and Several Liability** provides the rule.

    Mary's hot dog stand provides our example. Suppose that Mary and Bob go into business together as partners in the hot dog stand. Mary serves a hot dog to a customer who then becomes violently ill and wins a judgment of $50,000 as a result of the illness. Both Bob and Mary are jointly and severally personally liable to satisfy the judgment because Mary served the bad food during the furtherance of partnership business. That means that all of the business assets, Mary's personal assets, and Bob's personal assets can be taken by the customer in order to satisfy the claim. Assuming that Mary has no or little personal assets, the customer could try and recover all of the damages from Bob, even though he personally did not serve the bad food. Bob could later attempt to recover some of his personal loss from Mary by **Contribution**, but he may not be successful. As the saying goes, you cannot get blood from a stone. If Mary had served that hot dog at a picnic at her house, clearly as a personal endeavor unrelated to the partnership, then Bob would not be liable as Mary's hot dog was not served in the furtherance of partnership business.

    Clearly joint and several personal liability is a great disadvantage to the partners in a partnership. There are ways to avoid personal liability by using the other business forms discussed in this chapter.

**Joint and Several Liability:**
Liability in which two or more parties are each entirely liable for a debt to a third party. The third party may collect on the debt from one party, the other, or both in any proportion necessary in order to satisfy the debt.

**Contribution:**
A companion legal theory to joint and several liability whereby when two or more parties are found jointly and severally liable for a debt, and the debt is collected from the debtor parties in an uneven manner, the party who paid more to satisfy the debt may collect from the parties who paid less in order to make the debt burden more fair.

But joint and several liability is part and parcel of a general partnership and must always be considered when determining which business form to use.

## Taxes

Partnerships are **Pass-Through Entities**. Essentially, partnerships are not subject to double taxation. Instead, the profits and losses of the partnership are reported on and paid by the partners in proportion to the partners' respective shares in the partnership. This is an advantage to a partnership and the partners because then a larger share of after-tax profits end up in the partners' personal pockets.

Each year the partnership files an **Information Return** with the federal government (the same thing happens on the state level in most states). The information return lists profits and losses to the partnership for the year, and it sets out how those profits or losses were divided between the partners. Each partner also files with the government and with the other partners a Schedule K-1, which acts as a notification to the partners of what partnership items must be reported to the government on each partner's personal return. The partners, then, on Schedule E of their personal tax returns, report their shares of partnership income or losses and pay taxes at their personal tax rates, or take deductions against their other income as appropriate.

## Control

Control is exercised by the partners as set out in the **Partnership Agreement**, if there is one, or by each partner equally if there is no agreement. A partnership agreement is the basic document that governs the relationship between the partners. It can set out what the parties' shares of the partnership are, what their respective duties are, and what their rights to bind the partnership to their actions are. **Actual Authority** is the authority expressly given by law or the partnership agreement or some other agreement between the partners permitting one partner to do things that will bind the entire partnership. **Apparent Authority** is the authority a partner has to bind the partnership to agreements with outsiders who do not have reason to know otherwise, even though the partner might not have actual authority to do so.

An example is in order:

Bob and Mary's hot dog stand is flourishing. Bob and Mary have a written partnership agreement that allows either partner to make purchases of hot dog buns from any supplier without first con-

**Pass-Through Entities:** Business entities that do not pay their own income taxes. Instead, they file information returns with the taxation authorities, and the owners pay the taxes on the income, once, as appropriate, at the owners' personal tax rates.

**Information Return:** A return filed with the taxing authority by a business entity that enjoys pass-through taxation. The information return lists profits and losses and other details of the business's performance for the year, and it sets out how those profits or losses were divided between the owners of the business.

**Partnership Agreement:** A contract (usually written, although it may be oral) between two or more partners in a general partnership, limited partnership, or limited liability partnership that sets out the basic parameters of the partners' relationship with each other. It may be very simple, or it may include formation, operating, and dissolution rules and be as extensive as the partners desire.

**Actual Authority:** Authority validly granted by the partners in a partnership to a partner or an agent to perform an act or enter into an agreement that will bind the entire partnership. The concept applies to other business forms as well.

**Apparent Authority:** Authority that is *not* validly granted by the partners in a partnership to a partner or an agent to perform an act or enter into an agreement that will bind the entire partnership. The act, however, *will* bind the entire partnership when

sulting the other partner. Bob makes a purchase of hot dog buns. Mary finds out, and is furious and wants to cancel the hot dog bun purchase contract because she has found buns much cheaper from another supplier. The bun contract will stand because Bob had actual authority under the partnership agreement to purchase the hot dog buns without consulting Mary first. Mary cannot challenge the contract on that basis.

a reasonable person in that time and place, dealing with the partner or agent as a third party, would have no reason to know that the partner or agent did not have authority. The concept applies to other business forms as well.

If, however, Bob and Mary never had such a purchasing agreement between themselves as partners, the agreement with the bun vendor would still be valid. Why? Because assuming that the hot dog vendor had no reason to know that Bob was defying Mary, he was acting with apparent authority to bind the partnership. Based on these facts, a reasonable third party who has no reason to know otherwise would assume that a partner entering into a contract with him has the authority to bind the partnership.

## Transferability of Interest

The transfer of a partnership interest terminates the partnership unless the remaining partners to the partnership elect to continue the partnership without the partner who transferred the interest or the partnership agreement specifies otherwise. Most partnership agreements provide some mechanism for transferring partnership shares, and a partnership agreement often will require the partners to offer their partnership shares to the remaining partners first before there is any attempt to sell off the partnership share to a third party. The transfer of a partnership share to a third party is more difficult than transferring corporate shares, discussed later in this chapter.

## Creation

A partnership is created and ended at will by the partners, unless the partnership agreement places restraints on how the partnership may end. In that way, it is much like a sole proprietorship. A partnership does not need to be put in writing either (although tax laws and licensing laws may require it for certain types of business). A partnership can last for a day, or a lifetime. In short, its creation is rather simple and one of its more attractive attributes.

## Continuity

As noted above, unless the remaining partners (if there were more than two originally) agree to continue the business or unless provided in the partnership agreement, the partnership terminates upon the death of a partner or if a partner decides to ends the partnership unilaterally. This is a disadvantage to operating a business in partnership form. In fact, partnerships can be created and ended almost at will.

## LIMITED PARTNERSHIPS

### Owners

The owners of a **Limited Partnership** are divided into two classes. The first is the **General Partner**, and the second is the **Limited Partner**. There are two key differences between general partners and limited partners. General partners are just like partners in a standard partnership. They can make decisions to run the business, and they have unlimited personal liability. A limited partner, by contrast, is a partner who cannot make any decisions regarding the management of the business, or participate in managing the business at all. In return the limited partner gets protection from personal liability for the liabilities of the partnership.

### Ownership

Like a standard partnership (discussed above), partners in a partnership have partnership shares. A limited partnership must have a written partnership agreement and must be registered with the state where it is created. These shares are presumed by the law to be equal among all the partners, but the partnership agreement can say otherwise as the partners may agree. Commonly, the general partner may hold a very small percentage interest in the partnership, and the limited partners will hold the lion's share.

### Liability

The general partner, just as in a sole proprietorship or a standard general partnership, is personally liable for the debts of the limited partnership. The general partner, however, can sidestep this rule if it is another business entity that already has liability protection. For instance, a general partner can be a corporation, which has liability protection for its shareholders. So, although the basic rule—that the general partner is liable—still applies, the corporation acting as a general partner in a limited partnership cannot pass on that liability to the shareholders. Therefore, there are multiple layers of protection provided here.

**Limited Partnership:**
An organization of partners with one or more general partners who control the business and have full liability and one or more limited partners who contribute capital and have limited liability but who cannot participate in management or operations in any way.

**General Partner:**
A partner in a standard partnership. Also a partner in a limited partnership who has full control of the management of the business as well as full personal liability.

**Limited Partner:**
A type of partner in a limited partnership who has no personal liability for the acts of the business but who cannot participate in its management or operations in any way.

Limited partners are protected from personal liability for the debts of the partnership. Sometimes limited partners are called "silent partners." In order to maintain their protection, limited partners must really remain silent. They cannot make management decisions, and in most states they cannot participate in the business at all—even to take out the trash. They may merely wait, silently, and collect the profits or losses from the limited partnership.

## Taxes

A limited partnership is taxed in the same way as a general partnership, via pass-through taxation to the partners as defined by the partnership agreement or as the partners may agree. If the partnership wishes to, or if it fails to meet certain requirements as to the management and form of a limited partnership, it will be taxed as a corporation. That could result in double taxation at both a corporate tax rate and a personal tax rate.

## Control

The control of a limited partnership, aside from the basic negotiation of the limited partnership agreement, the selection of the general partner, and some other minor items, rests solely with the general partner. Limited partners are severely limited in the amount of control that they can exert over the operations of the limited partnership. They risk their protection from personal liability if they stray past those limits.

## Transferability of Interest

A limited partnership interest is transferable without terminating the partnership. It is generally transferable to third parties, but that transfer must conform to the partnership agreement's requirements. Most partnership agreements will require that the selling limited partner offer the interest for sale to the other limited partners first, before that interest is sold to a third party. This is known as a **Right of First Refusal**.

## Creation

A limited partnership is not created automatically. This is unlike a sole proprietorship or a general partnership, where the business can be created or destroyed at will. Instead, a limited partnership must be created by following the requirements of state law. Usually this

**Right of First Refusal:**
A right given to other owners of a business, family members, or whomever is designated by contract or law, requiring that the person holding the right be offered *first* for purchase any assets that another person who is party to the contract wishes to transfer to a third party. This right prevents business partners and shareholders from selling part of a business to third parties before the other current owners have the opportunity to purchase it.

means that paperwork creating the limited partnership must be filed with and accepted by the secretary of state for the state in which the limited partnership is created.

## Continuity

A limited partnership lasts past the lifetimes of any individual partner. It will last until the partnership agreement specifies, until the partners agree to terminate it, or until state law ends the partnership. This is an advantage as it provides continuity of business.

## CORPORATIONS

### Owners

The owners of a **Corporation** are called **Shareholders**. There can be one shareholder of a corporation, or millions in the case of publicly traded stocks of international corporations.

### Ownership

Ownership by the shareholders is signified by **Shares**. A person, a group, or another business, corporation, or partnership may own shares in a corporation (with some minor exceptions). A corporation may have **Issued Shares** numbering only 1 share, or 100, or 10 million. In the past all corporations actually did issue share certificates that signified a shareholder's stake in the company. That still occurs with many smaller companies. However, publicly traded companies that have millions of issued shares traded daily in tremendous volume cannot issue share certificates practically or cost effectively. So, in many cases stocks are held in "street name" by large brokerage houses on behalf of the individual investor in order to get around this problem.

**Corporation:**
A legal entity independent from its owners that is usually formed to do business. It exists under state law and has most of the rights, duties, and obligations of a flesh-and-blood person.

**Shareholders:**
The owners of a corporation.

**Shares:**
The units used to designate a shareholder's ownership rights in a corporation.

**Issued Shares:**
A term used to designate shares of stock that are actually held by shareholders.

### Liability

The greatest and first advantage to a corporation's shareholder is that of limited liability. The shareholder's personal assets are not subject to the debts and liabilities of the corporation. Instead, a shareholder is liable only up to the value of his shares.

Assume that Bob's and Mary's hot dog stand is a corporation worth $30,000. Bob owns half the stock, and Mary owns the other half. The hot dog incident mentioned earlier in this chapter occurs, and the corporation, Bob & Mary's Inc., is found to be liable to the customer for $50,000. The entire value of the $30,000 corporation is subject to the customer's judgment—and the customer could force a sale of those assets, or a transfer of the business to the customer, to satisfy part of the judgment. But Bob's and Mary's personal assets are protected. The customer can take the investment that Bob and Mary have in the corporation—making their stock worthless—but the customer cannot go beyond that and take personal bank accounts, cars, homes, and the like owned by either Bob or Mary.

It is important to note that **Corporate Formalities** must be followed in order for shareholders to maintain liability protection. In short, they must look like a corporation, act like a corporation, and be a corporation. They must follow all rules, regulations, and state codes. If the shareholders begin to mix personal and corporate assets (like depositing corporate money in personal bank accounts, or personally signing corporate contracts), they could short-circuit the personal liability protection otherwise built into the corporate form.

**Corporate Formalities:**
A term used to describe the actions that a corporation must take in order to be considered a corporation in good standing and to remain as a corporation in good standing with the relevant state government.

## Taxes

Corporations are taxed in two different ways.

**C Corporation** income is double-taxed and does not enjoy the benefits of pass-through taxation. Profits from the corporation's business are first taxed at the corporate rate. The current corporate tax rates range from 15 percent to 35 percent. Then any profits distributed to the shareholders as **Dividends** are taxed currently at 5 percent or 15 percent rates (15 percent for most taxpayers). Thus, the combination of a 35 percent tax rate at the corporate level and 15 percent at the shareholder's personal level could add up to a 50 percent tax rate on the corporation's profits. Taxation of C corporations is discussed in detail in a later chapter.

**S Corporations** are not double-taxed. They have the advantage of pass-through taxation. As such, the corporation avoids paying any corporate income taxes. Instead, the shareholders each pay taxes at their personal income tax rates on their allocated share. The Internal Revenue Service puts it this way: "On their tax returns, the S corporation's shareholders include their share of the corporation's separately stated items of income, deduction, loss, and credit, and their share of nonseparately stated income or loss." This avoids the double taxation problem, and lowers the tax paid in many cases. Thus, more profit goes to the shareholders.

Of course, most corporations would opt for S corporation status. However, there are specific limits on when a corporation can elect S corporation status based on size and shareholder type that are discussed in detail in a later chapter. Generally, only smaller, non–publicly traded corporations are eligible for S corporation treatment.

**C Corporation:**
A type of corporation that pays taxes at the corporate level and whose stock may be publicly traded. Most large corporations are required to have C corporation status. C corporations may retain earnings within the corporation or distribute them to shareholders as dividends.

**Dividends:**
The share of C corporation earnings and profits distributed to the shareholders.

**S Corporations:**
A type of corporation that does not pay corporate taxes. Rather, it files an information return with the taxing authority, and the shareholders proportionally pay taxes on profits, actually paid to the shareholders or not, at their personal tax rates. Only smaller corporations not publicly traded are eligible for S corporation status if they meet a series of guidelines.

## Control

Control in all corporations is divided between shareholders, the **Board of Directors**, and the **Officers**. Individuals may serve in multiple capacities. For instance, a shareholder may also serve on the board and as president of the corporation. Although ethics rules may prohibit this in some cases, quite commonly in smaller corporations the shareholders, board, and officers may all be the same people—or person.

The shareholders are the owners of the corporation. They exert control over the development and administration of the corporation by electing the board of directors. This election occurs regularly, usually once a year—although the actual timing may vary.

The board of directors provides overall direction to the corporation. It approves large changes in vision and direction, and it appoints the officers of the corporation.

The officers are charged with the day-to-day running of the corporation. Typically, there are four officers: president, vice president, secretary, and treasurer. Other positions exist (for example, the chief executive officer (CEO) and chief operating officer (COO)), but that is a matter of form and division of duties. It is not fundamental to the business itself. In most states, one person can hold all of the officer positions. In fact, not all officer positions need to be filled and sometimes are not in smaller corporations.

**Board of Directors:**
A group elected by the shareholders of a corporation for a fixed term of office and that provides overall direction to the corporation. It approves large changes in vision and direction, and it appoints the officers of the corporation.

**Officers:**
Those charged with the day-to-day running of a corporation. The officers are appointed by the board of directors.

## Transferability of Interest

Transfer of ownership in a corporation is accomplished by the sale or trade of some or all of the shares of a shareholder to another shareholder or to a third party. The shareholder's agreement or state law may restrict who may own shares. But any restrictions aside, a share may be sold privately or publicly through a national exchange. Billions upon billions of shares are bought and sold every day across the world.

## Creation

A corporation, like a limited partnership, is a creature of state law. In fact, it is a legal entity—almost a fictional person that the law recognizes as an entity with rights and obligations much like a natural person's. It must be created by the filing and acceptance of **Articles of Incorporation** in the office of the Secretary of State in the state where the corporation is set up. The corporation must then maintain its corporate status by filing periodic reports with the state, paying

**Articles of Incorporation:**
The filing paperwork submitted to and accepted by the department of state in the state where a corporation is created that are the founding documents of a corporation and that give the corporation its legal status as a separate entity.

corporate fees, and taking any other administrative action required by the state government. If the corporation fails to meet these requirements, it legally falls out of existence.

## Continuity

The corporation lasts forever, at least in theory. So long as the corporation is compliant with state laws that allow it to exist, it will continue to exist—far after the lifetimes of the shareholders that may have founded it.

## LIMITED LIABILITY PARTNERSHIPS

### Owners

Limited Liability Partnerships (LLPs) are owned by the partners. It is unlike a limited partnership where ownership is divided between general and limited partners. The limited liability partnership is owned like a general partnership—by the partners. However, many states limit the ownership of LLPs to professionals—so a law firm run as an LLP may only be owned by attorneys, a medical practice by doctors, and so forth.

### Ownership

Ownership of an LLP is essentially held the same way as ownership of a general partnership—by partnership shares.

### Liability

The major advantage of an LLP is that it short-circuits the rule of joint and several liability that applies to partners in a general partnership. Although partners will be generally liable for all the debts of the partnership in an LLP, partners are protected from liability for the professional errors of the other partners. This is a profound advantage of the LLP over the general partnership for professionals.

For instance, if doctors Smith and Jones each are partners in the same medical practice run as an LLP, Smith and Jones will still be liable, as in a general partnership, if the partnership is sued for non-professional liabilities such as a broken lease. However, if Smith commits medical malpractice, even though Smith is still personally liable (and the partnership assets are subject to seizure to pay the judgment), Jones will not be personally liable for Smith's professional malpractice.

**Limited Liability Partnerships (LLPs):** A variation on the general partnership in which partners are personally liable for the debts of the partnership as in a general partnership, but they are not personally liable for the torts (professional malpractice, usually) of the other partners. Many states restrict use of the LLP business form to professional businesses like those of attorneys, doctors, architects, and the like.

## Taxes

Taxes are allocated in the same pass-through through manner as in general partnerships.

## Control

Another differentiator between an LLP and general and limited partnerships is that in the LLP, the partner may still act as a general partner would in a standard general partnership. However, the LLP partner still will maintain partial liability protection—as in the limited partnership. Thus, it is a hybrid. Control is therefore exercised by the partners as they determine by the partnership agreement and amongst themselves. The partners may be directly and intimately involved in the business and not sacrifice that measure of personal liability protection as would be the case if a limited partner in a limited partnership was actively involved in management of the business.

## Transferability of Interest

Transfer of an LLP interest is essentially the same as transfer in a general partnership. However, in many states state law prohibits a transfer to a person who is not licensed in the profession in which the LLP is engaged. Thus, there is no transfer of a doctor's interest in an LLP to a third party who is not a doctor.

## CREATION

An LLP is a business format created by state laws that only began to be implemented in the early to mid 1990s. They are purely a creature of state law. They are created by filing and acceptance of the appropriate forms with the state secretary of state to form a new partnership, or they are created by the conversion of an existing general partnership to an LLP by the filing of forms with the state.

## CONTINUITY

The continuity of an LLP is essentially the same as in a limited partnership. An LLP may extend past the lifetimes of any individual partner. It will last until the partnership agreement specifies, until the partners agree to terminate it, or until state law ends the partnership.

## LIMITED LIABILITY COMPANIES

### Owners

Limited Liability Companies (LLCs) are owned by **Members**. Some states allow an LLC to have only one member, but many require at least two members. LLCs can be very large and have scores or hundreds of members, depending on the law of the state where an LLC is created.

**Limited Liability Companies (LLCs):** A relatively new form of legal business entity that combines the limited liability of a corporation with the pass-through taxation features and ease of management of a partnership.

### Ownership

A member's ownership is signified by shares, or **Units** of the LLC. They are analogous to the shares held by shareholders of a corporation.

**Members:** The owners of an LLC.

**Units:** A term used to designate a member's ownership rights in an LLC.

### Liability

A member is fully protected from personal liability for the acts of other members or the LLC itself. In this way, an LLC is analogous to a corporation. This is a tremendous advantage to an LLC.

### Taxes

Unless the members elect otherwise or in very rare circumstances, taxes are pass-through, as they are in a partnership. Thus, the LLC avoids the double-taxation problem and enjoys both the limited liability of a corporation and the advantageous tax treatment of a partnership.

### Control

LLCs have far more flexibility in control than a corporation (even an S corporation) has. For instance, the LLC can be managed directly by the members, without the layers of administration (shareholders, board, officers) that a corporation has, and without having to block the involvement of partners as a limited partnership does. Thus, the convenience of control provided by an LLC brings it beyond the advantages of an S corporation in many instances. The LLC is controlled through an **Operating Agreement**, which is analogous to a partnership agreement or shareholder's agreement. In manager-managed LLCs (which most companies choose to create), a board of managers, which functions very much like a corporation's board of directors, runs the company. All of the management decisions are

**Operating Agreement:** A written contract between the members of an LLC which sets out the basic parameters of the members' relationship with each other.

set out in the operating agreement signed by all of the members during the formation of the LLC.

### Transferability of Interest

LLCs are not publicly traded on exchanges as stocks are, although interest in them can be bought and sold by third parties. An interest in an LLC may be sold without terminating the LLC and is generally transferable to third parties, but any transfer must conform to the LLC's operating agreement and state law.

### Creation

LLCs only became popular in the mid 1990s, but every state now recognizes them. They are created under state law by filing the appropriate forms with the secretary of state of the relevant state, which then must be accepted by the secretary of state. The LLC must conform to state law in order to maintain its existence, as corporations and other state entities must do.

### Continuity

Like a corporation, the LLC will last indefinitely unless state law has put a specific limit on its existence and as long as it complies with state law regarding licensing fees, reporting, and so forth. However, if it chooses, the LLC may put a fixed term on its existence even though it has an option of existing in perpetuity.

## CHAPTER SUMMARY

This chapter has reviewed the basic types of business formats. There are sole proprietorships, partnerships, limited partnerships, corporations, limited liability partnerships, and limited liability companies. Although each business format shares much in common with the others, each of these business types has different attributes that must be weighed as a business makes decisions about how it will be structured.

What the owners are called, how they show ownership of the business, the extent of personal liability of owners of the business, the methods and limits of control by owners, ownership transfer tools, methods of business creation, and methods of ensuring business continuity all vary according to the type of business form. None is the same as any other, and each borrows ideas and elements from the others.

## ETHICAL ISSUES

● ● ●

The business laws in every state allow a large and varied spectrum of business types. Many of these business formats can create very large businesses in which owners can be divorced from any real responsibility for the conduct and activities of the business, and at the same time shield them from the consequences of their actions. Are there any ethical issues with the creation of "impersonal" businesses where there is no real human presence in the day-to-day operations? Some would say that this is an ethical tragedy that allows businesses to engage in activities that they would never do if there was a closer legal and personal connection between the owners and the business itself. Others defend these business structures as necessary and useful tools that allow businesses to grow, to achieve economies of scale that bring faster and cheaper products and services to the public, and to encourage entrepreneurs to take risks and to undertake ventures that they never would have considered in a world of sole proprietorships. Explain.

### Relevant Web Sites

http://www.dos.state.ny.us/corps/llcfaq.asp

http://sunbiz.org/

http://www.azsos.gov/business_services/partner ships/Partnerships_FAQ.htm

### Exercises

1. Find the state government agency that is responsible for the creation and tracking of business entities in the state where you are located.
2. List three benefits of pass-through taxation.
3. Describe one drawback of the partnership form of business.
4. Describe why personal liability protection is important as a business owner chooses a form of business.
5. List one advantage that a limited liability company has over a corporation.

### Questions

1. Why is a sole proprietorship so attractive to many businesspeople? List three reasons why.
2. What function does the board of directors of a corporation fulfill?
3. What function do the officers of a corporation fulfill?
4. Why would a business choose to be taxed on profits twice, once at the business (corporate) level and once at the owner's personal level?
5. What is the main difference between a limited liability partnership and a general partnership?
6. What must limited partners do in order to maintain their personal liability protection in a limited partnership?
7. What is the function of a general partner in a limited partnership?
8. What are the owners of a corporation called?
9. What happens to a business upon the death of a sole proprietor of that business?
10. What does it mean when a business is a "creature of the state"?

### Hypotheticals

1. Arden is a limited partner in a limited partnership and is independently wealthy. The partnership plows driveways and roadways in snowy weather in Arden's county. One January a tremendous blizzard hits the region. One of the usual snowplow drivers is ill. Arden is asked by the general partner to drive one of the trucks because the snowfall is such that the limited partnership needs every truck on the road plowing snow. Arden agrees and plows during that one storm. A week later another driver for the

company loses control of his plow and causes several hundred thousand dollars in damage to a house near the road. What is the best argument by the homeowner's attorney in a lawsuit against the limited partnership to get to Arden's personal assets?

2. Tammy is a member of Snuggles, L.L.C. One of the other members of the LLC breaches a contract worth more than a million dollars. What is Tammy's potential liability for the breached contract?

3. Hansel and Gretel decide to go into business. They hire a sign-making company to make up signage saying, "Candy Houses, Incorporated," which they use in all of their business dealings. Are they a corporation with all of the benefits of that status?

4. Lisa has decided that she wants to take her corporation public, so that it is traded on the stock exchanges. She wants to avoid double taxation though. Is it possible for her corporation to be classified as a subchapter S corporation and be publicly traded?

5. Lynda, Jason, and Meredith are partners in a house-painting business. Lynda passes away. The partnership is an oral agreement. What is the status of the partnership if Jason and Meredith do nothing after Lynda's death?

## Sample Cases

1. Ingram and Deere had a 1997 oral agreement whereby Deere would serve as the medical director for a multidisciplinary pain clinic. Deere believed he would receive one-third of the clinic's revenues and that Ingram would receive one-third. The final one-third would be used to pay the clinic's expenses. Ingram told Deere that it "was a joint venture." Ingram believed that Deere would receive one-third of the clinic's revenues and that there was no other agreement. Deere never contributed money to the clinic. He did not participate in the hiring of any employees. He did not know any of the clinic staff's names. He never purchased any of the clinic's equipment. His name was not on the clinic's bank account. His name was not on

the lease agreement for the clinic space. Was there a partnership?

*Ingram v. Deere*, 288 S.W.3d 886 (Tex. 2009).

2. Does a corporation's provision of an e-mail address with the corporation's domain name to an individual person who shared an office with the corporation give that individual the apparent authority to enter into contracts on the corporation's behalf?

*CSX Transp., Inc. v. Recovery Express, Inc.*, 415 F. Supp. 2d 6 (D. Mass. 2006).

## Key Terms

**Actual Authority:** Authority validly granted by the partners in a partnership to a partner or an agent to perform an act or enter into an agreement that will bind the entire partnership. The concept applies to other business forms as well.

**Apparent Authority:** Authority that is not validly granted by the partners in a partnership to a partner or an agent to perform an act or enter into an agreement that will bind the entire partnership. The act, however, will bind the entire partnership when a reasonable person in that time and place, dealing with the partner or agent as a third party, would have no reason to know that the partner or agent did not have authority. The concept applies to other business forms as well.

**Articles of Incorporation:** The filing paperwork submitted to and accepted by the department of state in the state where a corporation is created that are the founding documents of a corporation and that give the corporation its legal status as a separate entity.

**Board of Directors:** A group elected by the shareholders of a corporation for a fixed term of office and that provides overall direction to the corporation. It approves large changes in vision and direction, and it appoints the officers of the corporation.

**Contribution:** A companion legal theory to joint and several liability whereby when two or more parties are found jointly and severally liable for a debt, and the debt is collected from the debtor parties in an uneven manner, the party who paid more to satisfy the debt may collect from the parties who paid less in order to make the debt burden more fair.

**C Corporation:** A type of corporation that pays taxes at the corporate level and whose stock may be publicly traded. Most large corporations are required to have C corporation status. C corporations may retain earnings within the corporation or distribute them to shareholders as dividends.

**Corporate Formalities:** A term used to describe the actions that a corporation must take in order to be considered a corporation in good standing and to remain as a corporation in good standing with the relevant state government.

**Corporation:** A legal entity independent from its owners that is usually formed to do business. It exists under state law and has most of the rights, duties, and obligations of a flesh-and-blood person.

**Dividends:** The share of C corporation earnings and profits distributed to the shareholders.

**General Partner:** A partner in a standard partnership. Also a partner in a limited partnership who has full control of the management of the business as well as full personal liability.

**Information Return:** A return filed with the taxing authority by a business entity that enjoys pass-through taxation. The information return lists profits and losses and other details of the business's performance for the year, and it sets out how those profits or losses were divided between the owners of the business.

**Issued Shares:** A term used to designate shares of stock that are actually held by shareholders.

**Joint and Several Liability:** Liability in which two or more parties are each entirely liable for a debt to a third party. The third party may collect on the debt from one party, the other, or both in any proportion necessary in order to satisfy the debt.

**Limited Liability Companies (LLCs):** A relatively new form of legal business entity that combines the limited liability of a corporation with the pass-through taxation features and ease of management of a partnership.

**Limited Liability Partnerships (LLPs):** A variation on the general partnership in which partners are personally liable for the debts of the partnership as in a general partnership, but they are not personally liable for the torts (professional malpractice, usually) of the other partners. Many states restrict use of the LLP business form to professional businesses like those of attorneys, doctors, architects, and the like.

**Limited Partner:** A type of partner in a limited partnership who has no personal liability for the acts of the business but who cannot participate in its management or operations in any way.

**Limited Partnership:** An organization of partners with one or more general partners who control the business and have full liability and one or more limited partners who contribute capital and have limited liability but who cannot participate in management or operations in any way.

**Members:** The owners of an LLC.

**Officers:** Those charged with the day-to-day running of a corporation. The officers are appointed by the board of directors.

**Operating Agreement:** A written contract between the members of an LLC that sets out the basic parameters of the members' relationship with each other.

**Partnership:** A form of business created when two or more persons or other legal entities (like corporations) join together with common purpose to accomplish a goal.

**Partnership Agreement:** A contract (usually written, although it may be oral) between two or more partners in a general partnership, limited partnership, or limited liability partnership that sets out the basic parameters of the partners' relationship with each other. It may be very simple, or it may include formation, operating, and dissolution rules and be as extensive as the partners desire.

**Pass-Through Entities:** Business entities that do not pay their own income taxes. Instead, they file information returns with the taxation authorities, and the owners pay the taxes on the income, once, as appropriate, at the owners' personal tax rates.

**Personal Liability:** Liability for which a person's personal assets—over and above his or her business assets—are subject to collection to satisfy a debt.

**Right of First Refusal:** A right given to other owners of a business, family members, or whomever is designated by contract or law, requiring that the person holding the right be offered first for purchase any assets that another person who is party to the contract wishes to transfer to a third party. This right prevents business partners and shareholders from selling part of a business to third parties before the other current owners have the opportunity to purchase it.

**S Corporations:** A type of corporation that does not pay corporate taxes. Rather, it files an infor-mation return with the taxing authority, and the shareholders proportionally pay taxes on profits, actually paid to the shareholders or not, at their personal tax rates. Only smaller corporations not publicly traded are eligible for S corporation status if they meet a series of guidelines.

**Shares:** The units used to designate a shareholder's ownership rights in a corporation.

**Shareholders:** The owners of a corporation.

**Sole Proprietorship:** The oldest form of business, formed by one person, and easily created and ended without interference from the state (excluding licensing and permit issues). It provides no liability protection for the sole proprietor.

**Units:** A term used to designate a member's ownership rights in an LLC.

## CHAPTER 12

# Formation of Corporations

## LEARNING OBJECTIVES

You will be able to answer the following questions after reading this chapter:

1. Who are the parties involved in the preincorporation stage of a corporation?
2. What are the differences between domestic, foreign, and alien corporations?
3. What is the role of a registered agent for a corporation?
4. What are the requirements for a corporate name?
5. What are the roles of bylaws and articles of incorporation?

## INTRODUCTION

This chapter addresses the beginning stages of a corporation's life. A corporation does not spring to life overnight. It is a creature of the state, an independent legal entity, in many ways like a natural person, who is born, lives, and dies. A corporation has "parents"— its promoters. It has a purpose. It has rules of life that are set out by the state. It has processes that it must follow. It also has articles of incorporation, bylaws, and governing documents that regulate its activities. It even, eventually, has a death.

The discussion that follows traces those stages, from the seminal idea for a corporation, to the point where the corporation is fully created, up and running, as an independent legal entity—an "adult," if you will, independent of its promoters.

## PREINCORPORATION

The **Preincorporation** stage is the beginning of a corporation's life cycle. The corporation does not immediately spring into existence, fully formed, at the behest of the state or its shareholders. Instead, it begins with an idea that must be given legal form and legitimacy.

**Preincorporation:**
The beginning of a corporation's life cycle, prior to the filing of articles of incorporation with the state.

**Promoters** are the people (or other legal entity entitled to do so) who perform the basic steps needed to create a corporation. Many times, especially in the small business world, the promoters are the future shareholders, officers, and directors of the corporation. In larger deals, however, the promoters may be a bank, stock brokerage house, attorneys, or even other representatives who are acting for the benefit of the corporation and the shareholders.

The **Prospectus** is a written description drawn up by the promoters or their representatives that gives detailed information about the new corporation. If the new corporation is to be publicly traded, there are very specific rules about the contents, statements, and disclosures that must be made as a part of the prospectus itself.

**Subscribers** are the people or legal entities (like other corporations) with whom the promoter contracts to sell to them for a specific price a specific number of shares of the new corporation. In short, the promoter is raising money to create the corporation through these promises of stock for cash. The agreement between the subscribers and the promoters is called a subscription agreement.

One of the primary reasons to form a corporation is to avoid liability. However, before the corporation is actually formed and endorsed by the state, the promoters are engaging in acts, entering into agreements, and generally acting in the new corporation's best interests. Sometimes the promoters' actions are successful, and the corporation is formed without any problems. Sometimes the corporation is formed, but a legal dispute arises from something a promoter did before the corporation was officially created. Finally, sometimes the promoter promotes, but the corporation never is properly formed.

In most states and in most cases, a promoter is personally liable for preincorporation activities. The promoter may avoid liability in three ways. First, the promoter could come to an agreement with the third party with whom the promoter is dealing that the promoter is not personally liable—only the corporation will be. The third party could also agree to release any liability of the promoter. Finally, the new corporation could agree (and this requires the assent of the third party) to take over the agreement and its liabilities from the promoter. If that agreement is by **Adoption**, both promoter and corporation are liable. If it is by **Novation**, the promoter is no longer liable, and the new corporation becomes solely liable.

## CHOICE OF JURISDICTION

Every corporation must be created pursuant to state law in the United States. That is, the corporate promoters must determine what

**Promoters:**
The persons who perform the basic steps needed to create a corporation.

**Prospectus:**
The written description of the new corporation for potential investors.

**Subscribers:**
People who agree to purchase shares of the new corporation.

**Adoption:**
Under contract law, the agreement by a third party to take on both the benefits and obligations of one of the parties to a contract, whereby the original party remains liable under the contract.

**Novation:**
Under contract law, the agreement by a third party to take on both the benefits and obligations of one of the parties to a contract, whereby the original party is no longer liable under the contract.

state law to use as the basic governing law—the law enabling the corporation's existence.

The obvious choice is for the corporation's creators to use the law of the state where the business and the shareholders will be located. A second choice for the state of incorporation, often made, is another state, even though the corporation is actually headquartered elsewhere. Usually promoters choose Delaware (although increasingly they are choosing Nevada and other states) as the state of incorporation.

Primarily, a promoter will choose the state where the business and shareholders are located for simple reasons. Ease of paperwork (only needing to account for one state's law), lowered costs, convenience, local comfort, and other factors all contribute to this choice.

**Domestic Corporations** are corporations doing business in the state where they are incorporated. Thus, an Illinois corporation, created under Illinois law, doing business in Illinois, is a domestic corporation.

**Foreign Corporations** are U.S. chartered corporations (chartered in a U.S. state) doing business in another U.S. state. Thus, a Delaware corporation, doing business in Illinois, is a foreign corporation for purposes of Illinois law.

**Alien Corporations** are corporations chartered under the laws of another country that are doing business in a U.S. state. Thus, a corporation created under the laws of Canada, doing business in the United States, is an alien corporation. This situation seldom occurs, however, because most alien corporations will create a subsidiary corporation in a U.S. state in order to do business in the United States. Thus, these corporations have foreign corporation status rather than alien corporation status.

As a practical matter, however, the Commerce Clause and Privileges and Immunities Clause of the United States Constitution eliminate virtually all differences aside from the technical paperwork requirements between a foreign and domestic corporation in the United States.

As noted above, a promoter may choose another state instead of the local, obvious choice. Delaware is the primary state used by promoters who are picking a state other than their home state. There are multiple reasons for this trend. Generally, if the corporation is large enough that it will do business outside a single state, it will consider using Delaware or Nevada as its home state.

Many choose Delaware because its corporation law is generally settled, the law is well understood, the state has specialized courts for business, and it has a tax-friendly environment. There is no sales tax in Delaware. No state corporate income tax is levied by Delaware on Delaware corporations operating outside Delaware. There is no

**Domestic Corporation:**
Corporation doing business in the state where it is incorporated.

**Foreign Corporation:**
A U.S. corporation that is doing business in a state different from its state of incorporation.

**Alien Corporation:**
Corporation chartered under the laws of another country that is doing business in a U.S. state.

state corporate tax on interest or other investment income in Delaware that is earned by a Delaware holding company. In addition, there is no Delaware inheritance tax on stock of Delaware corporations operating outside Delaware (so long as the stock is held by nonresidents of Delaware).

## REGISTERED AGENTS

A corporation is an artificial entity. Many corporations have large factories, office buildings, and physical presences that make it obvious that a corporate representative is available to receive official notifications from the state, service of lawsuits, and the like (but even then, who do you serve? The doorman? The president of the corporation?). Many other corporations have no such physical presence. They exist on paper. Finding them to process paperwork and to satisfy other legal requirements could be a real problem without the registered agent.

**Registered Agents** are required by every state for every corporation that does business within that state. The rule applies to domestic corporations and to foreign corporations. The registered agent is designated by the corporation as the legal representative of that corporation in that particular state for acceptance of legal notifications and for **Service of Process**. Many domestic corporations will merely designate a person at their corporate offices in the state as their registered agent.

A problem arises if a small domestic corporation does not have offices. The corporation could designate the home address of an officer, but there are drawbacks to that strategy in terms of privacy, security, and availability. A problem also presents itself if a foreign corporation is doing business in a given state. That foreign corporation may just be doing business in the state on a very superficial level—no factories—no offices—no hard-and-fast, obvious place for a registered agent.

The solution is provided by an entire industry—the registered agent industry. Essentially, for a nominal fee corporations of all stripes (indeed, other business forms like limited liability companies, too) can hire a company to act as their registered agent in each particular state where it is necessary for them to have a registered agent. Then, that hired registered agent is listed as such in all paperwork with the state. The state, and anyone else giving any sort of legal notification, may then send notifications and service of process to the hired agent—eliminating all uncertainty and ambiguity and providing a level of convenience and security to all parties concerned.

**Registered Agent:**
The agent named by the corporation to accept legal notifications and service of process in the state.

**Service of Process:**
The formal procedure whereby notice of a lawsuit or other legal process is given to a defendant.

## CORPORATE NAME

One of the most important decisions that a corporation's promoters must make is the choice of the corporate name. Like naming a baby, the corporate name sends signals to the outside world about the corporation. In some industries, the corporate name is fundamentally important—and it can have tremendous value.

The corporate naming process follows several well-established steps. First, the promoters will select a name, or, to be prepared, a slate of names in descending order of preference. Names have some obvious requirements, and some more obscure limitations. For instance, the name cannot be vulgar, and it cannot be an already used name, or a name that is very close to another used name— which would cause confusion. All states require that the corporation have some sort of corporate indicator in the name, to advertise its status to the outside world. Delaware is a representative example. It requires that the name of the corporation contain one of the following words or its abbreviation: "'association,' 'company,' 'corporation,' 'club,' 'foundation,' 'fund,' 'incorporated,' 'institute,' 'society,' 'union,' 'syndicate,' or 'limited.'" Del. Code tit. 8, §102(a)(1).

Thus, the name "Bob" is not acceptable for a corporation, but "Bob, Incorporated" is. The corporate terminology alerts third parties that the entity with which they are dealing is a corporation, an artificial legal entity created by the state, rather than a natural person.

The name selection process does not end there. The business must be, essentially, granted the use of the name by the secretary of state in the state of incorporation. That is accomplished first by a reservation of corporate name. The promoters confirm with the state that the name is available, and for a fee, they reserve the name so that no other party may use it. That reservation usually lasts several months—120 days in Delaware. If the reservation expires without the corporation's creation, the name reservation ends and another party (absent copyright issues or other externalities) may use it. If the reservation is accepted, that name then becomes the corporate name.

## PROCESS

Every state has a set procedure by which the corporation is created. The state usually first becomes involved at the corporate name stage, and then the process unfolds from there. In most states the requirements are as follows:

First:    Reservation of corporate name.
Second: Filing and acceptance of articles of incorporation and

any required accompanying forms with the state secretary of state.

Third:   Payment of all fees attendant to filing of the articles.

Fourth:  Publication as required by the state.

## ARTICLES OF INCORPORATION

The **Articles of Incorporation** are the charter documents of a corporation. They found the corporation, and they are filed with the state secretary of state along with supporting documentation and fees. They have become relatively simple to file, as most states have now created preprinted forms that corporate promoters may use to complete their articles.

All states have minimum requirements that must be met for the articles of incorporation to be accepted. Below are items common in every state.

**Articles of Incorporation:** The filing paperwork submitted to and accepted by the secretary of state in the state where a corporation is created that are the founding documents of a corporation and that give the corporation its legal status as a separate entity.

### Purpose

Articles of incorporation require a **Declaration of Purpose**. This declaration indicates what the corporation is being founded to do. Most states allow, and most corporations use, a very simple statement like "this corporation is founded for all legal purposes." Variations on that language exist, but the idea is the same—the corporation is there in order to do whatever the shareholders, board, and officers steer it to do, so long as it is legal. This provides enormous flexibility in the operations and long-term direction of the corporation.

**Declaration of Purpose:** A legal description of the purposes of a corporation's founding that is required to be included in the articles of incorporation.

A more restrictive declaration of purpose might make sense in the short term, but it could cause problems later on. Suppose that Bob's & Mary's Hot Dogs, Inc., had a declaration of purpose stating that the purpose of the corporation was to "sell hot dogs." That's fine, so long as all that the owners want to do is sell hot dogs. What if they decide they want to sell hamburgers? Make their own chili? Then problems arise because any step outside the purpose stated in the articles is then outside the authority granted the corporation by the state. That can lead to problems of authority and to the loss of the protection of the corporate form for those involved in the corporation.

Some states require that professional corporations (doctors, attorneys, and the like) limit their purpose to the furnishing of services within that profession. In virtually all other cases, however, it is advisable for a corporation to use the broadest language possible in its declaration of purpose.

## Duration

In most states, articles of incorporation also require a declaration of the duration of the corporation. A corporation is an artificial legal entity, and it may last long beyond the lifetime of its human founders. Generally, there are two options. First, the articles could list the corporation as existing "in perpetuity"—that is, as long as the corporation fulfills the basic requirements to be a corporation that are set up by the state. Second, the corporation could declare that it has a limited existence—5 years or 50 years—essentially forecasting its own death.

## Capital Stock

A corporation must include in its articles of incorporation both a listing of its authorized stock and the classes of stock that it is permitted to issue. It also must declare the **Par Value** of the stock. Par value is the nominal value assigned to the stock as a part of the issuance process.

**Par Value:**
The nominal value assigned to a stock.

## BYLAWS

**Bylaws**, in this context, are the basic individualized rules and regulations internal to a corporation that govern those internal workings and the relationships between all of the shareholders, directors, and officers of the corporation.

**Bylaws:**
The basic rules and regulations internal to a corporation that govern those internal workings and the relationships between all of the shareholders, directors, and officers of the corporation.

Bylaws are often "boilerplate," meaning that they are standardized for many types of corporations. That means that many attorneys begin working from the same template as they draft bylaws for their corporate clients. Thus, even though that template may get customized, it still has a baseline that is common and recognizable.

Most bylaws should and do cover the number of meetings required of the shareholders and the board, the method and terms of voting, the number of persons that constitute a quorum for voting, the status and makeup and operations of the board of directors, the designation of any committees, and the creation of offices and control, election, and rights of officers.

The bylaws, in essence, are the "constitution" of the corporation. They are generally not filed with the state. They are drafted with provisions that permit amendments, changes, and adaptations as circumstances change, too.

## DE JURE CORPORATIONS

State corporation law imposes certain requirements that corporations must fulfill in order to be validly formed and entitled to do business within a state. When a corporation has been formed in accordance with all applicable laws, it is called a **De Jure Corporation** (a "corporation in law").

**De Jure Corporation:**
A corporation that has been formed in accordance with all applicable laws.

## DEFECTIVE CORPORATIONS

Sometimes a corporation is **Defective** because one of the legal requirements for its formation has not been satisfied. It could be that the articles of incorporation were incorrectly filed, or never filed, or there was some other error that did not allow the corporation and the secretary of state to dot the appropriate "i's" and cross the appropriate "t's".

**Defective Corporation:**
An attempted corporation that has failed to complete all the requirements for legal corporate status successfully.

### De Facto Corporation

A **De Facto Corporation** (a "corporation in fact") is a corporation that has failed to meet some legal requirement for valid existence but that otherwise looks, acts, and performs like a corporation. However, the courts in most states have determined that they will treat a de facto corporation as a true validly created and existing corporation if (1) the corporation could have been formed if all proper steps were followed; (2) the persons involved in the corporation did not know of the corporate defect; (3) the persons involved in the corporation did try to form the corporation; and (4) the persons involved in the corporation have acted as if the corporation was in fact validly formed. In short, the courts give a mechanism to save the corporation and its attributes from failure when the parties surrounding it are innocent. This doctrine applies to the entire world as it relates to the corporation.

**De Facto Corporation:**
A corporation that acts as a corporation for all intents and purposes but has failed to meet a legal requirement.

### Corporation by Estoppel

A **Corporation by Estoppel** is an otherwise defective corporation that the courts treat as if it is a valid corporation for the purposes of that corporation's relationship with one specific third party. The doctrine is not often applied, but the concept does exist. Essentially, the concept behind corporation by estoppel is fairness. In this case if a third party acted as if an otherwise defective corporation were valid, the third party has lost essentially nothing because of the defect in the corporation. Therefore, the courts will declare that the

**Corporation by Estoppel:**
An otherwise defective corporation that the courts treat as if it is a valid corporation for the purposes of that corporation's relationship with one specific third party.

## ETHICAL ISSUES

●●●

A registered agent accepts service of process for a corporation in any state where the company conducts business. It acts as the officially designated place of notice for all legal communications with the company. Is there an ethical issue with designating a third party to accept service of process where a corporation is located within a state, when the corporation could just as conveniently have its own name, address, and personnel to handle the task? That is, is it unethical for a corporation to "hide" behind a third party?

third party is **Estopped**, or prevented, from denying the existence of the corporation. The doctrine works in the opposite way as well— the corporation will be prevented from using its defective status to avoid its obligations to that third party.

**Estoppel:**
A legal doctrine that prevents a person from asserting a claim that contradicts what that person has said or done before or what has been established as true. Here, it refers to a doctrine that prevents a defective corporation and a third party from denying the existence of the corporation. *See also* Corporation by Estoppel.

## CHAPTER SUMMARY

A corporation is a legal entity that is created by its promoters with the approval of the state. It is classified in each state as a domestic corporation, a foreign corporation, or an alien corporation. There is a defined process in each state to create a corporation. The corporation's charter—its articles of incorporation—has required elements, and sometimes even a required form, in each state. Bylaws are the basic internal governing rules of the corporation. Even corporations that are defective can be treated as fully formed corporations when they are treated as de facto corporations or corporations by estoppel.

### Relevant Web Sites

http://business.ohio.gov/starting/
http://www.sos.state.tx.us/corp/registeredagent
  faqs.shtml
http://www.wdfi.org/corporations/fees/foreign.asp
http://www.maine.gov/sos/cec/corp/helpful.html

### Exercises

1. Determine the requirements of articles of incorporation in your state.
2. Find and describe a promoter's prospectus on the Internet.
3. Find a Delaware registered agent service on the Internet.
4. Determine the naming requirements for corporations in your state.
5. Describe the differences between a de facto corporation and a corporation by estoppel.

### Questions

1. What is a domestic corporation?
2. What is a foreign corporation?
3. What is an alien corporation?
4. What is the liability of a promoter for the contracts she makes before the corporate formation process is complete?
5. What is par value?
6. What are bylaws?

7. Why does it make sense to have a broadly defined declaration of purpose for a corporation?

8. What is a subscriber?

9. Why is a prospectus necessary as a part of the preincorporation process?

10. What is the purpose and importance of a registered agent?

## Hypotheticals

1. Cole and Maria formed Anchovy, Inc., under their state's law. Unknown to them, they forgot to file page 27(b) of the articles of incorporation. This page is a minor part of the incorporation process in their state. In all other respects, Anchovy, Inc., followed every requirement of the incorporation law in their state. Several years later, Anchovy, Inc., is sued. What is Cole's and Maria's best argument to avoid personal liability here?

2. Emma, Inc., is a Delaware corporation. It is entirely owned by Carolina Foodstuffs, Inc., which is a Canadian corporation. Emma, Inc., does business in Illinois. In Illinois, is Emma, Inc., a domestic, foreign, or alien corporation?

3. George and Logan create a new corporation. They assign a face value of $20,000 to each share of stock. They issue 500 shares. Does this mean that the corporation is now worth $10 million?

4. Janelle and Liz are the sole shareholders of Snapcool, Inc. They fundamentally disagree regarding how Snapcool, Inc., should be run. What is the first authority they should look to in order to help decide these questions?

5. The declaration of purpose for Matt's Surf Shop, Inc., states that the corporation is authorized to "carve, polish and sell classic wooden surfboards." The corporation later decides to expand to sell fiberglass surfboards made in China. Is there any legal issue as a result of the change in product?

## Sample Cases

1. Blaszak signed the articles of incorporation for his corporation, Consumers Land Title Agency, Inc., and filed them on December 27, 1996. Prior to that he signed an agency agreement on or about December 12, 1996, with Commonwealth Land Title Company. Consumers Land Title was not yet incorporated when Blaszak signed the agency agreement with Commonwealth Land Title Company. Was he personally liable as a promoter for the agency agreement?

*In re Blaszak*, 397 F.3d 386 (6th Cir. 2005).

2. A foreign corporation does business in New York state in two places, the county where the principal office is located, as designated in its application for authority to conduct business filed with New York state, and the location where it provides medical services. These locations are in different counties located far across the state. Where is the business sited for the purposes of a lawsuit?

*DeMichael v. Jaeger*, 70 A.D.3d 759 (N.Y. App. Div. 2d Dep't 2010).

## Key Terms

**Adoption:** Under contract law, the agreement by a third party to take on both the benefits and obligations of one of the parties to a contract, whereby the original party remains liable under the contract.

**Alien Corporation:** Corporation chartered under the laws of another country that is doing business in a U.S. state.

**Articles of Incorporation:** The filing paperwork submitted to and accepted by the secretary of state in the state where a corporation is created that are the founding documents of a corporation and that give the corporation its legal status as a separate entity.

**Bylaws:** The basic rules and regulations internal to a corporation that govern those internal workings and the relationships between all of the shareholders, directors, and officers of the corporation.

**Corporation by Estoppel:** An otherwise defective corporation that the courts treat as if it is a valid corporation for the purposes of that corporation's relationship with one specific third party.

**De Facto Corporation:**  A corporation that acts as a corporation for all intents and purposes but has failed to meet a legal requirement.

**De Jure Corporation:**  A corporation that has been formed in accordance with all applicable laws.

**Declaration of Purpose:**  A legal description of the purposes of a corporation's founding that is required to be included in the articles of incorporation.

**Defective Corporation:**  An attempted corporation that has failed to complete all the requirements for legal corporate status successfully.

**Domestic Corporation:**  A corporation doing business in the state where it is incorporated.

**Estoppel:**  A legal doctrine that prevents a person from asserting a claim that contradicts what that person has said or done before or what has been established as true. Here, it refers to a doctrine that prevents a defective corporation and a third party from denying the existence of the corporation. *See also* Corporation by Estoppel.

**Foreign Corporation:**  A U.S. corporation that is doing business in a state different from its state of incorporation.

**Novation:**  Under contract law, the agreement by a third party to take on both the benefits and obligations of one of the parties to a contract, whereby the original party is no longer liable under the contract.

**Par Value:**  The nominal value assigned to the stock as a part of the issuance process.

**Preincorporation:**  The beginning of a corporation's life cycle, prior to the filing of the articles of incorporation with the state.

**Promoters:**  The persons who perform the basic steps needed to create a corporation.

**Prospectus:**  The written description of the new corporation for potential investors.

**Registered Agent:**  The agent named by the corporation to accept legal notifications and service of process in the state.

**Service of Process:**  The formal procedure whereby notice of a lawsuit or other legal process is given to a defendant.

**Subscribers:**  People who agree to purchase shares of the new corporation.

## CHAPTER 13

# Corporate Financial Structure

**LEARNING OBJECTIVES**

You will be able to answer the following questions after reading this chapter:

1. What is the Securities Act of 1933?
2. What are the differences between common and preferred stock?
3. What are bonds and their role in financing the corporation?
4. What is the role of the Securities and Exchange Commission?
5. What is the importance of the disclosure of material facts and registration of publicly traded stocks?

## INTRODUCTION

This chapter provides a brief overview of the financial structure that underlies every corporation. The details vary from corporation to corporation, but the basic concepts remain the same. Every business, every corporation, requires funds—money—to operate. Corporations generally obtain funds through several methods— equity securities (like stocks), debt securities (like bonds), and traditional business loans or retention of profits (earnings) for future operations. This chapter gives a concise overview of debt securities and equity securities, and of how they are regulated.

## FINANCING THE CORPORATION

Securities have a precise definition given by law. The **Securities Act of 1933** defines *security* as:

> [a]ny note, stock, treasury stock, security future, bond, debenture, evidence of indebtedness, certificate of interest or participation in any profit-sharing agreement, collateral-trust certificate, preorganization certificate or subscription, transferable share, invest-

**Securities Act of 1933:**
A federal statute enacted in 1933 in the midst of the Great Depression as a response to the market crash of 1929 and some of the faults that were exposed in the market trading system at that time.

185

ment contract, voting-trust certificate, certificate of deposit for a security, fractional undivided interest in oil, gas, or other mineral rights, any put, call, straddle, option, or privilege on any security, certificate of deposit, or group or index of securities (including any interest therein or based on the value thereof), or any put, call, straddle, option, or privilege entered into on a national securities exchange relating to foreign currency, or, in general, any interest or instrument commonly known as a "security", or any certificate of interest or participation in, temporary or interim certificate for, receipt for, guarantee of, or warrant or right to subscribe to or purchase, any of the foregoing.

In essence, a security issued by a corporation represents a right of ownership, or a right to a share of profits, or a right to payment on a debt from the corporation to the holder of the security.

## EQUITY SECURITIES

**Equity Securities** are easily recognizable as stocks. Stocks are ownership shares in a corporation. Indeed, stocks are often called shares, and the owners are called shareholders. These stocks are the primary way a corporation obtains financing—directly from its owners. There are multiple types of stock available and authorized under the law. They are generally divided into two types—common stock and preferred stock. All corporations issue stock, and so all issue equity securities.

**Equity Securities:**
A security issued by a corporation that represents a right of ownership or a right to a share of profits in the corporation.

## COMMON STOCK

**Common Stock** provides the shareholder who owns that stock several rights.

First, the shareholder has the right to vote (usually one vote per share). As discussed in previous chapters, the shareholders elect the board of directors of the corporation. Here, they "vote their shares" for that purpose—one vote per share. Consequently, a shareholder who owns multiple shares may be able to exert an extraordinary amount of control over the corporation itself.

Second, the shareholder has the right to the dividends (the distributed profits) of the corporation. Dividends are distributed on a per-share basis, so the more shares a shareholder owns, the more dividends the shareholder is entitled to receive. Dividends are profits, not gross earnings, so all creditors, preferred stockholders, and any other party having a higher priority of payment than the com-

**Common Stock:**
The standard stock issued by a corporation that provides the right to vote, to dividends, and to a share of the assets of the corporation upon dissolution.

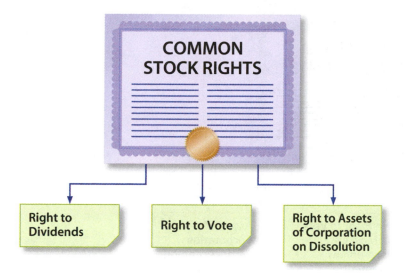

**Figure 13-1**
Common Stock

mon stockholder gets paid first from the corporate earnings. Thus, sometimes—many times—the common stockholders will receive nothing.

Third, the shareholder has the right to the assets of the corporation in proportion to the number of shares that she holds if the corporation is liquidated and its assets are passed out to the shareholders.

## PREFERRED STOCK

**Preferred Stock** is another type of equitable security. It differs from common stock in several ways. It does represent an ownership share in the corporation as common stock does. Many types of preferred stock have one disadvantage, and several advantages.

The disadvantage is that a holder of preferred stock usually does not have any voting rights in the corporation. It is possible for a holder of the preferred stock to be granted voting rights, but the default is that no such rights exist.

The fundamental advantage of preferred stock is that preferred stock is just that—preferred—over the common stock of the corporation. The holders of preferred stock will receive dividends first, and often at a higher rate, than holders of common stock, and holders of preferred stock also will receive a share of the corporate assets first when the corporation terminates.

Not every corporation has preferred stock. It is often seen, but the majority of corporations have only common stock. Why would a corporation elect to have preferred stock? There are several reasons.

**Preferred Stock:**
A second type of stock issued by a corporation that generally does not provide the right to vote (although it may) but that does provide dividends and a share of the assets of the corporation to preferred shareholders before holders of common stock.

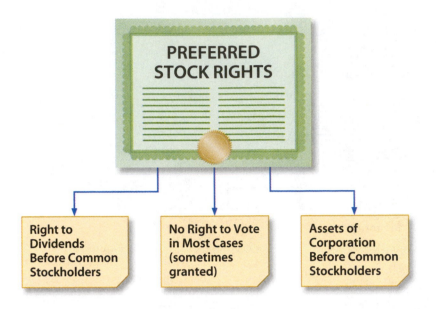

**Figure 13-2**
Preferred Stock

There may be good internal reasons—for instance, the corporation may have a deep family history—the family gives up control to common shareholders, but retains earnings priority through their preferred shares. Or the preferred shares may be worth a premium on the open market—the corporation will receive more for the preferred shares when they are offered than common shares would bring.

## DEBT SECURITIES

**Debt Securities** differ from stocks in a fundamental way: while equity securities represent ownership, debt security represents debt. That debt is issued by the corporation in order to borrow money. Debt securities do not carry voting rights in the corporation because they do not reflect an ownership interest.

## BONDS

**Bonds** are a very common way for corporations to raise funds. They are a debt security and a form, really, of a **Promissory Note**. Essentially the company, in exchange for borrowed money, agrees to pay back investors holding the bonds a set amount of interest throughout the life of the bond, and then the **Principal** amount at the bond's **Maturity**. Bondholders hold a higher priority to receive corporate assets than other creditors, and shareholders, too, if the corporation is dissolved.

**Debt Securities:**
Securities issued by a corporation in order to raise funds. They represent a debt of the corporation, but not an ownership interest.

**Bonds:**
A debt security whereby the company, in exchange for borrowed money, agrees to pay back investors holding the bonds a set amount of interest either periodically or at the end of the bond's term, and then the principal amount at the bond's maturity.

**Promissory Note:**
A contract whereby one party agrees to pay a sum of money to another party.

**Principal:**
The amount borrowed under a loan that remains unpaid, excluding interest.

**Maturity:**
The end date for a bond at which the principal and outstanding interest are repaid.

## Bonds

- Investor buys bond from corporation.
- Bonds may be bought and sold on open market.
- Corporation pays interest to bond holders at set intervals or at end of bond period as per bond terms.
- Corporation pays principal back to bond holder at maturity date.

## REGULATION

Both stocks and bonds existed long before 1933, when the Securities Act of 1933 was first enacted. The major reason for the legislation was the stock market crash of 1929 and the business and bank collapses that followed in the Great Depression. The Securities Act was a direct reaction to these problems.

The **Securities and Exchange Commission** (SEC) has enforcement powers under the Securities Act. The Act, according to the SEC, "has two basic objectives, [to] require that investors receive financial and other significant information concerning securities being offered for public sale; and [to] prohibit deceit, misrepresentations, and other fraud in the sale of securities."

One of the major problems before the Securities Act was the fact that many stocks were publicly traded without full disclosure of all the important, **Material Facts** that would help an investor to make a decision. Material facts are the information that a reasonable person needs in order to make a decision on a particular subject. The Securities Act details what material facts must be disclosed, and it provides through the SEC the forms and procedure to make those disclosures.

Essentially, if a stock is publicly traded, the corporation must **Register** its stock with the SEC in a manner that provides "a description of the company's properties and business; a description of the security to be offered for sale; information about the management of the company; and financial statements certified by independent accountants." This information provides a level of transparency that allows the investor to make educated decisions regarding which stock to buy and which stock to sell.

**Securities and Exchange Commission:**
The administrative agency of the federal government that is responsible, in part, for enforcing the securities laws of the United States.

**Material Facts:**
The information that a reasonable person needs in order to make a decision on a particular subject.

**Registration:**
For these purposes, a requirement of the SEC that a publicly traded company disclose a description of the company's properties and business; a description of the security to be offered for sale; information about the management of the company; and financial statements certified by independent accountants.

## CHAPTER SUMMARY

This chapter introduced the financing of the corporation. The Securities and Exchange Act of 1933 and the Securities and Exchange

## ETHICAL ISSUES

●●●

In 2009 (and in 2011) Apple CEO Steve Jobs took medical leave from his company. Jobs is the driving force behind Apple's success. Warren Buffett, a prominent investor in Apple through his company Berkshire Hathaway, stated in 2009 that Apple and Jobs were withholding material facts necessary for investors in Apple to make decisions about their Apple investments. He said, "If I have any serious illness, or something coming up of an important nature, an operation or anything like that, I think the thing to do is just tell the American, the Berkshire shareholders about it. I work for 'em. Some people might think I'm important to the company. Certainly Steve Jobs is important to Apple. So it's a material fact. Whether he is facing serious surgery or not is a material fact. Whether I'm facing serious surgery is a material fact. Whether [General Electric CEO] Jeff Immelt is, I mean, so I think that's important to get out. They're going to find out about it anyway so I don't see a big privacy issue or anything of the sort." Has Apple or Jobs broken any ethical rules or legal requirements by withholding Job's health status from the public?

Commission are important in regulating investments in public corporations. Before a stock may be publicly traded, the corporation must register the stock and the corporation must disclose any material facts that a reasonable investor would need in order to evaluate her investment in the corporation. Equity securities, including preferred stock with special rights and common stock, signify ownership rights in a corporation. Debt securities like bonds are the primary method for corporations to raise funds without transferring ownership rights.

### Relevant Web Sites

http://www.sec.gov/index.htm
http://www.sec.gov/edgar/quickedgar.htm.
http://www.nyse.com/
http://www.chx.com/

### Exercises

1. Identify an SEC registration statement through the SEC's EDGAR database at http://www.sec.gov/edgar/quickedgar.htm.
2. Name three stocks that are publicly traded and describe where you found them. Note their latest trading prices.
3. Describe the purpose of the Securities and Exchange Commission.
4. Determine why it is critically important for a corporation to have financing and describe how both equitable and debt securities fulfill that need.
5. Research and describe the terms of issuance for one bond publicly available for purchase today.

### Questions

1. What is the primary difference between common stock and preferred stock?
2. What is one advantage of common stock over preferred stock?
3. What is one advantage of preferred stock over common stock?
4. Why was the Securities Act of 1933 enacted?
5. What is one advantage of a bond over a stock?
6. What is one disadvantage of a bond as compared to a stock?

7. What does it mean when a bond reaches maturity?

8. What is the function of the SEC?

9. What is commercial paper?

10. What are dividends and how do they relate to shares of a corporation?

## Hypotheticals

1. Susan owns 1,000 shares of Townhouse Builders, Inc. She has the right to priority over other stockholders on earnings and assets if liquidation of the corporation ever happens, and she has a fixed dividend that is always paid prior to other stockholders. Is it more likely that Susan has preferred stock or common stock in Townhouse Builders, Inc.? Why?

2. Mohammed and Reza are shareholders and officers of Maple Tree, Inc. The corporation is publicly traded. They are in a position to know that the corporation is about to lose a government contract that constitutes at least half of the business's income. Is this a material fact that should be disclosed to investors? Discuss.

3. Jennifer holds bonds worth $1 million issued by Streetwise, Inc. The bonds are guaranteed to pay a fixed return of 10 percent of the face amount of the bond at maturity. Maturity is in August 2030. Jennifer is in desperate need of funds and demands that the corporation pay her the bond amount today. Is Jennifer's demand enforceable, and if not, what other options might she have to generate funds from that bond?

4. Alonso wishes to sell stock in his new corporation on the national stock exchanges. However, he does not want to obtain government permission or to let outsiders know much about the new corporation. Can he do so? What legal requirements of the Securities and Exchange Act of 1993 may affect him? Explain.

## Sample Cases

1. Basic, Incorporated, was a publicly traded company. Beginning in September 1976, representatives of Combustion Corporation had meetings and telephone conversations with Basic officers and directors concerning the possibility of a merger. During 1977 and 1978, Basic made three public statements denying that it was engaged in merger negotiations. At the end of 1978 Basic asked the New York Stock Exchange to suspend trading in its shares and issued a release stating that it had been "approached" by another company concerning a merger. Were the three public statements denying the merger material facts within the meaning of the Securities Act of 1933?

*Basic, Inc. v. Levinson,* 485 U.S. 224 (1988).

2. On March 2, 2006, UnitedHealth Group, Inc., publicly issued $850 million of 5.800 percent bond notes due on March 15, 2036. Throughout the life of the notes, all required interest payments were made and the debt had been continuously rated as investment grade. As a publicly traded company, UnitedHealth Group, Inc., is required to make periodic financial disclosures, including quarterly filings on SEC Form 10-Q. It filed a required Form 10-Q on March 6, 2007, almost seven months late. The holders of the bond notes demanded early redemption of the bonds because of the late filing. Is that late filing enough to accelerate the bond by 29 years?

*UnitedHealth Group, Inc. v. Wilmington Trust Co.,* 548 F.3d 1124 (8th Cir. 2008).

## Key Terms

**Bond:** A debt security whereby the company, in exchange for borrowed money, agrees to pay back investors holding the bonds a set amount of interest either periodically or at the end of the bond's term, and then the principal amount at the bond's maturity.

**Common Stock:** The standard stock issued by a corporation that provides the right to vote, to dividends, and to a share of the assets of the corporation upon dissolution.

**Debt Securities:** Securities issued by a corporation in order to raise funds. They represent a debt of the corporation, but not an ownership interest.

**Equity Securities:** A security issued by a corporation that represents a right of ownership or a right to a share of profits in the corporation.

**Material Facts:** The information that a reasonable person needs in order to make a decision on a particular subject.

**Maturity:** The end date for a bond at which the principal and outstanding interest are repaid.

**Preferred Stock:** A second type of stock issued by a corporation that generally does not provide the right to vote (although it may) but that does provide dividends and a share of the assets of the corporation to preferred shareholders before holders of common stock.

**Principal:** The amount borrowed under a loan that remains unpaid, excluding interest.

**Promissory Note:** A contract whereby one party agrees to pay a sum of money to another party.

**Registration:** For these purposes, a requirement of the SEC that a publicly traded company dis- close a description of the company's properties and business; a description of the security to be offered for sale; information about the manage- ment of the company; and financial statements certified by independent accountants.

**Securities Act of 1933:** A federal statute enacted in 1933 in the midst of the Great Depression as a response to the market crash of 1929 and some of the faults that were exposed in the market trading system at that time.

**Securities and Exchange Commission:** Also called the SEC, the administrative agency of the federal government that is responsible, in part, for en- forcing the securities laws of the United States.

## CHAPTER 14

# Qualification of Corporations in Foreign Jurisdictions and Piercing the Corporate Veil

**LEARNING OBJECTIVES**

You will be able to answer the following questions after reading this chapter:

1. What is the importance of jurisdiction to corporations?
2. Why must a corporation obtain authorization to do business in a state?
3. What are some common prohibitions imposed on unauthorized corporations doing business in a state?
4. How is the doctrine of piercing the corporate veil used in legal actions against corporate shareholders?

## INTRODUCTION

This chapter addresses two major themes within corporate law. The first theme is the treatment of foreign corporations doing business in a state. The second is the important theme of what happens to a corporation when it fails to act as a corporation. Both themes have intricate sets of rules. Nevertheless, the overall concepts are simply explained.

## JURISDICTION

**Jurisdiction** is the geographical area and subject matter within which a given governmental entity has power. For instance, the Pennsylvania Department of Agriculture has jurisdiction over all agricultural products produced or purchased within the boundaries of the Commonwealth of Pennsylvania. For purposes of this chapter, the term *jurisdiction* refers to the authority and control exercised by a state through the requirements of its Department of State over corporations that do business within the state.

**Jurisdiction:**
The geographical area and legal field within which a given governmental entity has power.

193

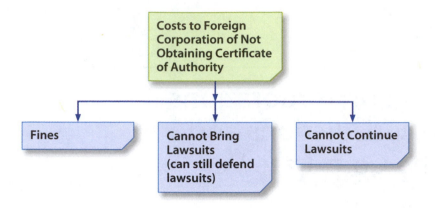

**Figure 14-1**
Consequences to a
Foreign Corporation of
Not Having a Certificate
of Authority

## QUALIFICATION OF CORPORATIONS IN FOREIGN JURISDICTIONS

A domestic corporation is a corporation created and doing business in the state of creation. The reality of today's economy is that few corporations do business solely in one state. Many are headquartered in one state, are registered domestically in another (usually Delaware), and do business in still more states. The question, then, is what happens to these corporations when they do business outside their domestic jurisdiction? Can it happen? How does it happen?

## AUTHORIZATION

Every corporation must obtain **Authorization** to do business as a foreign corporation in a state. The state Department of State dispenses these authorizations. In most cases, the authorizations provide that the foreign corporation has the same rights and obligations as a domestic corporation does after authorization. To do otherwise, to discriminate between foreign and domestic corporations, would violate the Commerce Clause of the United States Constitution.

For instance, in section 1301 of the New York Business Corporations law, the New York legislature provides that:

> (a) A foreign corporation shall not do business in this state until it has been authorized to do so as provided in this article. A foreign corporation may be authorized to do in this state any business which may be done lawfully in this state by a domestic corporation, to the extent that it is authorized to do such business in the jurisdiction of its incorporation, but no other business.

**Authorization:**
Permission to do business as a foreign corporation in a state, granted by the Department of State in that state.

Thus, in New York a foreign corporation has all the rights of a domestic corporation, so long as it is authorized, and not prohibited by its home state. The requirements in other states are similar.

## STATUTORY PROHIBITIONS

Foreign corporations that fail to register and obtain authorization in a state will suffer some legal repercussions as "punishment" to encourage registration and authorization. These **Statutory Prohibitions** are quite common in every state. Vermont, for example, provides as follows in its laws on the subject:

> §15.02. **Consequences of transacting business without authority**
>
> (a) A foreign corporation transacting business in this state without a certificate of authority may not maintain a proceeding in any court in this state until it obtains a certificate of authority.
>
> (b) The successor to a foreign corporation that transacted business in this state without a certificate of authority and the assignee of a cause of action arising out of that business may not maintain a proceeding on that cause of action in any court in this state until the foreign corporation or its successor obtains a certificate of authority.
>
> (c) A court may stay a proceeding commenced by a foreign corporation, its successor, or assignee until it determines whether the foreign corporation or its successor requires a certificate of authority. If it so determines, the court may further stay the proceeding until the foreign corporation or its successor obtains the certificate.
>
> (d) A foreign corporation is liable for a civil penalty of $50.00 for each day, but not to exceed a total of $1,000.00 for each year, it transacts business in this state without a certificate of authority, an amount equal to all fees that would have been imposed under this chapter during the years, or parts thereof, it transacted business in this state without a certificate of authority, and such other penalties as are imposed by law. The attorney general may collect all penalties due under this subsection.
>
> (e) Notwithstanding subsections (a) and (b) of this section, the failure of a foreign corporation to obtain a certificate of authority does not impair the validity of its corporate acts or prevent it from defending any proceeding in this state.
>
> —Vt. Stat. Ann. tit. 11B, §15.02.

**Statutory Prohibitions:** In this context, provisions penalizing unauthorized corporations for doing business in a state.

In short, a foreign corporation doing business in Vermont without obtaining a certificate of authority is fined, it cannot bring a new lawsuit in Vermont courts, it may not be able to continue a lawsuit in the Vermont courts that is already under way, but it can defend itself if sued. Every other state has similar provisions.

Thus, the prudent rule of thumb is for all foreign corporations, in whatever state, to obtain the appropriate certificate of authority for that state.

## PIERCING THE CORPORATE VEIL

Remember that one of the primary purposes of a forming a corporation is to shield its investors from **Personal Liability**. That is, the corporation acts as a barrier between the corporation itself, and its liabilities, and the personal assets of the shareholders.

As Figure 14-2 illustrates, the corporation's liabilities will not reach the shareholder. That means, for example, that a creditor of the corporation will not be able to take a shareholder's personal house, car, or bank account to satisfy the corporation's debt. This shield from personal liability, however, is neither free, nor magic. The shareholders and the officers and directors running the corporation must follow all the **Corporate Formalities** in order to maintain corporate status and protection from personal liability for the shareholders. In short, the corporation must look and act like a corporation in order to keep these corporate benefits.

It is not enough for a corporation to merely file its articles of incorporation, place the word "Inc." or another corporate indicator behind its name, and call the job finished. A corporation must

**Personal Liability:**
Liability for which an individual is personally responsible and for which a harmed party can seek recompense from that individual's personal assets.

**Corporate Formalities:**
In this context, the requirements that a corporation must satisfy to look and act like a corporation as required by law.

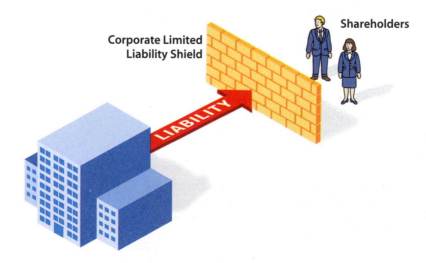

**Corporate Limited
Liability Shield**

**Shareholders**

LIABILITY

**Figure 14-2**
Corporations and
Shareholder Liability

always be in good standing with the relevant state (which means that it must pay the yearly fees required by the state, and it must file the reports the state also requires).

A corporation also must operate on a daily basis as a corporation. Most large corporations do not really struggle with satisfying this requirement because of their size and the inherent distance between the individual shareholder and the decision making at the corporate level. Smaller, closely held corporations are far more susceptible to this issue.

Essentially, the shareholders and the corporation (its officers, directors, and representatives) must maintain their assets separately from each other. A shareholder cannot commingle her personal funds with corporate funds. The corporation must operate as a corporation, too, with each part of the management structure of the corporation acting as it is required to act. The shareholders cannot directly manage the corporation. The board of directors cannot do so either. The officers must act as the management of the corporation and act, through resolutions, meetings, instructions from the board, and so forth. The board cannot make everyday management decisions that officers should make. The board must meet as required by law (usually at least once per year). The corporate records must be maintained. The shareholders must meet as required, too.

When the shareholders of a corporation fail to follow the corporate formalities, they create a hole in the usual personal liability protection from corporate acts that they commonly enjoy.

Every state has, usually through caselaw, a provision for **Piercing the Corporate Veil** that allows creditors of the corporation to move past the corporation, and its liability shields, and go directly to the personal assets of the officers, directors, and shareholders of the

**Piercing the Corporate Veil:** A legal theory in every state that allows creditors of the corporation to move past the corporation, and its liability shields, and go directly to the personal assets of the officers, directors, and shareholders of the corporation.

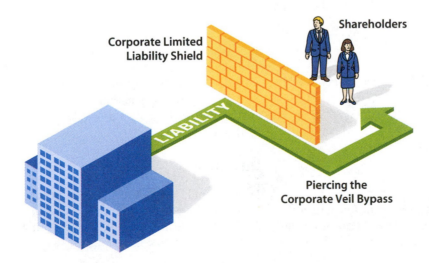

**Figure 14-3**
Piercing the Corporate Veil

## ETHICAL ISSUES

●●●

The doctrine of piercing the corporate veil allows a plaintiff to access a business owner's personal assets, not only the assets of the business, if the plaintiff is successful in a lawsuit. Quite often plaintiffs will bring a veil-piercing claim when the corporation's shareholders have assets and the company does not have enough to pay the judgment to the plaintiff, regardless of whether there is any evidence that the shareholders treated the corporate assets as their own, or that the corporation was not in good standing with the state and regarding its corporate records. Is it ethical to use a legal tool like piercing the corporate veil in cases like this in order to intimidate shareholders? Why or why not? Explain.

corporation. The rationale is that if a corporation is just a corporation in name only, it does not retain the attributes, including liability protection, of a corporation in its full form.

## CHAPTER SUMMARY

Foreign corporations doing business in a state must obtain authorization to do business from the secretary of state of that state. If the corporation fails to do so, it faces fines, is unable to bring lawsuits, and cannot continue lawsuits within that state. Most states follow this rule.

If a corporation fails to follow corporate formalities, and the shareholders do not treat the corporation as a separate entity, but instead treat it as an extension of the shareholders themselves, the corporation's creditors may go after the personal assets of the officers, directors, and shareholders of the corporation.

### Relevant Web Sites

http://www.corp.delaware.gov/faqs.shtml#forqual
http://www.state.tn.us/sos/bus_svc/forms.htm
https://www1.state.nj.us/TYTR_COARS/JSP/
   page1.jsp
http://sos.mt.gov/Business/Forms/

### Exercises

1. Find the authorization forms for foreign corporations doing business in your state from the appropriate Department of State Web site.

2. Explain what the consequences are, in your state, of a corporation's failure to obtain authorization to do business as a foreign corporation.

3. Explain how a corporation's shareholders could lose personal liability protection from acts of the corporation.

### Questions

1. How would you advise a corporate shareholder to act with respect to corporate assets?

2. What is the importance of the authorization process to foreign corporations?

3. How is the concept of piercing the corporate veil implemented in practice?

## Hypotheticals

1. Allan and Carol own Lightbulbs, Inc. They have one bank account that holds both their personal funds and their business funds. Lightbulbs, Inc., is sued, and the company loses the lawsuit. What is the best legal argument for the plaintiff's attorney to make in order to take Allan's and Carol's personal assets to pay Lightbulb's debt?

2. Snowfall, Inc., is a Delaware corporation doing business in New York. Snowfall, Inc., is involved in a contract dispute and wishes to sue a New York defendant. Snowfall, Inc., has never made any filings with the New York authorities to do business there. May Snowfall, Inc., sue? If not, what must it do to successfully file the lawsuit?

3. Treeline, Inc., wishes to sell tree-trimming tools in New York. A competitor wants to prevent Treeline from selling in New York on the basis that it is not a New York corporation. May the competitor stop Treeline, Inc., from doing business on that basis? Explain.

## Sample Cases

1. Walensky was a shareholder in Jonathan Royce International, Inc. Purcell was the majority stockholder in the corporation. Purcell used his position with the corporation to make sure that the corporation only benefited him and his business interests, to the detriment of all the other shareholders. The corporation was his "personal business conduit." Should Walensky be permitted to pierce the corporate veil and access Purcell's personal assets?

*Walensky v. Jonathan Royce Int'l, Inc.*, 624 A.2d 613 (N.J. Super. Ct. 1993).

2. Clearwater Artesian Well Co., Inc., was a New Hampshire corporation. It installed a $2,850 well and pump package on LaGrandeur's property in Maine. Clearwater was engaged in interstate commerce but never filed an application for authority with Maine to do business within the state. Was Clearwater doing business in Maine without the proper authorization and therefore not entitled to maintain its lawsuit against LaGrandeur in Maine?

*Clearwater Artesian Well Co. v. LaGrandeur*, 912 A.2d 1252 (Me. 2007).

## Key Terms

**Authorization:** Permission to do business as a foreign corporation in a state, granted by the Department of State in that state.

**Corporate Formalities:** In this context, the requirements that a corporation look and act like a corporation as required by law.

**Jurisdiction:** The geographical area and subject matter within which a given governmental entity has power.

**Personal Liability:** Liability for which an individual is personally responsible and for which a harmed party can seek recompense from that individual's personal assets.

**Piercing the Corporate Veil:** A legal theory in every state that allows creditors of the corporation to move past the corporation, and its liability shields, and go directly to the personal assets of the officers, directors, and shareholders of the corporation.

**Statutory Prohibitions:** In this context, provisions penalizing unauthorized corporations for doing business in a state.

# Corporate Meetings

## INTRODUCTION

This chapter addresses the basics of corporate meetings, shareholder agreements, and fundamental corporate changes.

There are several different types of corporate meetings as well as substitutes for those meetings. Each group that is central to overall corporate governance has its own separate meeting requirements. This chapter covers shareholder and director meeting requirements.

Shareholder agreements provide basic guidance for shareholders, describing how shareholders vote, manage their relationships, govern the corporation, and enter and leave shareholder status.

This chapter also addresses how fundamental corporate changes affect the corporation. Fundamental corporate changes include the following: amendments to agreements, mergers and consolidations, and dissolution of the corporation—the end of corporate existence.

## CORPORATE MEETINGS

### Types of Meetings

There are two different types of meetings for each of the main groups involved in the ownership and management of the corporation. There are also various permissible methods of holding the meeting.

The significant corporate meetings are the **Annual Meetings** of the shareholders and board of directors of the corporation. **Special Meetings** are also permitted, at times other than the regularly scheduled annual meetings.

State law governing corporations requires that the shareholders and directors meet together at least annually. The United States Supreme Court, in the case of *Cort v. Ash*, 422 U.S. 66 (1975), said the following:

> Corporations are creatures of state law, and investors commit their funds to corporate directors on the understanding that, except where federal law expressly requires certain responsibilities of directors with respect to stockholders, state law will govern the internal affairs of the corporation.

State laws concerning annual meetings vary between the states, and the requirement for an annual meeting can be changed in the corporation's own bylaws. For corporations incorporated in the state of Delaware, Delaware Code tit. 8, §211, entitled Meetings of Stockholders, governs the details of meetings.

Although meetings sometimes can be inconvenient or redundant, the annual meetings should be held, regardless of other facts, in order to observe corporate formalities and to elect members to the board of directors if necessary. Additionally, most state laws require that records of the meeting be maintained. These meeting minutes are typically required to be kept at the corporation's registered or principal office along with other corporate records such as articles of incorporation and amendments to those articles.

If no annual meeting is to be held, something must take its place. Otherwise, the corporation's failure to observe corporate formalities can be cause for a veil-piercing claim by a plaintiff in a case against the corporation, which means that the personal assets of the directors, officers, and shareholders of the corporation can be reached directly. In these cases, where a meeting might not be practical but is still required, the shareholders or board may use a **Unanimous Consent** in lieu of the relevant meeting.

For example, a corporation's shareholders all agree in advance to what should occur at a shareholder's meeting, so they may unanimously consent—that is, sign off—on a document that sets forth what the meeting would have accomplished if the meeting had actually been held. But the consent must be unanimous. If there is even a single dissenting shareholder authorized to attend and vote at the meeting, there is no unanimous consent.

**Annual Meetings:**
Meetings that state statutes require corporations to hold for the board of directors to discuss corporate business with shareholders.

**Special Meetings:**
Meetings called to discuss urgent but non-regular business of the corporation.

**Unanimous Consent in Lieu of Annual Meeting:**
Consent that may be given by shareholders in place of holding a meeting but that must be given by all shareholders in order to be effective.

## Requirements

Any meeting, annual or special, requires a **Quorum** before any business addressed at the meeting can be effective. A quorum is the minimum number of persons eligible to vote that must attend the meeting. A quorum can be defined as the corporation sees fit, but most corporations require a minimum of 50 percent of the eligible voting membership. It is common to see other ratios (66 percent or 33 percent, for instance). The quorum requirement is written into the corporation's bylaws.

An example of the quorum rules in action is as follows: Suppose that a corporation has ten shareholders. Its quorum requirements are set at 50 percent of the eligible shareholders. So, in order for the shareholders to meet and conduct business, at least five of the shareholders (50 percent) must attend the meeting to be counted toward the quorum. A unanimous consent is precluded here, as all ten shareholders are not involved.

Another requirement of a meeting of shareholders or the board of any given corporation is **Notice**. It stands to reason that the shareholders or board members need to know about a meeting before they can attend it. They also need a reasonable amount of time to plan their attendance. Therefore, every state has requirements that notices of a meeting (annual or special) of the board or shareholders of a corporation must be given to all the eligible board members or shareholders.

**Quorum:**
The minimum number of persons eligible to vote that must attend the meeting.

**Notice:**
A legal requirement that corporate meetings must be announced and declared in such a way as to notify all persons eligible to attend the meeting.

**NOTICE OF SHAREHOLDER MEETING**

To the shareholders of _____

[Choose one:]          ☐ An Annual   ☐ A Regular   ☐ A Special
                     Meeting of shareholders will be held as follows:

1. Date _____
2. Time _____
3. Place _____
4. Purpose _____
    ☐ To transact any business that properly comes before the meeting.

[Optional clause:]

☐  5.  This special meeting has been called by:
       ☐ the president
       ☐ another authorized officer: _____
       ☐ the following directors: _____
       ☐ the following shareholders: _____

[End optional clause]

Dated _____

**Figure 15-1**
Sample Notice

**SPECIAL MEETING WAIVER OF NOTICE**

We, the undersigned, being all the _____

in _____ ,
Name of Corporation

hereby waive notice of a Special Meeting of said Corporation, held at the offices of the Corporation located at

_____ ,
Address of Corporation

on _____ , 20 ____ , for the transaction of any and all business that may legally come before the meeting.

Executed this _____ day of _____ , 20 ____ .

_____

_____

**Figure 15-2**
Sample Waiver of Notice

Pennsylvania, for example, requires at least five days' notice of a meeting (and ten days' notice in some cases). The relevant Pennsylvania statute provides in part:

> Written notice of every meeting of the shareholders shall be given by, or at the direction of, the secretary or other authorized person to each shareholder of record entitled to vote at the meeting at least:
>
> 1. ten days prior to the day named for a meeting that will consider a fundamental change under Chapter 19 (relating to fundamental changes); or
>
> 2. five days prior to the day named for the meeting in any other case.
>
> —15 Pa. Cons. Stat. Ann. §1704(b).

There are exceptions to the notice requirement. Directors or shareholders can **Waive** notice. Waiving notice means it is no longer necessary to inform shareholders about the meeting. Waiver can be accomplished by a shareholder's doing one of two things—signing a document saying that the shareholder does not need notice—or actually attending the meeting. Waiver occurs most frequently in smaller, close corporations and in unanimous consents.

**Waiver of Notice:**
An act by a party entitled to notice of a meeting indicating that it is not necessary to notify him of the meeting's time and place.

There are also other circumstances in which the corporation need not give notice—for example, if the person who would get the notice has not provided a forwarding address (making notice tough, if not impossible) or where giving notice is illegal.

## The Future of Annual Meetings

Public companies must send annual reports to shareholders in advance of the annual meeting. Furthermore, if there will be a shareholder vote at the meeting, companies must offer proxy materials and forms to shareholders who will not be able to attend the meeting but want to vote. The proxy will allow the shareholder to vote *in absentia*. All of these materials and mailings cost the corporation and hence the shareholder. There has been some discussion of using the Internet more effectively in order to facilitate shareholder participation in the business of the corporation as well as to save everyone money. An additional savings that would result from more use of the Internet would be less impact on the environment.

Currently, many corporations allow shareholders to choose to receive communications, such as annual reports and proxy information, electronically, via e-mail. Another possibility would be to run annual meetings on the World Wide Web—a virtual shareholder meeting (VSM). New technologies make that more feasible. Canada has a corporate law that allows VSM. *See* Can. Bus. Corp. Act §132(5).

Delaware corporate law also allows for corporations to determine that the annual meeting will be a VSM. However, few U.S. corporations take advantage of this.

> If [...] the board of directors is authorized to determine the place of a meeting of stockholders, the board of directors may, in its sole discretion, determine that the meeting shall not be held at any place, but may instead be held solely by means of remote communication as authorized by paragraph (a)(2) of this section.
>
> —Del. Code tit. 8, §211(a)(1).

## SHAREHOLDER AGREEMENTS

### Purposes and Requirements

**Shareholder Agreements** also provide basic guidance for the relationships among and between the shareholders, describing how shareholders vote, manage their relationships, govern the corporation, and enter and leave shareholder status. These contracts can contain a wide variety of provisions.

**Shareholder Agreements:** Contracts that provide basic guidance for the relationships among and between the shareholders.

### Share Transfer Restrictions

**Share Transfer Restrictions** prevent shareholders from selling their shares to third parties in certain circumstances. These types of restrictions are very common in closely held corporations. The restrictions prevent shareholders, many of whom may have worked closely together for years, from being forced to have strangers as

**Share Transfer Restrictions:** Shareholder agreement provisions that restrict share transfer.

business partners, and to avoid other problems that could ensue from an uncontrolled transfer of ownership.

Typically, share transfer restrictions require rights of first refusal for the remaining shareholders when a shareholder decides to sell her shares. These restrictions are sometimes called a *buy-sell* agreement. In this situation, the non-selling shareholders have the opportunity to purchase the shares from the selling shareholder at or above the price a third party is willing to pay.

In the case of *Salt Lake Tribune Publishing Co. v. AT & T Corp*, 320 F.3d 1081 (10th Cir. 2003), the parties had a dispute over a share transfer restriction found in a shareholder agreement. In 1952 two newspapers, *The Salt Lake Tribune* and the *Deseret News*, entered into a joint operating agreement (JOA) in order to share the overhead expenses of running their respective operations. The *Salt Lake Tribune* was owned by a corporation whose shareholders were primarily members of one family, the Kearns-McCarthey family. The JOA created a new corporation. That corporation was called the Newspaper Agency Corporation (NAC). Each of the newspapers owned 50 percent of the shares of NAC, and the JOA prohibited the transfer of shares by shareholders of either corporation to anyone else.

Years later in 2000 and after several mergers and sales, a party with an interest in outright ownership of *The Salt Lake Tribune* asked a court in Utah to declare the 1952 JOA, with its stock transfer restriction, invalid. The court refused and more specifically stated that close corporations, with few shareholders, have very good reasons for creating restrictions on the transfer of those shares. Hence, the court in *Salt Lake Tribune Publishing Co. v. AT & T Corp.* upheld the validity and enforceability of the JOA share transfer restriction.

**Buyout Agreements** are agreements that more broadly cover what happens to stock when a shareholder parts ways with the corporation. The reasons for buying out a shareholder can include death, bankruptcy, divorce, or incapacity. The buyout agreement covers all of these eventualities so there can be an orderly sale of shares.

**Buyout Agreement:**
Agreements that detail what happens to a shareholder's stock when the shareholder parts ways with a corporation.

**Figure 15-3**
Share Transfer Restrictions: *Salt Lake Tribune Publishing Co. v. AT & T Corp.*

The agreement will specify if a departing shareholder must be bought out and who can buy those shares. The agreement can determine what price will be paid for those shares as well.

## FUNDAMENTAL CORPORATE CHANGES

There are particular events or corporate activities that are described by the law as fundamental corporate changes. Usually, these are changes to corporate structure. They require the agreement of shareholders and often members of the board of directors as well as other procedural requirements. These requirements protect the corporation and its shareholders. This discussion covers the fundamental corporate changes of amendments to the articles of incorporation, mergers and consolidations, the disposition of assets, and dissolution of the corporation.

### Amendments to the Articles of Incorporation

A corporation may make changes to the articles of incorporation through an amendment. State statutes describe the types of amendments that are permissible. Amendments can be very simple, such as changing the corporation's name, or can be much more complicated, such as changing shareholder voting rights.

The board of directors must approve the fundamental change. Then shareholders must vote on and approve the amendment by a majority or two-thirds vote, depending on the statute. The vote typically takes place at a meeting with the usual notice requirements. Once approval has been obtained, a certificate of amendment is filed with state officials.

### Mergers and Consolidations

A **Merger** is the combination of corporations that results in the continued existence of one of the merging corporations—the surviving corporation. Corporation A merges with Corporation B. It is decided that A will absorb B. Once the merger is complete, only Corporation A exists. Corporation B is terminated or dissolved. Corporation A is the surviving corporation.

**Merger:**
The combining of corporate assets whereby one corporation is absorbed by another.

The surviving corporation acquires all of the rights and obligations of the other corporation. This is significant when a financially secure corporation merges with one that has debts or outstanding legal judgments against it.

A **Consolidation**, on the other hand, involves the combining of two corporations whereby a new corporation is formed. Both con-

**Consolidation:**
The combining of corporate assets whereby two corporations form a new, successor third corporation.

solidating corporations cease to exist. Corporation A consolidates with Corporation B. That consolidation creates Corporation C.

For both mergers and consolidations, the board must first approve the change, then shareholders must vote to approve the action because it is a fundamental corporate change. There are some types of mergers—short-form mergers—that do not require a shareholder vote, but the majority of mergers do.

Some shareholders will not agree to a merger or consolidation. In that situation, the shareholders are called dissenting shareholders and are paid fair value for their shares.

## Disposition of Assets

A **Disposition of Assets** is a transfer of corporate assets, such as inventory or property, outside the corporation. It is considered a fundamental corporate change if the transfer takes place outside the regular course of business for the corporation. Whether a transfer is outside the regular course of business is sometimes defined by statute and can be determined by reference to the articles of incorporation. The change must be approved by shareholders. In this situation, dissenting shareholders are not given fair value for their shares.

**Disposition of Assets:**
A transfer of corporate assets outside the corporation.

## Dissolution of a Corporation

**Dissolution of a Corporation** terminates its existence. Dissolution can be voluntary through the actions of shareholders and directors. It can also be involuntary through a court order.

Voluntary dissolution follows the winding up of corporate affairs. Creditors must be notified and assets liquidated. Finally, an articles of dissolution is filed with the state, and a certificate of dissolution is issued. Involuntary dissolution most commonly follows a judgment received by the state's attorney general or a creditor of the corporation for some bad act of the corporation.

**Dissolution of a Corporation:**
The legal process of terminating the existence of a corporation.

## CHAPTER SUMMARY

Corporations are required by law to have meetings between shareholders and the board of directors. Statutes require one annual meeting, but corporations can call occasional special meetings, too. At these meetings corporate business is voted on and approved or not. This procedure is one way that shareholders participate in the corporation.

## ETHICAL ISSUES

●●●

| | |
|---|---|
| The RAND Institute has a Center for Corporate Ethics and Governance (CCEG). Go to http://www.rand.org/icj/centers/corporate_ethics.html. | What are the three objectives of the CCEG? |

Shareholder agreements manage and govern the relationships among and between shareholders. They can cover a multitude of transactions and like all contracts are consensual.

Corporate law addresses fundamental corporate changes by requiring a shareholder vote on them before corporations can make them. These changes alter the corporation in a fundamental way, such as terminating its existence in a merger, consolidation, or dissolution.

### Relevant Web Sites

http://www.berkshirehathaway.com/
http://www.suez-environment.com/en/finance/
  general-meeting/2009-agm/2009-agm/

### Exercises

1. Find the annual report requirements for the state of New York.
2. Research the changes to corporate governance after Enron and Worldcom. Describe the focus of those changes in five well-written paragraphs.
3. Find and cite the state of Oregon revised statute regarding corporate records and reports.
4. Describe the proxy voting changes that have been suggested or implemented since the global financial crisis.
5. Look up *Persson v. Smart Inventions*, 125 Cal. App. 4th 1141, 23 Cal. Rptr. 3d 335 (2d Dist. 2005). Describe the facts of this dispute between shareholders in a California corporation.
6. Look up *Scott v. Trans-System, Inc.*, 148 Wash. 2d 701, 64 P.3d 1 (2003). Prepare a case summary of the legal issues.
7. Prepare a one-page memorandum critically assessing the use of virtual shareholder meetings

(VSM) in the United States. To critically assess means to analyze the pros and cons—describing both and then drawing conclusions.
8. What countries allow VSMs?
9. Research the Organisation for Economic Cooperation and Development (OECD) Principles of Corporate Governance.
10. Identify two large corporate mergers in the last five years. Identify the surviving corporation.

### Questions

1. Why do corporations have an annual meeting?
2. What is a meeting called when it is held at a time other than the annual meeting?
3. What is a merger?
4. What is a consolidation?
5. What is it called when a corporation is dissolved against its will?

### Hypotheticals

1. ABC Corp. holds an annual shareholder meeting. It fails to send notice to a majority shareholder. Will votes at this meeting be valid?
2. XYC Corp. produces widgets. It has had a very profitable year. XYC Corp. would like to merge

with QVW Corp. QVW Corp. has an extensive distribution system for widgets, and the merger makes a great deal of business sense. What is required before this change can occur?

## Sample Cases

1. Iraj owned a 25 percent interest in a mini-mart along with his three cousins, Ajmal, Amood, and Bilal. Iraj was also an employee of the mini-mart, and he was the secretary of the corporation that owned the mini-mart, AMBI Corp. One day, the cousins held a corporate meeting. Iraj attended. At the meeting the cousins voted to terminate Iraj's employment at the mini-mart and his position as secretary of the corporation AMBI Corp. Subsequently, a new corporation was formed, AMA Corp. All of the assets of AMBI Corp. were transferred to AMA Corp. for $5. Does Iraj have any interest in the new corporation?

   *Mazloom v. Mazloom*, 675 S.E.2d 746 (S.C. Ct. App. 2009).

2. Jack Link and his sons Jay and Troy owned a meat and snack company. The company they formed is Links Snacks, a Wisconsin company. LSI is a South Dakota company that produced snacks exclusively for Links Snacks. Jay is employed by Link Snacks and LSI. After years of conflict with Jack and Troy, Jay wants to terminate his employment with the companies. The parties were unable to negotiate a buyout agreement. How will they value Jay's shares in LSI?

   *Link v. L.S.I., Inc.*, 793 N.W.2d 44 (S.D. 2010).

## Key Terms

**Annual Meetings:** Meetings that state statutes require corporations to hold for the board of directors to discuss corporate business with shareholders.

**Buyout Agreement:** Agreements that detail what happens to a shareholder's stock when the shareholder parts ways with a corporation.

**Consolidation:** The combining of corporate assets whereby two corporations form a new, successor third corporation.

**Disposition of Assets:** A transfer of corporate assets outside the corporation.

**Dissolution of a Corporation:** The legal process of terminating the existence of a corporation.

**Merger:** The combining of corporate assets whereby one corporation is absorbed by another.

**Notice:** A legal requirement that corporate meetings must be announced and declared in such a way as to notify all persons eligible to attend the meeting.

**Quorum:** The minimum number of persons eligible to vote that must attend the meeting.

**Share Transfer Restrictions:** Shareholder agreement provisions that restrict share transfer.

**Shareholder Agreements:** Contracts that provide basic guidance for the relationships among and between the shareholders.

**Special Meetings:** Meetings called to discuss urgent but non-regular business of the corporation.

**Unanimous Consent in Lieu of Annual Meeting:** Consent that may be given by shareholders in place of holding a meeting but that must be unanimous.

**Waiver of Notice:** An act by a party entitled to notice of a meeting indicating that it is not necessary to notify him of the meeting's time and place.

## CHAPTER 16

# Limited Liability Companies

**LEARNING OBJECTIVES**

You will be able to answer the following questions after reading this chapter:

1. What is a limited liability company?
2. How is an LLC formed?
3. What are the advantages and disadvantages of this form of business?
4. How is an LLC terminated?

## INTRODUCTION

A limited liability company (LLC) is a hybrid organization, having characteristics of both a corporation and a partnership. This chapter reviews in depth the characteristics of the LLC and considers why it is among the most popular of business organizations.

England has allowed for companies with limited liability since the turn of the 19th century. Also, in Brazil, a company designated as *limitada* is an LLC. In the United States the LLC is a relatively recent business organization development. IRS rules regarding LLCs came into effect in 1997. In 2010, the European Union began a phased rollout of plans to allow member countries to permit the formation of a company of limited liability, or European Private Company. The acronym for this type of entity will be SPE after the Latin *Societas Privata Europaea*.

An LLC is governed by state law. In 1995 the National Conference of Commissioners on Uniform State Laws drafted the Uniform Limited Liability Company Act in an effort to get uniformity among the states, but few states have adopted that uniform law.

An LLC functions in many ways just like a corporation yet also has advantageous tax treatment. An owner of an LLC, called a **Member**, can be an individual, a corporation, or a foreign investor, members of the LLC contribute money to the entity, and their

**Member:**
An owner of an LLC.

211

liability is typically limited to the amount of that investment. The entity itself is not taxed; instead, the tax passes through to the members individually as in a partnership.

Tax status is only one of the advantages of an LLC. This form of business organization is very flexible in terms of how it operates. State statutes on LLCs have fewer requirements than statutes governing corporations. There are some disadvantages to operating a business in the form of an LLC. State law that governs LLCs is not uniform. This means that when an LLC conducts business in several states, it will need to conform to potentially conflicting but certainly different rules. Additionally, because the LLC is relatively new, there is very little caselaw concerning LLCs, which has been so instrumental in the recent development of corporate law.

An LLC is formed by the filing of articles of organization with the state. Members decide how to operate the LLC through an **Operating Agreement**. This agreement usually provides for the division of profits, transfer of membership, as well as dissolution of the LLC.

**Operating Agreement:**
A written contract between the members of a limited liability company that sets out the basic parameters of the members' relationships with each other.

This chapter discusses how LLCs are managed. LLC statutes presume that members will be managing the business, but some LLCs are managed by a group of individuals designated by the members. The operating agreement often describes the procedures to follow should a manager need to be removed.

This chapter also details the rights and duties of the company as well as the members. The LLC is an individual under state law and can do all the things an individual can do: sue, be sued, lease or own real property, enter into contracts, lend money, and acquire debt. Members can manage the company, receive distributions, disassociate from the company, and wind up the business.

## OVERVIEW OF LIMITED LIABILITY COMPANIES

As a hybrid business organization, the LLC has aspects of both a corporation and and a partnership. Like a corporation, members of the company are not personally liable for the obligations of the company. Like a partnership, members are responsible for taxes assessed on the profits of the company. They are unlike corporations in that manner because corporations are subject to **Double Taxation,** meaning that the corporation is taxed on corporate profits and the shareholders are also taxed on corporate distributions such as dividends.

**Double Taxation:**
A taxation scheme whereby business profits are taxed and distributions to shareholders are also taxed.

**Member-Managed LLC:**
An LLC managed by its members.

**Manager-Managed LLC:**
An LLC managed by hired managers chosen by the members.

Management of the company is structured in any manner chosen by the members. In **Member-Managed LLCs** the members govern the company directly. In **Manager-Managed LLCs** (which most companies choose to create), a board of managers, which functions very much like a corporation's board of directors, runs the company. Rules regarding management of the LLC are set out in the operating agreement signed by all of the members during the formation of the LLC.

The operating agreement may also provide for future dissolution of the company, or not at all. If dissolution is anticipated at a particular future time, the entity is a **Term LLC.** Alternatively, the LLC could be an **LLC at Will,** operating until the members agree to dissolve it.

At some point a member may want to transfer his interest in the LLC. The **Transferability of Interest** may be restricted by the operating agreement or by state statute. Typically, the transferee does not become a member of the company and only has the right to receive distributions from the company. However, all of this will depend on what the operating agreement provides and whether the pertinent state statute addresses this issue.

**Term LLC:**
An LLC whose operating agreement states the date for dissolution of the LLC.

**LLC at Will:**
An LLC that is created without a date of dissolution.

**Transferability of Interest:**
The ability of an LLC member to transfer her interest in the LLC to another but only within state LLC statute restrictions.

## ADVANTAGES AND DISADVANTAGES OF LLCS

### Advantages

**Limited Liability** is a huge advantage for LLCs. Limited liability means that investors are investing with less risk. Companies that limit risk offer at least the opportunity for greater reward from an investment. LLCs typically have more than one investor/member, although they can be formed with just one investor. An LLC that is formed with a single investor is called a **Single-Member LLC.**

Flexibility of management structure is another advantage of the LLC. The operating agreement allows members to create the exact type of management structure that will suit the company's purpose. This flexibility is unheard of in corporate law. Although there is no requirement that shareholder meetings be held, state filings can be required. Therefore, state statutes should be consulted.

The **Pass-Through Taxation** feature of the LLC is another advantage. The entity does not pay tax, only members do. Furthermore, in the operating agreement members can decide how distributions will be made. Members may make a large capital investment in the company but only have a small distribution on which the member would owe income tax. The operating agreement could also provide that distribution amounts can be altered from time to time. This tax flexibility is an advantage for investors.

LLCs are frequently used by professionals such as doctors and lawyers. Many states have special statutes governing professional

**Limited Liability:**
A limitation of personal financial responsibility for the debts and obligations of a business.

**Single-Member LLC:**
An LLC that has only one member.

**Pass-Through Taxation:**
A method of taxation in which certain legal business entities do not pay their own income taxes, instead filing information returns with the taxation authorities, and in which the owners pay the taxes on the income, once, as appropriate, at the owners' personal tax rates.

LLCs. Frequently in these professions, the doctor or lawyer is personally liable for malpractice by law, so using a corporation as a business structure would simply complicate matters without limiting liability further.

## Disadvantages

LLCs do not have many disadvantages. The primary disadvantage of using the LLC business structure is the lack of uniformity between state LLC statutes. This creates problems when companies conduct business activities in several states.

Companies will need to spend the time and energy to determine whether they are in compliance with state laws in each state in which they do business. That can mean high legal fees. Of course, if LLCs do repeat business in only a few states, once they determine the laws, the work is done.

## ORGANIZATION AND CONTROL OF THE LIMITED LIABILITY COMPANY

To form an LLC, the articles of organization must be filed with the proper state authority, usually the secretary of state. By statute, the name of the LLC must contain the letters LLC or the words "Limited Liability Company" so that the entity is designated and recognized as an LLC. What exactly should be contained in the articles will be found in the statute. Typically, statutes require the following:

1. Name and address of the initial designated office;
2. Initial agent for service of process;
3. Names and addresses of company organizers; and
4. Names and addresses of company managers if there will be managers.

The operating agreement of the LLC is used to detail how the company will be run. The agreement may be general or very specific. When the operating agreement is specific, parties to the agreement are bound to perform under those specific provisions. The agreement may include provisions regarding the contribution of capital or the payment of salary. There may also be provisions regarding continuing capital contributions or explanations of various members' different duties to the LLC. In the absence of such provisions, typically the state LLC statute will act as a gap-filler. An LLC that is organized in one state is considered a **Foreign LLC** in all other states.

**Foreign LLC:**
An LLC doing business in a state other than the state where it was formed.

**Sample State Statute on LLC Operating Agreement**
Arizona Revised Statutes §29-682

### Operating Agreement

**A.** The members of a limited liability company may adopt an operating agreement containing provisions they deem appropriate. All or part of an operating agreement may be subsequently repealed or amended by agreement or consent of all of the members or, to the extent an operating agreement so provides, by all of the managers or a specified portion of the members or managers.

**B.** An operating agreement governs relations among the members and the managers and between the members and managers and the limited liability company and may contain any provision that is not contrary to law and that relates to the business of the limited liability company, the conduct of its affairs, its rights, duties or powers and the rights, duties or powers of its members, managers, officers, employees or agents including:

**1.** Whether the management of the limited liability company is vested in one or more managers and, if so, the powers to be exercised by managers.

**2.** Providing for classes or groups of members with various rights, powers and duties and providing for the future creation of additional classes or groups of members with relative rights, powers and duties superior, equal or inferior to existing classes and groups of members.

**3.** The exercise or division of management or voting rights among different classes or groups of members or managers on a per capita or other basis.

**4.** With respect to any matter requiring a vote, approval or consent of members or managers, provisions relating to notice of the time, place and purpose of any meeting at which the matter is to be voted on, waiver of notice, action by consent without a meeting, the establishment of a record date, quorum requirements, authorizations by proxy or any other matter concerning the exercise of any voting or approval rights.

**5.** Restrictions on the transfer of and option rights to acquire or sell any member's interest in the limited liability company.

**C.** A court may enforce an operating agreement by injunction or by any other relief that the court in its discretion determines to be fair and appropriate in the circumstances.

**Figure 16-1**
Sample State Statute on LLC Operating Agreement

The operating agreement will provide for how the company is managed. There are two choices for LLC governance—member-management or manager-management.

In member-managed companies, each member has a vote in business decisions for the LLC. This structure functions very much like a general partnership with all partners equally involved in management of the company. Along the same lines, no one member can bind the LLC in a contract or other agreement without the approval of all of the other members. Use caution when applying the partnership analogy to the LLC, however. Remember, each member is working for the benefit of the LLC as a company and not for himself or for one another. This is why the LLC is considered a hybrid.

In manager-managed arrangements, the members have agreed to "outsource" the management of the LLC to a manager or management team called a **Board of Managers**. The manager could also be another corporation or LLC.

The manager is an **Agent** of the LLC. An agent is the servant of another only authorized to act in a capacity designated by someone else. The manager of an LLC is authorized to act on behalf of the members, but the manager is not a member. The manager owes a **Fiduciary Duty** to the members, meaning she must act in good faith while taking care of the affairs of the members just as bankers owe a fiduciary duty to account holders.

**Board of Managers:**
A group of individuals chosen to manage the LLC in manager-managed LLCs. The board of managers functions like a board of directors.

**Agent:**
A person acting under instruction from another for the other's benefit.

**Fiduciary Duty:**
The duty to act in good faith and reasonable dealing when handling the affairs of another.

## Dissolution of the LLC

One member's leaving the LLC will not dissolve the LLC unless the LLC is a single-member LLC. Many state statutes provide for the disassociation of a member upon the occurrence of certain events. For example, such event could be the transfer of an interest in violation of a restriction on transfers or the transfer of an interest on a member's death.

The dissolution of the LLC may be planned for and described in the operating agreement. Also, the LLC members may mutually decide to dissolve the company. After the decision has been made to wind up the company, members may participate in the distribution of assets and the payment of debts and obligations. **Articles of Termination** are then filed with the proper state authority.

**Articles of Termination:**
The formal paperwork filed with the state authority that ends an LLC's existence.

## CHAPTER SUMMARY

The LLC is a hybrid business structure that has some characteristics of a corporation and some characteristics of a partnership, even

## ETHICAL ISSUES

●●●

Country Club Partners, LLC, was formed with the purpose of acquiring the debts and assets of a local country club. The golf club was located in upstate New York and had fallen on hard times during the recent recession. A local law firm Sol, Goldman, Mangioni and Sachs (SGMS) was retained to create the LLC, draft the operating agreement, and assist with the sale of some property owned by the club. Additionally, the LLC wanted to purchase a more desirable parcel of property, part of a larger piece of land, adjacent to the club and owned by Mari-

lyn Kline. The LLC was unsuccessful in acquiring the parcel. Subsequently, after representation of the LLC was terminated, a lawyer and partner at SGMS, Goldman, made an offer on the entire piece of land owned by Kline and purchased it. Country Club Partners, LLC, sued the lawyer for breach of fiduciary duty and sought damages. Did the lawyer breach an ethical responsibility to the LLC? What additional information might you need in order to determine whether a breach occurred?

beyond tax treatment. This chapter considered some of the advantages and disadvantages of using the LLC as a business form. It covered the formalities for creating the LLC and cautioned about the diversity of laws that govern these entities.

The LLC can be managed and operated in a number of ways that can be agreed upon by the members. This flexibility of operation provides members maneuverability that the corporate business form does not give. The LLC is a popular form of business organization.

### Relevant Web Sites

http://ec.europa.eu/enterprise/entrepreneurship/
   sba_en.htm
http://www.irs.gov/businesses/small/article/
   0,,is=98277,00.html
http://www.llcproject.org/

### Exercises

1. Determine the state law requirements for the articles of organization in your state.
2. Find your state's LLC statute and describe its provisions for the LLC operating agreement.
3. Describe the difference between a member-managed and manager-managed LLC.
4. Describe how LLCs are different from general partnerships.
5. Find one case from any state that concerns a dispute regarding any aspect of an LLC.

### Questions

1. What is a foreign LLC?
2. Who agrees to an LLC operating agreement?
3. What name must go on the LLC?
4. How are LLCs taxed?
5. Where are the articles of organization filed?
6. What is filed when an LLC dissolves?
7. What is a disadvantage of an LLC?
8. Can an interest in an LLC be transferred?
9. What kind of duty does a manager of an LLC, who is a non-member, owe to members?
10. What is the owner of an LLC called?

### Hypotheticals

1. Frank, Terry, and Ann want to open a nursery and sell shrubbery. They form an LLC called Mountain Home Nursery, LLC, each contributing $25,000 in capital. The Nursery, which

is located in Arkansas, obtains a mortgage of $1 million from Arkansas National Bank and uses it to buy an excellent piece of property. Business is good after the opening, and Frank, Terry, and Ann each share in the responsibilities of running the business. They sell shrubbery, garden tools, and garden accessories. They expand their business to neighboring states. A dispute arises with a business customer in Texas who ordered shrubbery to landscape an apartment complex. Frank tells Terry and Ann not to worry since they are in compliance with Arkansas LLC requirements and that is all that matters. Is Frank correct?

2. Ron and Ellen are married. They both are very famous, she as an actress and he as a Wall Street tycoon. Ellen has a very lazy brother Barry. She wants to start a film company with him to keep him busy and keep her hand in the industry. Ron reluctantly agrees, and the three—Ron, Ellen, and Barry—form an LLC called Apple-Sauce Pictures, LLC. It is run out of the home of Ron and Ellen, which is quite large. Barry is required under the operating agreement to work full-time on film development, for which he receives an annual salary. Eventually, Ron and Ellen separate. In the separation agreement they state that AppleSauce will need to move out of the house and that all divorce negotiations will be private and confidential. The operating agreement of AppleSauce is amended, and Ron agrees to pay capital contributions quarterly to the LLC even during the pending divorce. AppleSauce moves out, but Ron never makes the payments mandated by the LLC's amended operating agreement. Applesauce LLC sues Ron for breaching the operating agreement. Ron argues that Barry as manager of the LLC never does the work he is required to do under the operating agreement and so he won't either. Who should prevail?

## Sample Cases

1. Olmstead and Connell operated a credit card scam, which was discovered by the Federal Trade Commission (FTC). Assets of the pair were frozen and placed in receivership. Among those assets were several single-member LLCs with either Olmstead or Connell as the sole member. The FTC obtained an order compelling Olmstead and Connell to surrender to the receiver all right, title, and interest in their LLCs. They were now judgment-debtors. Olmstead and Connell objected to this action, arguing that the operating agreements of their LLCs had a restriction on the transfer of ownership rights. They argued that the FTC could only obtain a charging order that would allow payment of debts from distributions or profits from the LLC but could not obtain title. Can title to an LLC be transferred in satisfaction of a debt created by a judgment?

*FTC v. Peoples Credit First, LLC*, 621 F.3d 1327 (11th Cir. 2010).

2. Jim and Christine Gordon decided to go into business with Joseph Kuzara to buy and sell cattle. They formed an LLC called Half Breed. The Gordons invested $26,000, and Kuzara was a managing member of the LLC. The operating agreement (OA) of the LLC contained an arbitration clause stating that disputes regarding the OA must be arbitrated rather than resolved by a court. Over time the Gordons became frustrated by Kuzara's activities. Kuzara did not file tax returns, failed to distribute profits from cattle sales to the Gordons, and failed to give them credit for their capital contribution to Half Breed. The Gordons sued for dissolution of the LLC under a Montana statute governing the dissolution of LLCs. Kuzara argued that all disputes must be arbitrated. Can the court compel arbitration? Which should be more controlling, the OA or a state statute governing dissolution?

*Gordon v. Kuzara*, No. DA-0251, 2010 MT 275 (Mont. 2010).

## Key Terms

**Agent:** A person acting under instruction from another for the other's benefit.

**Articles of Termination:** The formal paperwork filed with the state authority that ends an LLC's existence.

**Board of Managers:**  A group of individuals chosen to manage the LLC in manager-managed LLCs. The board of managers functions like a board of directors.

**Double Taxation:** A taxation scheme whereby business profits are taxed and distributions to shareholders are also taxed.

**Fiduciary Duty:**  The duty to act in good faith and reasonable dealing when handling the affairs of another.

**Foreign LLC:** An LLC doing business in a state other than the state where it was formed.

**Limited Liability:** A limitation of personal financial responsibility for the debts and obligations of a business.

**LLC at Will:**  An LLC that is created without a date of dissolution.

**Manager Managed LLC:**  An LLC managed by hired managers chosen by the members.

**Member:**  An owner of an LLC.

**Member-Managed LLC:** An LLC managed by its members.

**Operating Agreement:**  A written contract between the members of an LLC that sets out the basic parameters of the members' relationships with each other.

**Pass-Through Taxation:** A method of taxation in which certain legal business entities do not pay their own income taxes, instead filing information returns with the taxation authorities, and in which the owners pay the taxes on the income, once, as appropriate, at the owners' personal tax rates.

**Single-Member LLC:** An LLC that has only one member.

**Term LLC:** An LLC whose operating agreement states its date for dissolution.

**Transferability of Interest:** The ability of an LLC member to transfer her interest in the LLC to another but only within state LLC statute restrictions.

# Partnerships and Limited Partnerships

## INTRODUCTION

A partnership is an association of two or more persons or other entities that are co-owners of a business carried on for profit. Partners share in those profits from the business. The extent to which partners share in profits is their **Partnership Interest**. Partners do not directly own assets of the partnership. Instead, the partnership owns the assets, and each partner owns an interest in the partnership according to his or her agreed-upon pro rata share. Absent an agreement, partners share in profits and losses equally and vote equally regarding management of the partnership. General partners all participate in the management of the business. Merely owning things as joint tenants does not make individuals partners. This chapter looks at the details of the partnership arrangement.

One particular type of partnership is a **Limited Partnership**. This is an advantageous business organization because it offers partners limited liability. In a limited partnership, there is one or more **General Partners** and one or more **Limited Partners**. The general partners act very much like those in a general partnership, with the same rights and duties. The limited partner is more like an investor, having limited liability but no authority to participate in management of the business without losing that limited liability. This chapter discusses the characteristics of the limited partnership.

**Partnership Interest:**
The proportional share of profits a partner will receive from the partnership.

**Limited Partnership:**
An organization of partners with one or more general partners who control the business and have full liability and one or more limited partners who contribute capital and have limited liability but who cannot participate in management of the business.

**General Partner:**
In a limited partnership, the partner who manages the partnership business and has full personal liability.

**Limited Partner:**
In a limited partnership, the partner who contributes capital and has personal liability only to the extent of that capital contribution but who cannot participate in management of the partnership.

221

## OVERVIEW OF PARTNERSHIPS

All states except for Louisiana have adopted the Uniform Partnership Act (UPA). The UPA was revised and is now referred to as the Revised Uniform Partnership Act (RUPA). The California Corporations Code, which incorporated the **Uniform Partnership Act of 1994**, defines a partnership in section 16101(9) as "[a]n association of two or more persons to carry on as co-owners a business for profit." This short simple definition belies the large number of disputes over whether a business enterprise is a partnership or not.

**Uniform Partnership Act of 1994:**
An Act adopted by individual states that governs the operation of partnerships where the partnership agreement has not addressed an issue.

## Partnership Agreement

In the case of *Fenwick v. Unemployment Compensation Commission*, 44 A.2d 172 (N.J. 1945), the court explained the factors to consider when determining whether a business arrangement was a partnership. Mr. Fenwick owned the United Beauty Shoppe. Mrs. Arline Chesire was a cashier at the shop. After working for most of one year Mrs. Chesire requested a raise in salary. Mr. Fenwick wanted to give her a raise as long as the business of the beauty shop could support the increase.

Mr. Fenwick and Mrs. Chesire entered into an agreement that provided for a bonus to Mrs. Chesire if the business warranted it. The agreement also stated that the parties were entering a partnership but that Mrs. Chesire would make no capital investment. It also stated that the partnership would continue until either party gave ten days' notice of termination.

Mrs. Chesire quit her cashier job. Mr. Fenwick refused to pay into the state-mandated unemployment fund for employees because he said that she was not an employee. The Unemployment Commission held that the agreement did not establish a partnership but rather was an agreement to set compensation. The New Jersey Supreme Court disagreed and held that the parties were partners. The Third Circuit Court of Appeals heard the appeal. The court stated that there are several elements to consider when determining the existence of a partnership. They are the following:

1. Intent of the parties;
2. Right to share in the profits;
3. Obligation to share the losses;
4. Ownership and control of the partnership property and business;
5. Community of power in administration (shared management duties);
6. Language of the agreement;

7. Holding themselves out as partners to third parties; and
8. Rights of the parties on dissolution.

The agreement failed on several elements to set up a partnership. To begin with, Mrs. Chesire did not share in the losses, and there was no sharing of management duties. Additionally, while a partnership tax return was filed, Mr. Fenwick and Mrs. Chesire did not hold themselves out as partners to other persons. Finally, when Mrs. Chesire quit, everything at the beauty shop continued as before except that Mr. Fenwick hired a new cashier. The court held that the agreement was simply a means for providing compensation out of the profits and not an attempt to create a partnership.

There are no formal requirements for creating a partnership. In order to prove a partnership was created, it is not necessary to show a written agreement. As the *Fenwick* case shows, even a written agreement that states that it creates a partnership may not create one. The courts look at how the parties act as well.

Individuals who are not partners may represent to third parties that they are partners. This could happen as a means to obtain credit or facilitate another business transaction. If something goes wrong and the partners are sued, they cannot defend themselves by claiming they are not partners. A court may determine that a **Partnership by Estoppel** exists and impose liability on the individuals as if they were partners. In effect, the persons are stopped—estopped—from claiming that there was no partnership.

> **Partnership by Estoppel:**
> A partnership implied by law when someone holds himself out as a partner to a third party, and the third party relies on that. In such cases, a court determines that a partnership exists for liability purposes but does not bestow partnership rights.

When there is a partnership agreement, the partners may include in it any provisions they want to include. The partnership agreement, written or oral, controls the partnership to the extent that it does not interfere with state law. As a contract, the agreement is also subject to contract law.

## Aggregate or Entity

The law may consider a partnership to be an aggregate of its members or an entity separate from the individual members. The **Entity Theory** allows treatment of a partnership as an entity for specific purposes such as capacity to sue or be sued, bankruptcy proceedings under federal law, and collection of judgments. The **Aggregate Theory** regards the partnership as not having an existence separate from the individual partners for purposes of the law.

> **Entity Theory:**
> A partnership theory stating that the partnership is an enterprise separate from the individual partners.
>
> **Aggregate Theory:**
> A partnership theory stating that the partnership enterprise does not have an existence separate from the individuals who are its partners.

## Agency

Partners may act on behalf of the partnership. An act will be considered on behalf of the partnership if it is in the ordinary course of business of the partnership. For example, a partnership that buys and sells real estate will be bound by transactions entered into by one of the partners when the transactions involve the sale or purchase of real estate because the partner is seen to be acting as an agent of the partnership.

## Fiduciary Duty

In the case of *Meinhard v. Salmon*, 249 N.Y. 458 (1928), the New York Court of Appeals considered a dispute between two partners in a real estate joint venture. The court held that "co adventurers" owe a fiduciary duty of the "finest loyalty" to one another.

Meinhard and Salmon entered into an agreement whereby Meinhard provided money and Salmon managed property for an agreed-upon share of the profits. Their collaboration did not make much money at first but over time made both men rich. Near the agreed-upon end of their joint enterprise, Salmon looked for new opportunities. He entered into an agreement concerning the same property as the Meinhard joint venture. He did not inform Meinhard of his new venture. When Meinhard did find out about it, he asked for a share of the profits and was refused. This case ensued.

The court held that the opportunity came to Salmon because of his position as agent on behalf of the joint venture with Meinhard. Thus, Salmon was under a duty to proceed with loyalty to his ties with Meinhard. The court likens their relationship to that of a trustee who owes a fiduciary duty.

## Liability

Section 15 of the UPA describes the liability of partners as joint and several. Most states have adopted the UPA. For example, Delaware law provides that all partners are liable jointly and severally for all obligations of the partnership unless they have agreed otherwise. Del. Code Ann. tit. 6, §15-306. **Joint and Several Liability** means that partners may be personally sued together (jointly) or individually (severally). This liability covers contract and tort claims.

## Dissociation

When a partner is no longer associated with a partnership, the partner's separation from the partnership is called **Dissociation.** Upon dissociation, the partner may have his or her interest purchased by the partnership. The dissociation means that the partner can no longer act on behalf of the partnership and can no longer participate in the management of the partnership. The partnership, after

**Joint and Several Liability:**
Liability that is apportioned among two or more parties or borne by only one or a few select members of the group. Under this legal principle, the plaintiff sues more than one defendant both together and separately and can recover the entire amount of damages from either one, both, or all of the multiple defendants. The plaintiff cannot recover more than the damages owed.

**Dissociation:**
A partner's separation from a partnership.

dissociation of the partner, continues functioning as before. Certain events can cause dissociation. UPA section 601 provides that a partner can be dissociated by unanimous vote of the other partners, by the occurrence of some event agreed upon in the partnership agreement, or by declaration of bankruptcy, among other events.

## Termination

Termination of a partnership occurs when partners no longer carry on the business of the partnership and dissolve it. The partnership agreement may state how and when the partnership is to be dissolved. It could be the happening of an event or the passage of a specified period of time. A partner can sue for dissolution and ask a court to order dissolution of the partnership.

In the case of *Owen v. Cohen*, 19 Cal. 2d 147 (1941), a partnership was dissolved by order of the court. In *Owen*, the partnership managed a bowling alley. Cohen financed the business, and Owen managed the bowling alley. Conflict arose when Cohen breached the partnership agreement. Owen proposed that Cohen buy him out or sell to him. Cohen rejected this offer.

Owen sued. The court found that Cohen wrongfully appropriated partnership funds, mismanaged the business, and persistently humiliated Owen in front of customers and employees. The court ordered the partnership dissolved and found Cohen at fault for his misdeeds.

In general, after dissolution all that remains to complete termination is to wind up the partnership. **Winding Up** includes such activities as accounting for assets, paying obligations, and providing each partner his or her interest in the partnership. This will complete termination of the partnership.

**Winding Up:**
The process of accounting for assets, paying obligations, and providing each partner his or her interest in the partnership before termination of a partnership.

## OVERVIEW OF LIMITED PARTNERSHIPS

A limited partnership (LP) is created by statute. It has two types of partners—general and limited. The general partner functions just like partners in a regular partnership with the same rights and duties. The limited partner, however, only contributes capital in exchange for a share in the profits of the partnership. The limited partner does not participate in the management of the business and is not personally liable for partnership obligations beyond his or her capital contribution.

LPs are governed by the Revised Uniform Limited Partnership Act (RULPA) of 1976. A newly revised ULPA was promulgated in 2001. The ULPA of 2001 provides that the LP is an entity separate from the individual partners. This does not affect the LP as a pass-through organization for tax purposes. Most states have incorporated the 1976 version of the RULPA into their statutes.

## Certificate of Limited Partnership

A LP must have at least one general partner and at least one limited partner. According to the RULPA, it must file a **Certificate of Limited Partnership** with the secretary of state. The certificate typically must include the following:

1. Partnership name;
2. Partnership address;
3. Information on the agents for service of process (names and addresses);
4. General partner name and address; and
5. Term of duration of the LP.

**Certificate of Limited Partnership:**
A certificate filed with the secretary of state to form a limited partnership.

## Limited Liability of the Limited Partner

The limited liability of the limited partner can erode if the limited partner participates in the management of the business. If a limited partner does participate in management, under the law she can be treated as a general partner with personal liability for partnership obligations. There is divergence in the law in this regard, however. The RULPA states that a limited partner will be treated as a general partner for liability purposes if the limited partner takes part in control of the business. Furthermore, the liability is extended only to the persons who were part of the transaction that gave rise to the involvement in the control of the business. On the other hand, the ULPA of 2001 states that even if a limited partner participates in the management of the partnership, she will not be personally liable for the obligations of the partnership. The ULPA of 2001 is not the rule followed in most states.

## CHAPTER SUMMARY

This chapter provided an overview of general partnerships and limited partnerships. General partnerships are informal business organizations. Partners participate in the management and control of the business and each has similar liability for partnership obligations. The partnership agreement can address any aspect of the duties and rights of the partners. In the absence of such provisions in the agreement, state law is applied to fill in the gaps.

## ETHICAL ISSUES

Diane formed a partnership with her sister Patricia. They formalized as a partnership Q Works. Q Works was a metal works business. Patricia and her husband loaned the partnership $65,000 so that the partnership could buy a lathe and milling machine. Eventually, Q Works dissolved, and Diane needed to find a new partner. She formed a new partnership with Steven. The oral partnership agreement of O Works was based upon Steven's working at the metal works business but also his providing the funds to repay the loan to Patricia and her husband. O Works would operate much as Q Works had, but the agreement was that the first payment made each month was to repay Steven, who had provided the funds to repay Patricia and her husband. Soon Steven began to see discrepancies in the accounting of O Works. He was being repaid, but the loan to Patricia was not and it appeared that Diane was taking profits out of the business for her own personal expenses. One day, Steven showed up at work, collected his belongings, and returned home, never to be seen at O Works again. Steven sued Diane for breach of contract and breach of fiduciary duty. Diane countersued Steven for breach of contract. Identify each of the actions, ethical and legal, that Diane and Steven may be liable for as partners.

The limited partnership is created by statute. General partners participate in the management of the business, and limited partners contribute capital. A limited partner's liability for obligations of the partnership is not greater than the amount of the limited partner's capital contribution, unless the limited partner participates in management.

## Relevant Web Sites

http://www.law.cornell.edu/uniform/vol7.html #partn

http://www.leginfo.ca.gov/cgi-bin/calawquery?co desection = corp&codebody = &hits = All

http://www.irs.gov/businesses/small/article/0,, id = 98214,00.html

## Exercises

1. Search the Internet for the Certificate of Limited Partnership for the State of Tennessee, Department of State. Describe what information is required.
2. Find your state's Partnership Code and describe its provisions for the termination of a partnership.
3. Find the Delaware Code provision concerning dissociation of a partnership. Identify four events causing a partner's dissociation.
4. Describe how general partnerships are different from limited partnerships.
5. Find one case from any state that concerns a dispute regarding any aspect of a general partnership.

## Questions

1. What is the entity theory of partnership?
2. What are the different statutes that govern limited partnerships?
3. What information must be included in the limited partnership certificate?
4. How is a partnership by estoppel created?
5. What kinds of things does a court look at when determining if a partnership exists?

6. How is a partnership terminated?

7. What is joint and several liability?

8. What did the court hold in *Fenwick v. Unemployment Compensation Commission*?

9. What did the court hold in *Meinhard v. Salmon*?

10. What did the court hold in *Owen v. Cohen*?

## Hypotheticals

1. Simon talked his friend Liz into starting a driving school together. Simon is pretty trustworthy, so Liz agrees. Simon tells everyone about the new partnership. Simon's best friend Eric has a car he no longer drives. He offers to sell the car to Simon and Liz. Eric agrees to allow Liz to try out the car over the weekend. Before the weekend, Simon and Liz have a row and decide to drop the new business venture. Liz still takes the car for a test drive and has a collision. Can Eric sue Simon for the loss?

2. Harry, Sally, and Conrad are partners. Harry works 80 hours a week at the partnership business. Sally does nothing, and Conrad contributed $10,000. There is no partnership agreement. How will profits be divided among the partners?

3. Assume the same facts as Hypo #2. There still is no partnership agreement. How many votes does each partner get?

## Sample Cases

1. Richard Cohen retired from his law firm. A Special Referee was appointed by the court to assist the firm in determining its assets and dividing them appropriately. The Special Referee was given all the power of the court to call for a trial if there were disputed issues between the partners. The remaining partners objected to the Special Referee's activities, however legal they were. In the absence of an agreement otherwise, partnership law permits a court or referee to order a buyout of a retiring partner's interest by the remaining partners. Is this equitable?

*Cohen v. Akabas & Cohen*, 2010 N.Y. Slip Op. 08993 (App. Div. 1st Dep't Dec. 7, 2010).

2. Desert Mountain Properties Limited Partnership builds homes. It contracted for the construction of 50 new homes in North Scottsdale, Arizona, with The Weitz Company. From the outset homes began to experience settlement and drainage problems. One patio sunk two to three inches, and most homes had cracks in the roof and interior walls. Desert Mountain hired a consultant to investigate all 50 properties. The consultant determined that the soil had poorly compacted fill material and that there were also construction defects in water and sewage lines. Desert Mountain began repairs and also filed for coverage under their insurance. Who is liable for the damages?

*Desert Mountain Prop. v. Liberty Fire Ins. Co.*, 236 P.3d 421 (Ariz. Ct. App. 2010).

## Key Terms

**Aggregate Theory:** A partnership theory stating that the partnership enterprise does not have an existence separate from the individuals who are its partners.

**Certificate of Limited Partnership:** A certificate filed with the secretary of state to form a limited partnership.

**Dissociation:** A partner's separation from a partnership.

**Entity Theory:** A partnership theory stating that the partnership is an enterprise separate from the individual partners.

**General Partner:** A partner in a standard partnership; also a partner in a limited partnership who has full control of the management of the business as well as full personal liability.

**Joint and Several Liability:** Liability that is apportioned among two or more parties or borne by only one or a few select members of the group. Under this legal principle, the plaintiff sues more than one defendant both together and separately and can recover the entire amount of damages from either one, both, or all of the multiple defendants.

**Limited Partner:** In a limited partnership, the partner who contributes capital and has personal liability only to the extent of that capital contribution but who cannot participate in management of the partnership.

**Limited Partnership:** An organization of partners with one or more general partners who control the business and have full liability and one or more limited partners who contribute capital and have limited liability but who cannot participate in management of the business.

**Partnership by Estoppel:** A partnership implied by law when someone holds himself out as a partner to a third party, and the third party relies on that. In such cases, a court determines that a partnership exists for liability purposes but does not bestow partnership rights.

**Partnership Interest:** The proportional share of profits a partner will receive from the partnership.

**Uniform Partnership Act of 1994:** An Act adopted by individual states that governs the operation of partnerships where the partnership agreement has not addressed an issue.

**Winding Up:** The process of accounting for assets, paying obligations, and providing each partner his or her interest in the partnership before termination of a partnership.

# The Constitution of the United States[*]

We the People of the United States, in Order to form a more perfect Union, establish Justice, insure domestic Tranquility, provide for the common defence, promote the general Welfare, and secure the Blessings of Liberty to ourselves and our Posterity, do ordain and establish this Constitution for the United States of America.

## ARTICLE I.

### Section 1.

All legislative Powers herein granted shall be vested in a Congress of the United States, which shall consist of a Senate and House of Representatives.

### Section 2.

The House of Representatives shall be composed of Members chosen every second Year by the People of the several States, and the Electors in each State shall have the Qualifications requisite for Electors of the most numerous Branch of the State Legislature.

No Person shall be a Representative who shall not have attained to the Age of twenty five Years, and been seven Years a Citizen of the United States, and who shall not, when elected, be an Inhabitant of that State in which he shall be chosen.

Representatives and direct Taxes shall be apportioned among the several States which may be included within this Union, according to their respective Numbers, which shall be determined by adding to the whole Number of free Persons, including those bound to Service for a Term of Years, and excluding Indians not taxed, three fifths of all other Persons. The actual Enumeration shall be made within three Years after the first Meeting of the Congress of the United States, and within every subsequent Term of ten Years, in such Manner as they shall by Law direct. The Number of Representatives shall not exceed one for every thirty Thousand, but each State shall have at Least one Representative; and until such enumeration shall be made, the State of New Hampshire shall be entitled to chuse three, Massachusetts eight, Rhode-Island and Providence Plantations one, Connecticut five, New-York six, New Jersey four, Pennsylvania eight, Delaware one, Maryland six, Virginia ten, North Carolina five, South Carolina five, and Georgia three.

When vacancies happen in the Representation from any State, the Executive Authority thereof shall issue Writs of Election to fill such Vacancies.

The House of Representatives shall chuse their Speaker and other Officers; and shall have the sole Power of Impeachment.

### Section 3.

The Senate of the United States shall be composed of two Senators from each State, chosen by the Legislature thereof for six Years; and each Senator shall have one Vote.

Immediately after they shall be assembled in Consequence of the first Election, they shall be divided as equally as may be into three Classes. The Seats of the Senators of the first Class shall be vacated at the Expiration of the second Year, of the second Class at the Expiration of the fourth Year, and of the third Class at the Expiration of the sixth Year, so that one third may be chosen every second Year; and if Vacancies happen by Resignation, or otherwise, during the Recess of the Legislature of any State, the Executive thereof may make temporary Appointments until the next Meeting of the Legislature, which shall then fill such Vacancies.

No Person shall be a Senator who shall not have attained to the Age of thirty Years, and been nine

*As annotated by the United States National Archives at http://www.archives.gov/

Years a Citizen of the United States, and who shall not, when elected, be an Inhabitant of that State for which he shall be chosen.

The Vice President of the United States shall be President of the Senate, but shall have no Vote, unless they be equally divided.

The Senate shall chuse their other Officers, and also a President pro tempore, in the Absence of the Vice President, or when he shall exercise the Office of President of the United States.

The Senate shall have the sole Power to try all Impeachments. When sitting for that Purpose, they shall be on Oath or Affirmation. When the President of the United States is tried, the Chief Justice shall preside: And no Person shall be convicted without the Concurrence of two thirds of the Members present.

Judgment in Cases of Impeachment shall not extend further than to removal from Office, and disqualification to hold and enjoy any Office of honor, Trust or Profit under the United States: but the Party convicted shall nevertheless be liable and subject to Indictment, Trial, Judgment and Punishment, according to Law.

## Section 4.

The Times, Places and Manner of holding Elections for Senators and Representatives, shall be prescribed in each State by the Legislature thereof; but the Congress may at any time by Law make or alter such Regulations, except as to the Places of chusing Senators.

The Congress shall assemble at least once in every Year, and such Meeting shall be on the first Monday in December, unless they shall by Law appoint a different Day.

## Section 5.

Each House shall be the Judge of the Elections, Returns and Qualifications of its own Members, and a Majority of each shall constitute a Quorum to do Business; but a smaller Number may adjourn from day to day, and may be authorized to compel the Attendance of absent Members, in such Manner, and under such Penalties as each House may provide.

Each House may determine the Rules of its Proceedings, punish its Members for disorderly Behaviour, and, with the Concurrence of two thirds, expel a Member.

Each House shall keep a Journal of its Proceedings, and from time to time publish the same, excepting such Parts as may in their Judgment require Secrecy; and the Yeas and Nays of the Members of either House on any question shall, at the Desire of one fifth of those Present, be entered on the Journal.

Neither House, during the Session of Congress, shall, without the Consent of the other, adjourn for more than three days, nor to any other Place than that in which the two Houses shall be sitting.

## Section 6.

The Senators and Representatives shall receive a Compensation for their Services, to be ascertained by Law, and paid out of the Treasury of the United States. They shall in all Cases, except Treason, Felony and Breach of the Peace, be privileged from Arrest during their Attendance at the Session of their respective Houses, and in going to and returning from the same; and for any Speech or Debate in either House, they shall not be questioned in any other Place.

No Senator or Representative shall, during the Time for which he was elected, be appointed to any civil Office under the Authority of the United States, which shall have been created, or the Emoluments whereof shall have been encreased during such time; and no Person holding any Office under the United States, shall be a Member of either House during his Continuance in Office.

## Section 7.

All Bills for raising Revenue shall originate in the House of Representatives; but the Senate may propose or concur with Amendments as on other Bills.

Every Bill which shall have passed the House of Representatives and the Senate, shall, before it become a Law, be presented to the President of the United States: If he approve he shall sign it, but if not he shall return it, with his Objections to that House in which it shall have originated, who shall enter the Objections at large on their Journal, and proceed to reconsider it. If after such Reconsideration two thirds of that House shall agree to pass the Bill, it shall be sent, together with the Objections, to the other House, by which it shall likewise be reconsidered, and if approved by two thirds of that House, it shall become a Law. But in all such Cases the Votes of both Houses shall be determined by yeas and Nays, and the Names of the Persons voting for and against the Bill shall be entered on the Journal of each House respectively. If any Bill shall not be returned by the President within ten Days (Sundays excepted) after it shall have been presented to him, the Same shall be a Law, in like Manner as if he had signed it, unless the Congress by their Adjournment prevent its Return, in which Case it shall not be a Law.

Every Order, Resolution, or Vote to which the Concurrence of the Senate and House of Representatives may be necessary (except on a question of Adjournment) shall be presented to the President of the United States; and before the Same shall take Effect, shall be approved by him, or being disapproved by him, shall be repassed by two thirds of the Senate and House of Representatives, according to the Rules and Limitations prescribed in the Case of a Bill.

### Section 8.

The Congress shall have Power To lay and collect Taxes, Duties, Imposts and Excises, to pay the Debts and provide for the common Defence and general Welfare of the United States; but all Duties, Imposts and Excises shall be uniform throughout the United States;

To borrow Money on the credit of the United States;

To regulate Commerce with foreign Nations, and among the several States, and with the Indian Tribes;

To establish an uniform Rule of Naturalization, and uniform Laws on the subject of Bankruptcies throughout the United States;

To coin Money, regulate the Value thereof, and of foreign Coin, and fix the Standard of Weights and Measures;

To provide for the Punishment of counterfeiting the Securities and current Coin of the United States;

To establish Post Offices and post Roads;

To promote the Progress of Science and useful Arts, by securing for limited Times to Authors and Inventors the exclusive Right to their respective Writings and Discoveries;

To constitute Tribunals inferior to the supreme Court;

To define and punish Piracies and Felonies committed on the high Seas, and Offences against the Law of Nations;

To declare War, grant Letters of Marque and Reprisal, and make Rules concerning Captures on Land and Water;

To raise and support Armies, but no Appropriation of Money to that Use shall be for a longer Term than two Years;

To provide and maintain a Navy;

To make Rules for the Government and Regulation of the land and naval Forces;

To provide for calling forth the Militia to execute the Laws of the Union, suppress Insurrections and repel Invasions;

To provide for organizing, arming, and disciplining, the Militia, and for governing such Part of them as may be employed in the Service of the United States, reserving to the States respectively, the Appointment of the Officers, and the Authority of training the Militia according to the discipline prescribed by Congress;

To exercise exclusive Legislation in all Cases whatsoever, over such District (not exceeding ten Miles square) as may, by Cession of particular States, and the Acceptance of Congress, become the Seat of the Government of the United States, and to exercise like Authority over all Places purchased by the Consent of the Legislature of the State in which the Same shall be, for the Erection of Forts, Magazines, Arsenals, dock-Yards, and other needful Buildings;—And

To make all Laws which shall be necessary and proper for carrying into Execution the foregoing Powers, and all other Powers vested by this Constitution in the Government of the United States, or in any Department or Officer thereof.

## Section 9.

The Migration or Importation of such Persons as any of the States now existing shall think proper to admit, shall not be prohibited by the Congress prior to the Year one thousand eight hundred and eight, but a Tax or duty may be imposed on such Importation, not exceeding ten dollars for each Person.

The Privilege of the Writ of Habeas Corpus shall not be suspended, unless when in Cases of Rebellion or Invasion the public Safety may require it.

No Bill of Attainder or ex post facto Law shall be passed.

No Capitation, or other direct, Tax shall be laid, unless in Proportion to the Census or enumeration herein before directed to be taken.

No Tax or Duty shall be laid on Articles exported from any State.

No Preference shall be given by any Regulation of Commerce or Revenue to the Ports of one State over those of another; nor shall Vessels bound to, or from, one State, be obliged to enter, clear, or pay Duties in another.

No Money shall be drawn from the Treasury, but in Consequence of Appropriations made by Law; and a regular Statement and Account of the Receipts and Expenditures of all public Money shall be published from time to time.

No Title of Nobility shall be granted by the United States: And no Person holding any Office of Profit or Trust under them, shall, without the Consent of the Congress, accept of any present, Emolument, Office, or Title, of any kind whatever, from any King, Prince, or foreign State.

## Section 10.

No State shall enter into any Treaty, Alliance, or Confederation; grant Letters of Marque and Reprisal; coin Money; emit Bills of Credit; make any Thing but gold and silver Coin a Tender in Payment of Debts; pass any Bill of Attainder, ex post facto Law, or Law impairing the Obligation of Contracts, or grant any Title of Nobility.

No State shall, without the Consent of the Congress, lay any Imposts or Duties on Imports or Exports, except what may be absolutely necessary for executing it's inspection Laws: and the net Produce of all Duties and Imposts, laid by any State on Imports or Exports, shall be for the Use of the Treasury of the United States; and all such Laws shall be subject to the Revision and Controul of the Congress.

No State shall, without the Consent of Congress, lay any Duty of Tonnage, keep Troops, or Ships of War in time of Peace, enter into any Agreement or Compact with another State, or with a foreign Power, or engage in War, unless actually invaded, or in such imminent Danger as will not admit of delay.

## ARTICLE II.

### Section 1.

The executive Power shall be vested in a President of the United States of America. He shall hold his Office during the Term of four Years, and, together with the Vice President, chosen for the same Term, be elected, as follows:

Each State shall appoint, in such Manner as the Legislature thereof may direct, a Number of Electors, equal to the whole Number of Senators and Representatives to which the State may be entitled in the Congress: but no Senator or Representative, or Person holding an Office of Trust or Profit under the United States, shall be appointed an Elector.

The Electors shall meet in their respective States, and vote by Ballot for two Persons, of whom one at least shall not be an Inhabitant of the same State with themselves. And they shall make a List of all the Persons voted for, and of the Number of Votes for each; which List they shall sign and certify, and transmit sealed to the Seat of the Government of the United States, directed to the President of the Senate. The President of the Senate shall, in the Presence of the Senate and House of Representatives, open all the Certificates, and the Votes shall then be counted. The Person having the greatest Number of Votes shall be the President, if such

Number be a Majority of the whole Number of Electors appointed; and if there be more than one who have such Majority, and have an equal Number of Votes, then the House of Representatives shall immediately chuse by Ballot one of them for President; and if no Person have a Majority, then from the five highest on the List the said House shall in like Manner chuse the President. But in chusing the President, the Votes shall be taken by States, the Representation from each State having one Vote; A quorum for this purpose shall consist of a Member or Members from two thirds of the States, and a Majority of all the States shall be necessary to a Choice. In every Case, after the Choice of the President, the Person having the greatest Number of Votes of the Electors shall be the Vice President. But if there should remain two or more who have equal Votes, the Senate shall chuse from them by Ballot the Vice President.

The Congress may determine the Time of chusing the Electors, and the Day on which they shall give their Votes; which Day shall be the same throughout the United States.

No Person except a natural born Citizen, or a Citizen of the United States, at the time of the Adoption of this Constitution, shall be eligible to the Office of President; neither shall any Person be eligible to that Office who shall not have attained to the Age of thirty five Years, and been fourteen Years a Resident within the United States.

In Case of the Removal of the President from Office, or of his Death, Resignation, or Inability to discharge the Powers and Duties of the said Office, the Same shall devolve on the Vice President, and the Congress may by Law provide for the Case of Removal, Death, Resignation or Inability, both of the President and Vice President, declaring what Officer shall then act as President, and such Officer shall act accordingly, until the Disability be removed, or a President shall be elected.

The President shall, at stated Times, receive for his Services, a Compensation, which shall neither be increased nor diminished during the Period for which he shall have been elected, and he shall not receive within that Period any other Emolument from the United States, or any of them.

Before he enter on the Execution of his Office, he shall take the following Oath or Affirmation:—"I do solemnly swear (or affirm) that I will faithfully execute the Office of President of the United States, and will to the best of my Ability, preserve, protect and defend the Constitution of the United States."

## Section 2.

The President shall be Commander in Chief of the Army and Navy of the United States, and of the Militia of the several States, when called into the actual Service of the United States; he may require the Opinion, in writing, of the principal Officer in each of the executive Departments, upon any Subject relating to the Duties of their respective Offices, and he shall have Power to grant Reprieves and Pardons for Offences against the United States, except in Cases of Impeachment.

He shall have Power, by and with the Advice and Consent of the Senate, to make Treaties, provided two thirds of the Senators present concur; and he shall nominate, and by and with the Advice and Consent of the Senate, shall appoint Ambassadors, other public Ministers and Consuls, Judges of the supreme Court, and all other Officers of the United States, whose Appointments are not herein otherwise provided for, and which shall be established by Law: but the Congress may by Law vest the Appointment of such inferior Officers, as they think proper, in the President alone, in the Courts of Law, or in the Heads of Departments.

The President shall have Power to fill up all Vacancies that may happen during the Recess of the Senate, by granting Commissions which shall expire at the End of their next Session.

## Section 3.

He shall from time to time give to the Congress Information of the State of the Union, and recommend to their Consideration such Measures as he shall judge necessary and expedient; he may, on extraordinary Occasions, convene both Houses, or either of them, and in Case of Disagreement between them, with Respect to the Time of Adjournment, he may adjourn them to such Time as he shall think proper; he shall receive Ambassadors and other public Ministers; he shall take Care that the Laws be faithfully executed, and shall Commission all the Officers of the United States.

### Section 4.

The President, Vice President and all civil Officers of the United States, shall be removed from Office on Impeachment for, and Conviction of, Treason, Bribery, or other high Crimes and Misdemeanors.

## ARTICLE III.

### Section 1.

The judicial Power of the United States shall be vested in one supreme Court, and in such inferior Courts as the Congress may from time to time ordain and establish. The Judges, both of the supreme and inferior Courts, shall hold their Offices during good Behaviour, and shall, at stated Times, receive for their Services a Compensation, which shall not be diminished during their Continuance in Office.

### Section 2.

The judicial Power shall extend to all Cases, in Law and Equity, arising under this Constitution, the Laws of the United States, and Treaties made, or which shall be made, under their Authority;—to all Cases affecting Ambassadors, other public Ministers and Consuls;—to all Cases of admiralty and maritime Jurisdiction;—to Controversies to which the United States shall be a Party;—to Controversies between two or more States;—between a State and Citizens of another State,—between Citizens of different States,—between Citizens of the same State claiming Lands under Grants of different States, and between a State, or the Citizens thereof, and foreign States, Citizens or Subjects.

In all Cases affecting Ambassadors, other public Ministers and Consuls, and those in which a State shall be Party, the supreme Court shall have original Jurisdiction. In all the other Cases before mentioned, the supreme Court shall have appellate Jurisdiction, both as to Law and Fact, with such Exceptions, and under such Regulations as the Congress shall make.

The Trial of all Crimes, except in Cases of Impeachment, shall be by Jury; and such Trial shall be held in the State where the said Crimes shall have been committed; but when not committed within any State, the Trial shall be at such Place or Places as the Congress may by Law have directed.

### Section 3.

Treason against the United States, shall consist only in levying War against them, or in adhering to their Enemies, giving them Aid and Comfort. No Person shall be convicted of Treason unless on the Testimony of two Witnesses to the same overt Act, or on Confession in open Court.

The Congress shall have Power to declare the Punishment of Treason, but no Attainder of Treason shall work Corruption of Blood, or Forfeiture except during the Life of the Person attainted.

## ARTICLE IV.

### Section 1.

Full Faith and Credit shall be given in each State to the public Acts, Records, and judicial Proceedings of every other State. And the Congress may by general Laws prescribe the Manner in which such Acts, Records and Proceedings shall be proved, and the Effect thereof.

### Section 2.

The Citizens of each State shall be entitled to all Privileges and Immunities of Citizens in the several States.

A Person charged in any State with Treason, Felony, or other Crime, who shall flee from Justice, and be found in another State, shall on Demand of the executive Authority of the State from which he fled, be delivered up, to be removed to the State having Jurisdiction of the Crime.

No Person held to Service or Labour in one State, under the Laws thereof, escaping into another, shall, in Consequence of any Law or Regulation therein, be discharged from such Service or Labour, but shall be delivered up on Claim of the Party to whom such Service or Labour may be due.

### Section 3.

New States may be admitted by the Congress into this Union; but no new State shall be formed or erected within the Jurisdiction of any other State; nor any State be formed by the Junction of two or more States, or Parts of States, without the Consent of the Legislatures of the States concerned as well as of the Congress.

The Congress shall have Power to dispose of and make all needful Rules and Regulations respecting the Territory or other Property belonging to the United States; and nothing in this Constitution shall be so construed as to Prejudice any Claims of the United States, or of any particular State.

### Section 4.

The United States shall guarantee to every State in this Union a Republican Form of Government, and shall protect each of them against Invasion; and on Application of the Legislature, or of the Executive (when the Legislature cannot be convened), against domestic Violence.

### ARTICLE V.

The Congress, whenever two thirds of both Houses shall deem it necessary, shall propose Amendments to this Constitution, or, on the Application of the Legislatures of two thirds of the several States, shall call a Convention for proposing Amendments, which, in either Case, shall be valid to all Intents and Purposes, as Part of this Constitution, when ratified by the Legislatures of three fourths of the several States, or by Conventions in three fourths thereof, as the one or the other Mode of Ratification may be proposed by the Congress; Provided that no Amendment which may be made prior to the Year One thousand eight hundred and eight shall in any Manner affect the first and fourth Clauses in the Ninth Section of the first Article; and that no State, without its Consent, shall be deprived of its equal Suffrage in the Senate.

### ARTICLE VI.

All Debts contracted and Engagements entered into, before the Adoption of this Constitution, shall be as valid against the United States under this Constitution, as under the Confederation.

This Constitution, and the Laws of the United States which shall be made in Pursuance thereof; and all Treaties made, or which shall be made, under the Authority of the United States, shall be the supreme Law of the Land; and the Judges in every State shall be bound thereby, any Thing in the Constitution or Laws of any State to the Contrary notwithstanding.

The Senators and Representatives before mentioned, and the Members of the several State Legislatures, and all executive and judicial Officers, both of the United States and of the several States, shall be bound by Oath or Affirmation, to support this Constitution; but no religious Test shall ever be required as a Qualification to any Office or public Trust under the United States.

### ARTICLE VII.

The Ratification of the Conventions of nine States, shall be sufficient for the Establishment of this Constitution between the States so ratifying the Same.

### THE BILL OF RIGHTS (Amendments 1–10)

Congress of the United States begun and held at the City of New-York, on Wednesday the fourth of March, one thousand seven hundred and eighty nine.

THE Conventions of a number of the States, having at the time of their adopting the Constitution, expressed a desire, in order to prevent misconstruction or abuse of its powers, that further declaratory and restrictive clauses should be added: And as extending the ground of public confidence in the Government, will best ensure the beneficent ends of its institution.

RESOLVED by the Senate and House of Representatives of the United States of America, in Congress assembled, two thirds of both Houses concurring, that the following Articles be proposed to the Legislatures of the several States, as amendments to the Constitution of the United States, all, or any of which Articles, when ratified by three fourths of the said Legislatures, to be valid to all intents and purposes, as part of the said Constitution; viz.

ARTICLES in addition to, and Amendment of the Constitution of the United States of America, proposed by Congress, and ratified by the Legislatures of the several States, pursuant to the fifth Article of the original Constitution.

## Amendment I

Congress shall make no law respecting an establishment of religion, or prohibiting the free exercise thereof; or abridging the freedom of speech, or of the press; or the right of the people peaceably to assemble, and to petition the Government for a redress of grievances.

## Amendment II

A well regulated Militia, being necessary to the security of a free State, the right of the people to keep and bear Arms, shall not be infringed.

## Amendment III

No Soldier shall, in time of peace be quartered in any house, without the consent of the Owner, nor in time of war, but in a manner to be prescribed by law.

## Amendment IV

The right of the people to be secure in their persons, houses, papers, and effects, against unreasonable searches and seizures, shall not be violated, and no Warrants shall issue, but upon probable cause, supported by Oath or affirmation, and particularly describing the place to be searched, and the persons or things to be seized.

## Amendment V

No person shall be held to answer for a capital, or otherwise infamous crime, unless on a presentment or indictment of a Grand Jury, except in cases arising in the land or naval forces, or in the Militia, when in actual service in time of War or public danger; nor shall any person be subject for the same offence to be twice put in jeopardy of life or limb; nor shall be compelled in any criminal case to be a witness against himself, nor be deprived of life, liberty, or property, without due process of law; nor shall private property be taken for public use, without just compensation.

## Amendment VI

In all criminal prosecutions, the accused shall enjoy the right to a speedy and public trial, by an impartial jury of the State and district wherein the crime shall have been committed, which district shall have been previously ascertained by law, and to be informed of the nature and cause of the accusation; to be confronted with the witnesses against him; to have compulsory process for obtaining witnesses in his favor, and to have the Assistance of Counsel for his defence.

## Amendment VII

In Suits at common law, where the value in controversy shall exceed twenty dollars, the right of trial by jury shall be preserved, and no fact tried by a jury, shall be otherwise re-examined in any Court of the United States, than according to the rules of the common law.

## Amendment VIII

Excessive bail shall not be required, nor excessive fines imposed, nor cruel and unusual punishments inflicted.

## Amendment IX

The enumeration in the Constitution, of certain rights, shall not be construed to deny or disparage others retained by the people.

## Amendment X

The powers not delegated to the United States by the Constitution, nor prohibited by it to the States, are reserved to the States respectively, or to the people.

## SUBSEQUENT AMENDMENTS

### Amendment XI

Passed by Congress March 4, 1794. Ratified February 7, 1795.

*Note:* Article III, section 2, of the Constitution was modified by amendment 11.

The Judicial power of the United States shall not be construed to extend to any suit in law or equity, commenced or prosecuted against one of the United States by Citizens of another State, or by Citizens or Subjects of any Foreign State.

## Amendment XII

Passed by Congress December 9, 1803. Ratified June 15, 1804.

*Note:* A portion of Article II, section 1 of the Constitution was superseded by the 12th amendment.

The Electors shall meet in their respective states and vote by ballot for President and Vice-President, one of whom, at least, shall not be an inhabitant of the same state with themselves; they shall name in their ballots the person voted for as President, and in distinct ballots the person voted for as Vice-President, and they shall make distinct lists of all persons voted for as President, and of all persons voted for as Vice-President, and of the number of votes for each, which lists they shall sign and certify, and transmit sealed to the seat of the government of the United States, directed to the President of the Senate;—the President of the Senate shall, in the presence of the Senate and House of Representatives, open all the certificates and the votes shall then be counted;—The person having the greatest number of votes for President, shall be the President, if such number be a majority of the whole number of Electors appointed; and if no person have such majority, then from the persons having the highest numbers not exceeding three on the list of those voted for as President, the House of Representatives shall choose immediately, by ballot, the President. But in choosing the President, the votes shall be taken by states, the representation from each state having one vote; a quorum for this purpose shall consist of a member or members from two-thirds of the states, and a majority of all the states shall be necessary to a choice. [And if the House of Representatives shall not choose a President whenever the right of choice shall devolve upon them, before the fourth day of March next following, then the Vice-President

shall act as President, as in case of the death or other constitutional disability of the President.—]* The person having the greatest number of votes as Vice-President, shall be the Vice-President, if such number be a majority of the whole number of Electors appointed, and if no person have a majority, then from the two highest numbers on the list, the Senate shall choose the Vice-President; a quorum for the purpose shall consist of two-thirds of the whole number of Senators, and a majority of the whole number shall be necessary to a choice. But no person constitutionally ineligible to the office of President shall be eligible to that of Vice-President of the United States.

## Amendment XIII

Passed by Congress January 31, 1865. Ratified December 6, 1865.

*Note:* A portion of Article IV, section 2, of the Constitution was superseded by the 13th amendment.

### Section 1.

Neither slavery nor involuntary servitude, except as a punishment for crime whereof the party shall have been duly convicted, shall exist within the United States, or any place subject to their jurisdiction.

### Section 2.

Congress shall have power to enforce this article by appropriate legislation.

## Amendment XIV

Passed by Congress June 13, 1866. Ratified July 9, 1868.

*Note:* Article I, section 2, of the Constitution was modified by section 2 of the 14th amendment.

### Section 1.

All persons born or naturalized in the United States, and subject to the jurisdiction thereof, are citizens of the United States and of the State wherein they reside. No State shall make or enforce any law which shall abridge the privileges or immunities of citizens of the United States; nor

---

*Superseded by section 3 of the 20th amendment.

shall any State deprive any person of life, liberty, or property, without due process of law; nor deny to any person within its jurisdiction the equal protection of the laws.

### Section 2.

Representatives shall be apportioned among the several States according to their respective numbers, counting the whole number of persons in each State, excluding Indians not taxed. But when the right to vote at any election for the choice of electors for President and Vice-President of the United States, Representatives in Congress, the Executive and Judicial officers of a State, or the members of the Legislature thereof, is denied to any of the male inhabitants of such State, being twenty-one years of age,* and citizens of the United States, or in any way abridged, except for participation in rebellion, or other crime, the basis of representation therein shall be reduced in the proportion which the number of such male citizens shall bear to the whole number of male citizens twenty-one years of age in such State.

### Section 3.

No person shall be a Senator or Representative in Congress, or elector of President and Vice-President, or hold any office, civil or military, under the United States, or under any State, who, having previously taken an oath, as a member of Congress, or as an officer of the United States, or as a member of any State legislature, or as an executive or judicial officer of any State, to support the Constitution of the United States, shall have engaged in insurrection or rebellion against the same, or given aid or comfort to the enemies thereof. But Congress may by a vote of two-thirds of each House, remove such disability.

### Section 4.

The validity of the public debt of the United States, authorized by law, including debts incurred for payment of pensions and bounties for services in suppressing insurrection or rebellion, shall not be questioned. But neither the United States nor any State shall assume or pay any debt or obligation incurred in aid of insurrection or rebellion against the

*Changed by section 1 of the 26th amendment.

United States, or any claim for the loss or emancipation of any slave; but all such debts, obligations and claims shall be held illegal and void.

### Section 5.

The Congress shall have the power to enforce, by appropriate legislation, the provisions of this article.

## Amendment XV

Passed by Congress February 26, 1869. Ratified February 3, 1870.

### Section 1.

The right of citizens of the United States to vote shall not be denied or abridged by the United States or by any State on account of race, color, or previous condition of servitude—

### Section 2.

The Congress shall have the power to enforce this article by appropriate legislation.

## Amendment XVI

Passed by Congress July 2, 1909. Ratified February 3, 1913.

*Note:* Article I, section 9, of the Constitution was modified by amendment 16.

The Congress shall have power to lay and collect taxes on incomes, from whatever source derived, without apportionment among the several States, and without regard to any census or enumeration.

## Amendment XVII

Passed by Congress May 13, 1912. Ratified April 8, 1913.

*Note:* Article I, section 3, of the Constitution was modified by the 17th amendment.

The Senate of the United States shall be composed of two Senators from each State, elected by the people thereof, for six years; and each Senator shall have one vote. The electors in each State shall have the qualifications requisite for electors of the most numerous branch of the State legislatures.

When vacancies happen in the representation of any State in the Senate, the executive authority of such State shall issue writs of election to fill such vacancies: Provided, That the legislature of any State may empower the executive thereof to make temporary appointments until the people fill the vacancies by election as the legislature may direct.

This amendment shall not be so construed as to affect the election or term of any Senator chosen before it becomes valid as part of the Constitution.

## Amendment XVIII

Passed by Congress December 18, 1917. Ratified January 16, 1919. Repealed by amendment 21.

### Section 1.

After one year from the ratification of this article the manufacture, sale, or transportation of intoxicating liquors within, the importation thereof into, or the exportation thereof from the United States and all territory subject to the jurisdiction thereof for beverage purposes is hereby prohibited.

### Section 2.

The Congress and the several States shall have concurrent power to enforce this article by appropriate legislation.

### Section 3.

This article shall be inoperative unless it shall have been ratified as an amendment to the Constitution by the legislatures of the several States, as provided in the Constitution, within seven years from the date of the submission hereof to the States by the Congress.

## Amendment XIX

Passed by Congress June 4, 1919. Ratified August 18, 1920.

The right of citizens of the United States to vote shall not be denied or abridged by the United States or by any State on account of sex.

Congress shall have power to enforce this article by appropriate legislation.

## Amendment XX

Passed by Congress March 2, 1932. Ratified January 23, 1933.

*Note:* Article I, section 4, of the Constitution was modified by section 2 of this amendment. In addition, a portion of the 12th amendment was superseded by section 3.

### Section 1.

The terms of the President and the Vice President shall end at noon on the 20th day of January, and the terms of Senators and Representatives at noon on the 3d day of January, of the years in which such terms would have ended if this article had not been ratified; and the terms of their successors shall then begin.

### Section 2.

The Congress shall assemble at least once in every year, and such meeting shall begin at noon on the 3d day of January, unless they shall by law appoint a different day.

### Section 3.

If, at the time fixed for the beginning of the term of the President, the President elect shall have died, the Vice President elect shall become President. If a President shall not have been chosen before the time fixed for the beginning of his term, or if the President elect shall have failed to qualify, then the Vice President elect shall act as President until a President shall have qualified; and the Congress may by law provide for the case wherein neither a President elect nor a Vice President shall have qualified, declaring who shall then act as President, or the manner in which one who is to act shall be selected, and such person shall act accordingly until a President or Vice President shall have qualified.

### Section 4.

The Congress may by law provide for the case of the death of any of the persons from whom the House of Representatives may choose a President whenever the right of choice shall have devolved upon them, and for the case of the death of any of the persons from whom the Senate may choose a Vice President whenever the right of choice shall have devolved upon them.

### Section 5.

Sections 1 and 2 shall take effect on the 15th day of October following the ratification of this article.

### Section 6.

This article shall be inoperative unless it shall have been ratified as an amendment to the Constitution by the legislatures of three-fourths of the several States within seven years from the date of its submission.

## Amendment XXI

Passed by Congress February 20, 1933. Ratified December 5, 1933.

### Section 1.

The eighteenth article of amendment to the Constitution of the United States is hereby repealed.

### Section 2.

The transportation or importation into any State, Territory, or Possession of the United States for delivery or use therein of intoxicating liquors, in violation of the laws thereof, is hereby prohibited.

### Section 3.

This article shall be inoperative unless it shall have been ratified as an amendment to the Constitution by conventions in the several States, as provided in the Constitution, within seven years from the date of the submission hereof to the States by the Congress.

## Amendment XXII

Passed by Congress March 21, 1947. Ratified February 27, 1951.

### Section 1.

No person shall be elected to the office of the President more than twice, and no person who has held the office of President, or acted as President, for more than two years of a term to which some other person was elected President shall be elected to the office of President more than once. But this Article shall not apply to any person holding the office of President when this Article was proposed by Congress, and shall not prevent any person who may be holding the office of President, or acting as President, during the term within which this Article becomes operative from holding the office of President or acting as President during the remainder of such term.

### Section 2.

This article shall be inoperative unless it shall have been ratified as an amendment to the Constitution by the legislatures of three-fourths of the several States within seven years from the date of its submission to the States by the Congress.

## Amendment XXIII

Passed by Congress June 16, 1960. Ratified March 29, 1961.

### Section 1.

The District constituting the seat of Government of the United States shall appoint in such manner as Congress may direct:

A number of electors of President and Vice President equal to the whole number of Senators and Representatives in Congress to which the District would be entitled if it were a State, but in no event more than the least populous State; they shall be in addition to those appointed by the States, but they shall be considered, for the purposes of the election of President and Vice President, to be electors appointed by a State; and they shall meet in the District and perform such duties as provided by the twelfth article of amendment.

### Section 2.

The Congress shall have power to enforce this article by appropriate legislation.

## Amendment XXIV

Passed by Congress August 27, 1962. Ratified January 23, 1964.

### Section 1.

The right of citizens of the United States to vote in any primary or other election for President or Vice President, for electors for President or Vice President, or for Senator or Representative in Congress, shall not be denied or abridged by the United States or any State by reason of failure to pay poll tax or other tax.

### Section 2.

The Congress shall have power to enforce this article by appropriate legislation.

## Amendment XXV

Passed by Congress July 6, 1965. Ratified February 10, 1967.

*Note:* Article II, section 1, of the Constitution was affected by the 25th amendment.

### Section 1.

In case of the removal of the President from office or of his death or resignation, the Vice President shall become President.

### Section 2.

Whenever there is a vacancy in the office of the Vice President, the President shall nominate a Vice President who shall take office upon confirmation by a majority vote of both Houses of Congress.

### Section 3.

Whenever the President transmits to the President pro tempore of the Senate and the Speaker of the House of Representatives his written declaration that he is unable to discharge the powers and duties of his office, and until he transmits to them a written declaration to the contrary, such powers and duties shall be discharged by the Vice President as Acting President.

### Section 4.

Whenever the Vice President and a majority of either the principal officers of the executive departments or of such other body as Congress may by law provide, transmit to the President pro tempore of the Senate and the Speaker of the House of Representatives their written declaration that the President is unable to discharge the powers and duties of his office, the Vice President shall immediately assume the powers and duties of the office as Acting President.

Thereafter, when the President transmits to the President pro tempore of the Senate and the Speaker of the House of Representatives his written declaration that no inability exists, he shall resume the powers and duties of his office unless the Vice President and a majority of either the principal officers of the executive department or of

such other body as Congress may by law provide, transmit within four days to the President pro tempore of the Senate and the Speaker of the House of Representatives their written declaration that the President is unable to discharge the powers and duties of his office. Thereupon Congress shall decide the issue, assembling within forty-eight hours for that purpose if not in session. If the Congress, within twenty-one days after receipt of the latter written declaration, or, if Congress is not in session, within twenty-one days after Congress is required to assemble, determines by two-thirds vote of both Houses that the President is unable to discharge the powers and duties of his office, the Vice President shall continue to discharge the same as Acting President; otherwise, the President shall resume the powers and duties of his office.

## Amendment XXVI

Passed by Congress March 23, 1971. Ratified July 1, 1971.

*Note:* Amendment 14, section 2, of the Constitution was modified by section 1 of the 26th amendment.

### Section 1.

The right of citizens of the United States, who are eighteen years of age or older, to vote shall not be denied or abridged by the United States or by any State on account of age.

### Section 2.

The Congress shall have power to enforce this article by appropriate legislation.

## Amendment XXVII

Originally proposed Sept. 25, 1789. Ratified May 7, 1992.

No law, varying the compensation for the services of the Senators and Representatives, shall take effect, until an election of representatives shall have intervened.

# Glossary

**Abandoned Property:** Property that is not owned by anyone because its former owner no longer exercises any general incident of ownership over the property.

**Abnormally Dangerous Activity:** An activity in which a defendant engages that cannot be performed safely and for which a defendant is held strictly liable for the harm caused if something goes wrong regardless of fault or precautions taken.

**Acceptance:** Manifestation of assent to the offer proposed.

**Accord and Satisfaction:** An agreement by one party to accept as full payment the other party's payment of less than the full sum of a debt owed.

**Actual Authority:** Authority that is given to the agent to act, either expressly given by the principal or inferred from words or conduct of the principal. For example, it is authority validly granted by the partners in a partnership to a partner or an agent to perform an act or enter into an agreement that will bind the entire partnership. The concept applies to other business forms as well.

**Administrative Agencies:** Agencies of the executive branch of federal and state governments. The administrative agencies are charged with enforcing the laws created by the executive branch of the government. These agencies sometimes exercise judicial power, having their own courts. They also exercise legislative power when they draft administrative rules and regulations under the direction and oversight of the legislative branch.

**Administrative Law:** Rules and regulations created by the administrative agencies. These administrative laws cannot contradict federal or state statutes or constitutions.

**Adoption:** Under contract law, the agreement by a third party to take on both the benefits and obligations of one of the parties to a contract, whereby the original party remains liable under the contract.

**Adversary System:** The procedural system for trying lawsuits in which each side through its attorney presents its respective legal case in the best possible light to the judge and jury as neutral decision makers. The theory is that the truth will come from this give-and-take of arguments. The U.S. system is derived from England and is common to most of her former colonies.

**Advisory Opinions:** Hypothetical opinions issued by courts when there is no matter in controversy. U.S. courts do not issue advisory opinions.

**Affirmative Action:** A policy that gives preference to protected individuals based on their race, color, religion, national origin, and gender, if the protected individuals are otherwise qualified for the position.

**Age Discrimination in Employment Act (ADEA):** A federal statute that makes it illegal to discriminate against an employee or job applicant over 40 years of age because of his or her age.

**Agency:** A fiduciary relationship in which a principal authorizes an agent to act on the principal's behalf, subject to the principal's control, as if the agent were the principal.

**Agent:** A person acting under instruction from another (the principal) for the other's benefit.

**Aggregate Theory:** A partnership theory stating that the partnership enterprise does not have an existence separate from the individuals who are its partners.

**Alien Corporation:** Corporation chartered under the laws of another country that is doing business in a U.S. state.

**Alienation:** Disposal or transfer of property in a manner of the owner's choosing.

**Allege:** To assert that a given fact is true or false in a lawsuit. An allegation is not yet proven. Proof that an allegation is true is determined by the trier of fact (usually a jury) in a case.

**Americans with Disabilities Act (ADA):** A federal statute that prevents employers from discriminating against qualified individuals with disabilities and that requires employers to make reasonable accommodations to applicants and employees with disabilities unless doing so would cause the employer undue hardship.

**Annual Meetings:** Meetings that state statutes require corporations to hold for the board of directors to discuss corporate business with shareholders.

**Anticipatory Repudiation:** Repudiation of a contractual duty by one party to a contract before performance is due when the other party to the contract makes clear statements or conducts himself in such a way as to indicate that he will not be performing under the contract. In such event, the former party may treat the latter conduct as a breach of contract, stop performance under the contract, and immediately sue for breach of contract.

**Apparent Authority:** The authority of the agent, as reasonably perceived by a third party, to act on behalf of the principal. For example, it is authority that is *not* validly granted by the partners in a partnership to a partner or an agent to perform an act or enter into an agreement that will bind the entire partnership. The act, however, *will* bind the entire partnership when a reasonable person in that time and place, dealing with the partner or agent as a third party, would have no reason to know that the partner or agent did not have authority. The concept applies to other business forms as well.

**Appeal:** A request to a higher court by an aggrieved party in a lawsuit to correct errors of law made by the judge at the lower court.

**Appeals Court:** A court superior to the court of original jurisdiction in any given court structure. The appeals court hears issues of law, not facts. It has no jury, and it decides matters by the majority vote of multiple judges hearing the case.

**Arbitration:** The resolution of a dispute outside the court system through an agreement of the parties that a third party will decide the dispute.

**Articles of Incorporation:** The filing paperwork submitted to and accepted by the secretary of state in the state where a corporation is created that are the founding documents of a corporation and that give the corporation its legal status as a separate entity.

**Articles of Termination:** The formal paperwork filed with the state authority that ends an LLC's existence.

**Assault:** An intentional, unexcused act that creates in another person a reasonable apprehension that he is about to suffer an immediate harmful or offensive physical contact.

**Assignment:** The transfer of a party's rights under a contract to someone else.

**Assumpsit:** A historical cause of action for recovery for breach of contract. It is based in tort law.

**Assumption of the Risk:** Under the law of torts, the act of assuming the risk of loss or injury by taking a dangerous job or engaging in a dangerous activity. The plaintiff knows the risk of harm in a given situation yet still participates in the behavior. It is a defense to certain tort claims.

**Attorneys:** The professional advocates for one side or the other in a legal transaction or lawsuit. Attorneys, like judges, are officers of the court. They are subject to a code of ethics and legal restrictions on their advocacy. For instance, they may not knowingly lie, they may not misrepresent law or facts, and they may not assist in the commission of a crime or its cover-up.

**Authorization:** Permission to do business as a foreign corporation in a state, granted by the Department of State in that state.

**Bailee:** Person granted possession and control of personal property by another for a temporary period.

**Bailments:** The willing or unwilling grant of possession and control of personal property by the owner to another party.

**Bailor:** Person granting possession and control of personal property to another for a temporary period.

**Bargaining Unit:** A group of employees who have been authorized to engage in collective bargaining on behalf of other employees.

**Battery:** An intentional tort in which there is a completed act of harmful or offensive contact.

**Benefit:** Something received as a part of a contract; the profits gained by a property owner because of a property's use.

**Beyond a Reasonable Doubt:** A balancing test used in criminal cases whereby the prosecution has met the standard of proof if all of the evidence on a given issue supports the prosecution's argument, with no room for a reasonable person to doubt the prosecution's version of events.

**Bilateral Contract:** A contract in which both parties make promises.

**Board of Directors:** A group elected by the shareholders of a corporation for a fixed term of office and that provides overall direction to the corporation. It approves large changes in vision and direction, and it appoints the officers of the corporation.

**Board of Managers:** A group of individuals chosen to manage the LLC in manager-managed LLCs. The board of managers functions like a board of directors.

**Bona Fide Occupational Qualification (BFOQ):** A job requirement that is reasonably necessary to the normal operation of the business.

**Bond:** A debt security whereby the company, in exchange for borrowed money, agrees to pay back investors holding the bonds a set amount of interest either periodically or at the end of the bond's term, and then the principal amount at the bond's maturity.

**Bricks and Mortar:** A physical location of a business where customers come to buy goods or consult with professionals.

**Burden of Proof:** A term used to describe a party's duty to prove any given element of a cause of action. Usually the plaintiff or prosecution has the burden of proof and must provide evidence that facts supporting an allegation in a lawsuit did or did not occur.

**Buyout Agreement:** An agreement that details what happens to a shareholder's stock when the shareholder parts ways with a corporation.

**Bylaws:** The basic rules and regulations internal to a corporation that govern those internal workings and the relationships between all of the shareholders, directors, and officers of the corporation.

**C Corporation:** A type of corporation that pays taxes at the corporate level and whose stock may be publicly traded. Most large corporations are required to have C corporation status. C corporations may retain earnings within the corporation or distribute them to shareholders as dividends.

**Capitalism:** An economic system that relies on competition in the free market and on the private ownership of goods and the means of production of goods. The theory of capitalism relies on the reinvestment of profits combined with the competition that results because of the free market. This combination results in increases in wealth for the owners of the capital. Legal restraints on the early excesses of capitalism have tempered the extreme inequities that can and have resulted from unregulated capitalist behavior and have allowed the increase in wealth to spread from the owners of the means of production themselves to the society at large.

**Caselaw:** Judge-made law coming out of the common law tradition. The decision made by a judge in a court case serves as precedent for other cases like it within that same jurisdiction. In that way, later cases are treated in the same manner as prior cases. Caselaw also can interpret the constitution, statutory law, administrative law, and prior cases from the deciding court or courts that are of a lower rank than the deciding court.

**Cause-in-Fact:** The subset of causation in negligence that holds that an injury would not have occurred but for the defendant's negligence.

**Cause of Action:** A reason to sue in a court of law. Each cause of action (there are thousands of types) has specific elements that must be alleged to remain in court, and proven in order for the plaintiff to recover.

**Certificate of Deposit:** A negotiable instrument entitling the bearer to receive a fixed sum of interest and principal from a bank on a deposit at the maturity date.

**Certificate of Limited Partnership:** A certificate filed with the secretary of state to form a limited partnership.

**Circuit Courts:** The appeals-level court in the federal court system.

**Civil Law:** One of two basic divisions of the law that governs the basic relationships between people and business in everyday activity. Violations of civil law are punished by fines, monetary damages, and other enforcement tools that do not involve the criminal court system of crime and punishment.

**Class Action Fairness Act of 2005 (CAFA):** A federal law that increased federal court jurisdiction over class actions where the amount in controversy was more than $5 million and there are plaintiffs who come from several different states.

**Class Action Lawsuits:** Cases in which one or more plaintiffs represent the interests of all the plaintiffs who have similar damages from a similar set of facts.

**Clear and Convincing Evidence:** A balancing test used in certain high-stakes civil cases whereby plaintiffs have met the standard of proof if a strong majority of the evidence on a given issue is in their favor. This standard falls between the preponderance of the evidence and the beyond a reasonable doubt standards.

**Code of Ethics:** A code, sometimes called a code of professional conduct, for attorneys that requires them to operate with strict limits on behavior in order to maintain the integrity of the legal profession, the legal process, and the legal system itself.

**Collective Bargaining Agreement:** A contract between an employer and a union that regulates employees' working conditions. Its terms are negotiated by the employer and representatives of the bargaining unit.

**Commercial Paper:** In this context, an alternative name for negotiable instruments.

**Common Law:** A system of law originating in England in the medieval period that is derived from judicial decisions. It is the basis of the legal systems in most countries that were colonized by England, including the United States (except Louisiana—which had French roots), Canada (except Quebec—which also has French heritage), Australia, and New Zealand. The common law system relies on judge-made law from similar cases in similar circumstances, so that the law in the jurisdiction is applied in "common" to all.

**Common Stock:** The standard stock issued by a corporation that provides the right to vote, to dividends, and to a share of the assets of the corporation upon dissolution.

**Community Property:** Ownership form in western states whereby any property acquired by either spouse during the course of a marriage (with the exception of property acquired by inheritance or gift to one spouse) is considered community property and both spouses have an undivided 50 percent interest in the property.

**Comparative Negligence:** A defense to unintentional torts that provides that if the plaintiff was negligent (as well as the defendant), the plaintiff can only recover a portion of his damages from the defendant because he caused some of his own injuries.

**Compensatory Damages:** Cash compensation for a breach of contract limited to the provable amount required to make the injured party whole.

**Condition Precedent:** A condition that must be met before a party's promise under a contract becomes absolute.

**Congress:** The governing assembly of the U.S. federal government. Congress is composed of two houses, the House of Representatives and the Senate. Each state sends two senators to Congress. Each state also sends representatives to Congress based upon the state's population. Congress is created by the United States Constitution and is empowered to create statutory law.

**Consequential Damages:** Damages that do not directly flow from the breach of contract but rather occur as a secondary result of the breach.

**Consideration:** The bargain of the contract—a benefit conferred by or detriment incurred at the request of the other party.

**Consolidation:** The combining of corporate assets whereby two corporations form a new, successor third corporation.

**Constitution:** The foundational document of the federal government. State governments also have constitutions. The United States Constitution is unique in that it generally provides limits on what the federal government can do, and it provides that all other rights, including the rights specifically listed in the Bill of Rights (the first ten Amendments to the Constitution), belong to the people (private individuals and state governments). All laws passed in the United States must conform to the limits of the Constitution, else they are unconstitutional and cannot be enforced.

**Constructive Condition:** A condition that is not agreed upon by the parties or mentioned in the contract but rather is supplied by the court in the interest of fairness.

**Contract:** An agreement or exchange of promises that is legally enforceable.

**Contractual Capacity:** The legal ability of a person to enter into a contractual relationship.

**Contractual Intent:** The purposefulness of forming a contractual relationship.

**Contribution:** A companion legal theory to joint and several liability whereby when two or more parties are found jointly and severally liable for a debt, and the debt is collected from the debtor parties in an uneven manner, the party who paid more to satisfy the debt may collect from the parties who paid less in order to make the debt burden more fair.

**Contributory Negligence:** A defense to unintentional torts that provides that if the plaintiff was negligent at all, she would not be able to recover for any of the injuries caused by the defendant.

**Control:** The mechanisms by which a business is governed.

**Controlling the Assault of Non-Solicited Pornography and Marketing Act (CAN-SPAM):** A federal law that places restrictions on bulk electronic marketing.

**Copyrights:** Property rights granted by a government to the author or creator of an original work.

**Corporate Formalities:** A term used to describe the actions that a corporation must take in order to be considered a corporation in good standing and to remain as a corporation in good standing with the relevant state government. The corporation must look and act as a corporation is required to by law.

**Corporation:** A legal entity independent from its owners that is usually formed to do business. It exists under state law and has most of the rights, duties, and obligations of a flesh-and-blood person.

**Corporation by Estoppel:** An otherwise defective corporation that the courts treat as if it is a valid corporation for the purposes of that corporation's relationship with one specific third party.

**Counteroffer:** A rejection of an offer and the creation of a new offer.

**Course of Dealing:** How the parties have done business in the past. It is a legal concept embodied in the UCC that recognizes that parties develop contractual habits after dealing with one another over the years. A court will interpret the pattern of business conduct between two parties over time across several contracts as an indication of what the parties meant for the written words of the present contract to mean.

**Course of Performance:** A legal concept embodied in the UCC that recognizes that parties develop contractual habits after dealing with one another over the years. A court will interpret the pattern of business conduct between two parties over time within one contract as an indication of what the parties meant for the written words of the contract to mean.

**Court of Original Jurisdiction:** The court that first hears a lawsuit in a jurisdiction. A court of original jurisdiction is a trial court.

**Courts of Equity:** Courts historically controlled by the church in England. Equity courts generally gave other forms of legal relief besides money in lawsuits (for example, injunctions, property, etc.).

**Courts of Law:** Courts historically controlled by the king in England. Law courts generally gave money damages in civil lawsuits.

**Covenants:** Promises that are attached to real property and contained in deeds.

**Criminal Law:** One of two basic divisions of the law that governs the behavior of individuals and the safety of the society as a whole. Violations of criminal law are punishable by fines, probation, community service, imprisonment, and even death, depending on the severity of the crime.

**Cyber Tort:** Use of the Internet and modern communications technologies like mobile phones that causes harm to others.

**Damages:** Money to be paid to the plaintiff for injuries or loss caused by the defendant.

**De Facto Corporation:** A corporation that has failed to meet some legal requirement for valid existence but otherwise—factually—looks, acts, and performs like a corporation.

**De Jure Corporation:** A corporation that has been formed in accordance with all applicable laws.

**Debt Securities:** Securities issued by a corporation in order to raise funds. They represent a debt of the corporation, but not an ownership interest.

**Declaration of Purpose:** A legal description of the purposes of a corporation's founding that is required to be included in the articles of incorporation.

**Deed:** A written document through which ownership and title to real property or an interest in real property is conveyed between parties.

**Defective Corporation:** An attempted corporation that has failed to complete all the requirements for legal corporate status successfully.

**Defendant:** The party who is accused of breaking a criminal law or causing civil damages to the plaintiff.

**Delegation:** A party's appointment of another person to fulfill the duties required of the party under the contract.

**Design Defect:** A products-liability defective condition that occurs when the product was poorly designed.

**Design Patents:** Patents granted to anyone who invents a new, original, and ornamental design for an article of manufacture.

**Destruction:** The ruination of a property owner's property. This incident of ownership gives property owners the right to destroy property they own.

**Detriment:** Loss or harm that comes from a person's acting based on wrong information, thereby placing him or her in a worse position than if no action had been taken.

**Disclosed Principal:** A principal who is known by and identified to the third party when the contract is made by the agent.

**Disparate Impact Discrimination:** A type of illegal discrimination in which nondiscriminatory actions, neutral on their face, can have a discriminatory impact on protected groups of people.

**Disparate Treatment Discrimination:** A type of illegal discrimination that is intentional and discriminatory on its face.

**Disposition of Assets:** A transfer of corporate assets outside the corporation.

**Dispute Resolution Clause:** A clause in a contract that describes how disputes that arise under the contract are to be resolved.

**Dissociation:** A partner's separation from a partnership.

**Dissolution of a Corporation:** The legal process of terminating the existence of a corporation.

**Dividends:** The share of C corporation earnings and profits distributed to the shareholders.

**Domestic Corporation:** Corporation doing business in the state where it is incorporated.

**Donee:** The recipient of a gift.

**Donor:** The maker of a gift.

**Double Jeopardy:** Being prosecuted twice for the same alleged crime, prohibited by the Fifth Amendment to the U.S. Constitution. The clause reads: "nor shall any person be subject for the same offence to be twice put in jeopardy of life or limb."

**Double Taxation:** Taxation of a business's profits twice—first, at the level of the business, and second, at the level of the owners/shareholders.

**Draft:** An order that payment be made, such as a check.

**Duress:** Improper pressure on another party in order to force the other party to do something against his or her will. Duress may be mental or physical.

**Duty of Loyalty:** The duty of the agent to act in the principal's interest, and not in the agent's own interest.

**Duty to Perform:** The duty of an agent to perform his or her duties under an agency agreement.

**E-Agent:** A computer program that works on behalf of a principal to execute instructions based on parameters ordered by the principal.

**E-Commerce:** Any commerce in electronic form.

**E-Contract:** A contract entered into electronically.

**Easements:** An interest in real property owned by another person which gives its holder the right to use the land for a specific purpose or prevent something from being done on it.

**Electronic Communications Privacy Act of 1986:** A federal statute that permits employers to monitor employee business-related electronic communications but not personal ones, unless by employee consent.

**Electronic Signatures in Global and National Commerce Act (E-SIGN Act):** A federal law that provides that all contracts, records, or signatures that are in electronic form are legally valid to the extent they would be legally valid if they were in printed form on paper.

**Eminent Domain:** A procedure whereby the government may take private property for a public use with just compensation.

**Employee:** The party to the employment relationship who is hired by an employer to perform work.

**Employee Retirement Income Security Act of 1974 (ERISA):** A federal statute that provides standards and controls for pension and retirement plans.

**Employer:** The party to the employment relationship who hires workers and pays their wages or salary in exchange for the workers' performance of work.

**Employment at Will:** A doctrine providing that either the employer or the employee has the power to terminate the employment relationship at any time and for any reason.

**Employment Discrimination Laws:** A set of laws that prohibits an employer from treating certain employees or applicants differently because of their status as a member of a protected group.

**Entity Theory:** A partnership theory stating that the partnership is an enterprise separate from the individual partners.

**Equal Employment Opportunity Act of 1972:** A federal statute that created the EEOC.

**Equal Employment Opportunity Commission (EEOC):** A federal agency that administers and enforces the provisions of Title VII and other employment discrimination laws.

**Equal Pay Act:** A federal statute requiring that men and women be paid the same for work that requires equal levels of skill, effort, and responsibility, performed under similar conditions.

**Equity Security:** A security issued by a corporation that represents a right of ownership or a right to a share of profits in the corporation.

**Estoppel:** A legal doctrine that prevents a person from asserting a claim that contradicts what that person has said or done before or what

has been established as true. Here, it refers to a doctrine that prevents a defective corporation and a third party from denying the existence of the corporation. *See also* Corporation by Estoppel

**Evidence:** Facts that are related to a case. Relevant evidence is evidence that will help prove or disprove an issue presented in a case. Admissible evidence is relevant evidence that will be considered by a judge or jury in a trial.

**Exclusion:** The state of being kept from using property that the owner holds. This incident of ownership of property that gives the property owner the right to exclude others from using the property.

**Exclusivity:** A legal theory that provides that a property owner has the right to exclude others from the property

**Executive Branch:** The branch of government headed by the President at the national level and by governors at the state level. The executive branch is responsible for enforcing the laws.

**Executory Promises:** Promises to be performed in the future.

**Express Condition:** A condition that the parties have agreed upon and that is explicitly stated in the contract.

**Failure to Warn:** A products-liability defective condition that occurs when there are dangers inherent in the products that are not obvious to the user and the defendant did not warn of those dangers.

**Family and Medical Leave Act of 1993 (FMLA):** A federal statute mandating that certain employers must provide an eligible employee up to a total of 12 weeks of unpaid leave during any 12-month period.

**Federal Insurance Contribution Act (FICA):** A federal statute that requires the employer and the employee to contribute tax dollars to Social Security and Medicare.

**Federal Unemployment Tax Act of 1935:** A federal statute that provides unemployment compensation to the involuntarily unemployed.

**Federalism:** A governmental system in which political and legal authority is split between a central government and other units of government that together make up the whole. In the United

States power is split between the 50 states and the national federal government.

**Fiduciary Duty:** The duty to act in good faith and reasonable dealing and in the other's best interest when handling the affairs of another person in a particular matter.

**Foreign Corporation:** U.S.-chartered corporation (chartered in a U.S. state) doing business in another U.S. state.

**Foreign LLC:** An LLC doing business in a state other than the state where it was formed.

**Forum Shopping:** A tactic used by plaintiffs to look for the state or court with the most favorable laws to bring a claim.

**Fraud:** A knowing misrepresentation of the truth or concealment of a material fact to trick someone into entering into a transaction that he or she would otherwise not have entered into.

**Frustration of Purpose:** Theory used to discharge a contract that has lost its purpose because of a change in circumstance, although performance is not technically impossible.

**General Incidents of Ownership:** The rights of control of property, which are possession, exclusion, alienation, use, benefit, and destruction.

**General Partner:** A partner in a standard partnership; also a partner in a limited partnership who has full control of the management of the business as well as full personal liability.

**Gift:** A transfer of property whereby a donor gives up all dominion over and control of a piece of property to a willing donee for no compensation.

**Good:** A movable item as defined by the UCC.

**Hostile Work Environment Harassment:** A type of sexual harassment that occurs when there is a work environment pervasive with sexual advances, or unwelcome sex-related humor or comments.

**Illusory Promise:** A promise that is based on the whim of the promisor but without the intention to really perform.

**Implied Agency Relationship:** Relationship created by the observed conduct of the principal that shows an intention to create an agency.

**Implied-in-Law Contract:** A contract implied by a court of law. It is the same as a quasi contract. The court will conclude that a contract exists based on what has transpired between the parties.

**Incidental Beneficiary:** A third-party beneficiary not mentioned in the contract.

**Indemnify:** To reimburse or promise to reimburse a party for a payment made.

**Independent Contractor:** A party hired to perform a specific service or who works independently to accomplish a specific goal or set of goals on behalf of a principal. How the independent contractor completes the task cannot be controlled by the person who hires him or her.

**Information Return:** A return filed with the taxing authority by a business entity that enjoys pass-through taxation. The information return lists profits and losses and other details of the business's performance for the year, and it sets out how those profits or losses were divided between the owners of the business.

**Injunction:** A court order requiring a party to a dispute to do or refrain from doing something.

**Intellectual Property:** The "intangible" personal property primarily made up of copyrights, trademarks, and patents.

**Intended Beneficiary:** A third-party beneficiary mentioned in the contract.

**Intent to Deceive:** The intent to obtain a thing of value through misrepresentation.

**Intentional Torts:** Torts in which a person acts with intention and as a result harms another person.

**Invitation to Deal:** An act that looks like an offer but is simply an invitation to start the negotiation process or to come in and buy.

**Issued Shares:** A term used to designate shares of stock that are actually held by shareholders.

**Joint and Several Liability:** Liability that is apportioned among two or more parties or borne by only one or a few select members of the group. Under this legal principle, the plaintiff sues more than one defendant both together and separately and can recover the entire amount of damages from either one, both, or all of the multiple defendants. The plaintiff cannot recover more than the damages owed.

**Joint Tenancy:** Property ownership form in which the owners all own equal undivided shares in the entire property. Each owner's share passes to the remaining owners upon her death.

**Judge:** An officer of the court who acts as the "umpire" of a case, in order to ensure that procedure is properly followed and the law is enforced. The judge also acts as the interpreter of the law in the case and issues rulings that may act as new law and have precedential value. Judges are also called justices if they sit on the highest court of their jurisdiction.

**Judicial Branch:** The branch of government made up of the courts at the state and federal levels. The judicial branch is responsible for interpreting existing law, although the very act of interpreting the law makes new caselaw.

**Judicial Review:** The power of the courts to review statutes, administrative rules and regulations, and other acts of government when those laws are brought before them in a lawsuit. The courts review these laws to determine if they violate the Constitution.

**Jurisdiction:** The geographical area and subject matter within which a given governmental entity has power.

**Jury:** The finders of fact in a lawsuit. The jury is usually composed of 12 people of legal age in the jurisdiction, although numbers may vary.

**Lawsuit:** A matter that is heard before a court, wherein one side is seeking money or property, or in some cases punishment, from the other side. Lawsuits in the United States must be "real world," that is, there must be a matter in controversy for the court to decide.

**Leases:** Contractual tools used by property owners to transfer the possession and use of a piece of property for a temporary time period.

**Legal Reporters:** Books that contain written opinions of appeals courts that may be used as precedent in later cases.

**Legality of Subject Matter:** One of the requirements of a valid contract, meaning that a contract can only be formed for a legal purpose.

**Legislative Branch:** The branch of federal and state governments made up of Congress and the state legislatures, respectively. The legislative branch is responsible for making the laws.

**Lessee:** Person granted possession and control of real property by another for a temporary period.

**Lessors:** Persons granting possession and control of real property to another for a temporary period.

**Liability:** Responsibility for the inappropriate action or the inaction of a person or an entity like a business.

**License:** Contractual tool that grants a licensee the right to use the property of a licensor for a specific purpose.

**Licensee:** Person granted the right to use property of another for a specific purpose for a specific period of time.

**Licensor:** Person granting another the right to use property for a specific purpose for a specific period of time.

**Limited Liability:** Liability that is restricted by law or by contract and that prevents the owner of a business from being held personally liable for business debts and obligations. The owner can only lose his or her investment in that company.

**Limited Liability Companies (LLCs):** A relatively new form of legal business entity that combines the limited liability of a corporation with the pass-through taxation features and ease of management of a partnership.

**Limited Liability Partnerships (LLPs):** A variation on the general partnership in which partners are personally liable for the debts of the partnership as in a general partnership, but they are not personally liable for the torts (professional malpractice, usually) of the other partners. Many states restrict use of the LLP business form to professional businesses like those of attorneys, doctors, architects, and the like.

**Limited Partner:** In a limited partnership, the partner who contributes capital and has personal liability only to the extent of that capital contribution but who cannot participate in management or operations of the partnership in any way.

**Limited Partnership:** An organization of partners with one or more general partners who control the business and have full liability and one or more limited partners who contribute capital and have limited liability but who cannot participate in management or operations of the business in any way.

**Liquidated Damages:** An amount agreed upon at the making of the contract to be recovered by one party if the other party breaches.

**LLC at Will:** An LLC that is created without a date of dissolution.

**Magna Carta:** A "great charter" signed in 1215 by John of England that granted, among other rights and privileges, the right to judgment of the accused by a jury of peers. Initially intended as a right for nobility, the right expanded over time to include the entire population.

**Manager-Managed LLC:** An LLC managed by hired managers chosen by the members.

**Manufacturing Defects:** A products-liability defective condition that occurs when a product was correctly and safely designed but there was an error in the manufacturing process on one, some, or all of the units.

**Material Facts:** The information that a reasonable person needs in order to make a decision on a particular subject.

**Matter in Controversy:** A real-world issue for a court to decide in a lawsuit.

**Maturity:** The end date for a bond at which the principal and outstanding interest are repaid.

**Mediation:** Process whereby a dispute is resolved outside the court system through an agreement of the parties that a third party will make non-binding recommendations to decide the dispute.

**Medicare:** A federal statute that provides health insurance for persons 65 years old and older and for disabled persons under age 65.

**Member-Managed LLC:** An LLC managed by its members.

**Member:** An owner of an LLC.

**Merchant:** A buyer or seller of goods with specialized knowledge about that good. This includes any commercial sellers of a product in the ordinary course of business.

**Merger:** The combining of corporate assets whereby one corporation is absorbed by another.

**Mirror Image Rule:** This common law concept providing that no terms of the offer can be changed in the acceptance. If the acceptance looks different from the offer, it will be considered a counteroffer.

**Misrepresentation:** A misstatement of fact.

**Mistake:** A misunderstanding that materially impacts the contract.

**Mitigation:** Reduction of damages through the efforts of the injured party. This is a self-help requirement.

**Mutual Assent:** A valid offer by the offeror and a valid acceptance by the offeree.

**Mutual Mistake:** A mistake on which both parties to the contract act.

**Mutual Rescission:** Agreement by both parties to relieve one another of the obligation to perform.

**National Institute for Occupational Safety and Health:** A federal agency that conducts research on workplace safety and makes recommendations to OSHA.

**National Labor Relations Board:** A federal agency that monitors employer-union relations.

**Negligence:** An unintentional tort in which a defendant breaches a duty that he owes to another, causing damages.

**Negotiable Instrument:** A written instrument of commerce that includes a promise to pay or order for payment to be made.

**Notary:** An individual who is authorized by the state to authenticate signatures on documents.

**Note:** A promise for payment in the future, such as a certificate of deposit.

**Notice:** A legal requirement that corporate meetings must be announced and declared in such a way as to notify all persons eligible to attend the meeting.

**Novation:** Under contract law, the agreement by a third party to take on both the benefits and obligations of one of the parties to a contract, whereby the original party is no longer liable under the contract.

**Occupational Safety and Health Act of 1970:** A federal statute that is meant to protect employees' safety and health while on the job through workplace safety standards.

**Occupational Safety and Health Administration (OSHA):** A federal agency that sets standards and regulations, enforces the relevant legislation, and makes workplace inspections.

**Occupational Safety and Health Review Commission:** A federal agency that acts as a review board to hear appeals from measures taken by OSHA.

**Offer:** A proposal by one party to another showing an intent to enter into a valid contract.

**Offeree:** The party to whom an offer is made.

**Offeror:** The party making an offer.

**Officers:** Those charged with the day-to-day running of a corporation. The officers are appointed by the board of directors.

**Operating Agreement:** A written contract between the members of an LLC that sets out the basic parameters of the members' relationships with each other.

**Oral Contract:** A contract created by verbal discussion but not memorialized in writing.

**Overruled:** A term used to describe the overturning or setting aside of precedent from one court, when it is voided and replaced by another precedent from the same or a higher-level court.

**Par Value:** The nominal value assigned to the stock as a part of the issuance process.

**Parol Evidence Rule:** A rule of contract construction that says a written agreement purporting to be the full and final expression of the parties' intentions may not be altered or contradicted by evidence that adds to, varies, or contradicts the agreement or by oral or written agreements made prior to the writing.

**Partial Integration:** Discussing the parties' agreement but not purporting to be a full expression of the agreement.

**Partially Disclosed Principal:** A principal who is known to exist by the third party, but is not identified, when the contract is made by the agent.

**Partnership:** A form of business created when two or more persons or other legal entities (like corporations) join together with common purpose to accomplish a goal for profit.

**Partnership Agreement:** A contract (usually written, although it may be oral) between two or more partners in a general partnership, limited partnership, or limited liability partnership that sets out the basic parameters of the partners' relationship with each other. It may be very simple, or it may include formation, operating, and dissolution rules and be as extensive as the partners desire.

**Partnership by Estoppel:** A partnership implied by law when someone holds himself out as a partner to a third party, and the third party relies on that. In such cases, a court determines that a partnership exists for liability purposes but does not bestow partnership rights.

**Partnership Interest:** The proportional share of profits a partner will receive from the partnership.

**Pass-Through Entities:** Business entities that do not pay their own income taxes. Instead, they file information returns with the taxation authorities, and the owners pay the taxes on the income, once, as appropriate, at the owners' personal tax rates.

**Pass-Through Taxation:** A method of taxation in which certain legal business entities do not pay their own income taxes, instead filing information returns with the taxation authorities, and in which the owners pay the taxes on the income, once, as appropriate, at the owners' personal tax rates.

**Past Consideration:** Something that was done previously without expectation of payment or receipt of something in return.

**Patent:** Property right that allows the inventor to prevent others from making, using, offering for sale, or selling the inventor's creation.

**Peers:** In a legal context, those on a jury drawn from a representative group of the citizenry of legal age and without a legal disability (a felony conviction, for example) in the jurisdiction where the trial takes place.

**Personal Liability:** Liability for which a person's personal assets—over and above his or her business assets—are subject to collection to satisfy a debt.

**Personal Property:** All other property that is not real property.

**Persuasive Law:** Precedent that a court is not required to observe as binding law. In most cases persuasive law originates in another state.

**Piercing the Corporate Veil:** A legal theory in every state that allows creditors of the corporation to move past the corporation, and its liability shields, and go directly to the personal assets of the officers, directors, and shareholders of the corporation.

**Plaintiff:** The party (either the government or a private person) who brings a civil lawsuit to court for the redress of damages and grievances.

**Plant Patents:** Patents granted to anyone who invents or discovers a new and distinct variety of asexually reproducing plant.

**Possession:** The property owner's right to have and hold property to the exclusion of others.

**Power of Attorney:** A document that creates written actual authority for the agent to act for specific purposes on behalf of the principal.

**Precedent:** A legal decision that binds later courts in certain circumstances to follow the logic and legal holdings of a previous court in the interests of fairness, justice, and clarity.

**Predominant Factor Test:** Test applied by the court to determine whether the UCC applies when a contract contains both a sales and a service element, with which the court identifies which of the two elements is the predominant factor in the contract.

**Preferred Stock:** A second type of stock issued by a corporation that generally does not provide the right to vote (although it may) but that does provide dividends and a share of the assets of the corporation to preferred shareholders before holders of common stock.

**Preincorporation:** The beginning of a corporation's life cycle, prior to the filing of the articles of incorporation with the state.

**Preponderance of the Evidence:** A balancing test used in most civil cases whereby plaintiffs have met the standard of proof if 50.1 percent of the evidence on a given issue points in their favor.

**Principal:** The amount borrowed under a loan that remains unpaid, excluding interest.

**Principal:** The party in an agency relationship who permits an agent to act on the principal's behalf.

**Products Liability:** A tort theory that holds manufacturers and sellers of defective products liable for harm that is caused by those products.

**Profit:** The money made for the business and its owners after all expenses, taxes, and costs are paid.

**Promissory Note:** A contract in which one party promises to pay or repay a specific amount on a given date or on demand by the holder of the note.

**Promoters:** The people (or other legal entity entitled to do so) who perform the basic steps needed to create a corporation.

**Prosecutor:** An attorney who acts as the representative of the government in bringing criminal actions against defendants as a part of the adversary system.

**Prospectus:** The written description drawn up by the promoters or their representatives that gives detailed information (sometimes legally required) about the new corporation.

**Proximate Cause:** The subset of causation in negligence that holds that an injury could be reasonably anticipated from the defendant's act.

**Public Domain:** Property that is no longer protected by intellectual property laws. Anyone is allowed to copy, make use of, or adapt the work.

**Publicly Traded:** Description given to shares that are available on public exchanges for the general public to buy and sell.

**Punitive Damages:** Compensation paid to a party not to make the injured party whole but rather to punish the wrongdoer for extreme or outrageous conduct.

**Quantum Meruit:** Remedy that provides the injured party with the value of the service provided to the other party.

**Quantum Valebant:** Remedy that provides the injured party with the value of the property provided to the other party.

**Quasi Contract:** A contract implied by a court of law.

**Quid Pro Quo Harassment:** A type of sexual harassment that occurs when an employment decision is conditioned on sexual activity or the basis for the decision is the satisfaction of a sexual demand.

**Quorum:** The minimum number of persons eligible to vote that must attend the meeting.

**Real Property:** Land, and any property attached to the land.

**Reasonable:** A term used to describe what a common person, at that place, at that time, would consider to be plausible and logical.

**Reasonable Accommodation:** An accommodation made by an employer to the known disabilities of an employee, done in such a way that the accommodation does not impose an undue hardship on the employer.

**Reasonable Person Standard:** A test used by the courts to determine if a reasonably prudent person in the same circumstances would have acted in the manner that the defendant did.

**Reasonably Foreseeable:** A legal standard that asks whether a reasonable person could foresee that there would be harm from the act or behavior.

**Reformation:** A remedy under which a court rewrites all or part of a contract.

**Registered Agent:** The agent designated by the corporation as the legal representative of that corporation in that particular state for acceptance of legal notifications and for service of process.

**Registration:** For these purposes, a requirement of the SEC that a publicly traded company disclose a description of the company's properties and business; a description of the security to be offered for sale; information about the management of the company; and financial statements certified by independent accountants.

**Reliance:** Depending on a fact to be true when taking an action.

**Requirements Contract:** A contract under which a buyer agrees to buy from a seller all that the buyer requires of a certain item or items.

**Res Ipsa Loquitur:** Latin for "the thing speaks for itself, "a tort theory holding that the fact that an accident took place means that the defendant had a duty to the plaintiff and breached it.

**Rescission:** A remedy whereby a party "takes back" any promise made under the contract.

**Restatement of Torts:** An important treatise on tort law that provides a measure of uniformity among most of the states.

**Restitution:** A remedy whereby a party is made whole under a contract by the return of lost property.

**Revocation:** The timely withdrawal of an offer.

**Right of First Refusal:** A right given to other owners of a business, family members, or whomever is designated by contract or law, requiring that the person holding the right be offered first for purchase any assets that another person who is party to the contract wishes to transfer to a third party. This right prevents business partners and shareholders from selling part of a business to third parties before the other current owners have the opportunity to purchase it.

**Rulings:** Decisions issued by a judge regarding issues of law that come up during the case. That is, the judge would decide if X law applies, or Y law, or if this statement can be heard by the jury, or if that bit of evidence must be excluded in any given case. These decisions become new law and have precedential value in many cases.

**S Corporations:** A type of corporation that does not pay corporate taxes. Rather, it files an information return with the taxing authority, and the shareholders proportionally pay taxes on profits, actually paid to the shareholders or not, at their personal tax rates. Only smaller corporations not publicly traded are eligible for S corporation status if they meet a series of guidelines.

**Sales Contract:** A contract concerning the sale of goods and not services.

**Securities Act of 1933:** A federal statute enacted in 1933 in the midst of the Great Depression as a response to the market crash of 1929 and some of the faults that were exposed in the market trading system at that time.

**Securities and Exchange Commission:** Also called the SEC, the administrative agency of the federal government that is responsible, in part, for enforcing the securities laws of the United States.

**Service of Process:** The formal procedure whereby notice of a lawsuit or other legal process is given to a defendant.

**Sexual Harassment:** Unwelcome sexual advances, requests for sexual favors, and other forms of unwelcome conduct in the workplace.

**Share Transfer Restrictions:** Shareholder agreement provisions that restrict share transfer.

**Shareholder Agreements:** Contracts that provide

basic guidance for the relationships among and between the shareholders.

**Shareholders:** The owners of a corporation through shares.

**Shares:** The units used to designate a shareholder's ownership rights in a corporation.

**Single-Member LLC:** An LLC that has only one member.

**Situs:** The legal and operating jurisdiction of a business.

**Social Security Act of 1935 (SSA):** A federal statute that provides for Social Security payments for the aged and disabled.

**Sole Proprietorship:** The oldest form of business, formed by one person, and easily created and ended without interference from the state (excluding licensing and permit issues). It provides no liability protection for the sole proprietor.

**Special Meetings:** Meetings called to discuss urgent but non-regular business of the corporation.

**Specific Performance:** A court-ordered requirement that a party perform an obligation under the contract.

**Standard of Proof:** A term describing the balancing test required to determine if the side holding the burden of proof on any given element of a case has actually met that burden.

**Statute of Frauds:** A set of state laws and UCC provisions that list contracts that must be in writing in order to be enforceable.

**Statutory Law:** Law created by the governing assembly of the federal government or a state government.

**Statutory Prohibitions:** In this context, provisions penalizing unauthorized corporations for doing business in a state.

**Strict Liability:** Liability of one who sells a defective product or engages in abnormally hazardous activities for any damages that may occur because of using that product or engaging in that activity even if there was no negligence or intent to harm.

**Strike Suits:** A term used for baseless lawsuits.

**Subscribers:** People or legal entities (for example, other corporations) with whom the promoter contracts to sell to them for a specific price a specific number of shares of the new corporation.

**Supremacy:** A legal concept under which federal law controls if federal and state law are in conflict.

**Tax Planning:** The advanced study of the tax consequences of a given business's configuration and operations. Tax planning also includes directing that configuration and operations in such a way so as to minimize or eliminate tax liabilities.

**Tax Rate:** The percentage of tax paid by an entity on every given dollar of taxable income received.

**Tenancy by the Entirety:** Property ownership form closely related to joint tenancy, but only available to married couples and only in some states. The entireties property is protected from the debts of one spouse.

**Tenancy in Common:** Property ownership form in which the owners all own equal undivided shares in the entire property unless they specify otherwise. Each owner designates to whom his share should go in the event of his death.

**Term LLC:** An LLC whose operating agreement states its date for dissolution.

**Third-Party Beneficiary:** Someone who receives a benefit under a contract that he or she is not a party to.

**Title:** The right to ownership of property and at the same time the written proof of ownership of property.

**Title VII of the Civil Rights Act of 1964:** A federal statute that prohibits discrimination in hiring, firing, promotion, compensation, or any other aspect of employment based on race, color, religion, national origin, and gender.

**Tort:** A civil wrongful act (other than breach of contract) causing harm or injury, for which relief may be obtained, usually in the form of damages.

**Tortfeasor:** A party who commits a tort.

**Total Integration:** Full expression of the parties' agreement.

**Trademarks:** Property rights that protect words, phrases, names, logos, symbols, sounds, or colors that distinguish goods and services from those manufactured or sold by others and to indicate the source of the goods.

**Transferability:** The ability of an owner of property to convey his property rights to another.

**Transferability of Interest:** The ability of an LLC member to transfer her interest in the LLC to another but only within state LLC statute restrictions.

**Trespass to Land:** The tort that results when a defendant invades the real property of another, such as a business or an individual, without permission.

**Trial Court:** A court that is usually composed of a judge and a jury and that tries both law and fact. It is the court of original jurisdiction in almost all cases.

**UCITA:** Uniform Computer Information Transactions Act, which governs contracts for pure software or software embedded in goods.

**Unanimous Consent in Lieu of Annual Meeting:** Consent that may be given by shareholders in place of holding a meeting but that must be unanimous.

**Unconditional Promise:** A promise to pay with no conditions and no reference to other agreements.

**Unconstitutional:** Status of any law, rule, caselaw decision, or regulation that goes outside the permitted bounds of government set out by the United States Constitution or a state constitution. Unconstitutional laws, rules, caselaw, and regulations are not enforceable.

**Undisclosed Principal:** A principal who is unknown to the third party when the contract is made by the agent.

**Undue Hardship:** The result when an accommodation by an employer to an employee's disability in the workplace in order to allow the employee to perform the essential functions of his or her position is unreasonable to the employer in terms of the time or money required.

**Unemployment Compensation:** Payments made to the involuntarily unemployed individuals.

**Uniform Commercial Code (UCC):** A model law that has been adopted separately by each state to facilitate making the law of sales and commercial transactions generally uniform across the different states so that these transactions would be easier to complete.

**Uniform Electronic Transactions Act (UETA):** A model law that was created in an attempt to make state governing of e-signatures more uniform. Under the UETA most contracts must be signed by the parties against whom enforcement is sought.

**Uniform Partnership Act of 1994:** An Act adopted by individual states that governs the operation of partnerships where the partnership agreement has not addressed an issue.

**Unilateral Contract:** A contract in which one party makes a promise and the other party performs in some way.

**Unilateral Mistake:** A mistake by only one party to the contract.

**Unintentional Torts:** Torts in which a person unintentionally acts in a way that causes harm to another.

**Union:** An organization composed of workers who have joined together to negotiate with an employer on behalf of its members' interests regarding working conditions and other job-related issues.

**Units:** A term used to designate a member's ownership rights in an LLC.

**Universality:** A legal theory that provides that every limited resource is owned by someone.

**Usage of Trade:** A legal concept embodied in the UCC that recognizes that the standard practice or set of practices in a particular type of business or trade in a certain region should guide the interpretation of what a contract means.

**Use:** The incident of ownership referring to the property owner's right to utilize property as the owner wishes.

**Utility Patents:** Patents granted to anyone who invents or discovers any new and useful process, machine, article of manufacture, or composition of matter, or any new and useful improvement thereof.

**Waiver of Notice:** An act by a party entitled to notice of a meeting indicating that it is not necessary to notify him of the meeting's time and place.

**Whistleblowing:** Reporting of illegal activities of the employer to authorities by an employee.

**Winding Up:** The process of accounting for assets, paying obligations, and providing each partner his or her interest in the partnership before termination of a partnership.

**Workers' Compensation Statutes:** State statutes in every state that provide that so long as an employee is injured during the course of employment, the employee is able to file a claim for specific damages for specific injuries without a lawsuit or proof of the employer's fault.

**Writ of Certiorari:** A formal request to the United States Supreme Court to hear a case.

**Wrongful Interference with a Business Relationship:** A business tort in which there is an established business relationship between the plaintiff and a third party; a defendant intentionally interferes with the business relationship, thereby causing the relationship to end; and the plaintiff suffers damage due to the interference.

**Wrongful Interference with a Contractual Relationship:** A business tort in which there is a valid, enforceable contract between two parties; a third party knows of the contract; and the third party intentionally interferes with the contract and causes one party to breach the contract.

**Zoning:** A device used to restrict the types of buildings and the uses available to an owner of a given piece of real property.

# Index